Contemporary architecture in Belgium

GEERT BEKAERT

Contemporary architecture
in Belgium

PHOTOGRAPHY CHRISTINE BASTIN AND JACQUES EVRARD

lannoo

The series ARCHITECTURE IN BELGIUM appears
thanks to the cooperation of Cimenteries CBR Cementbedrijven

This book is published simultaneously
in Dutch by Lannoo as
HEDENDAAGSE ARCHITECTUUR IN BELGIE

in French by éditions Racine as
ARCHITECTURE CONTEMPORAINE EN BELGIQUE

In the same series:
(in English, French, Dutch, and German)

Jos Vandenbreeden & Françoise Dierkens-Aubry
ART NOUVEAU IN BELGIUM

Jos Vandenbreeden & Françoise Dierkens-Aubry
THE 19th CENTURY IN BELGIUM

In preparation:
Jos Vandenbreeden & France Vanlaethem
ART DECO & MODERNISM

© Uitgeverij Lannoo nv, Tielt
ISBN 90 209 2724 8
D/1995/45/274

Graphic design: Geert Verstaen
English translation: Ferdinand du Bois

Typeset, printed, and bound by
Drukkerij Lannoo nv, Tielt - 1995

DUST-JACKET:
front: Mark Belderbos, Astene/Deinze,
Own house, 1990-'91
backside: Charles Vandenhove, Liège,
Hors-Château, renovation and new
elements, 1978

FRONTISPIECE:
Antwerp, Wilmarsdonk, Container-port,
1994

ENDPAPERS:
Constantin Brodzki and Marcel Lambrichs,
Brussels, CBR Offices

Contents

A. Hardy
Grimbergen, hangar, 1948-1950
(Bastin/Evrard)
The elegant concrete construction with
its daring corbelling, intended as a
hangar for small sports planes, is one of
the few Belgian post-war buildings that
has received attention from abroad.
It was included in the 'Twentieth Century
Engineering' exhibition in the MOMA in
New York.

The realm
of the commonplace

A country without architecture

Belgium has never been a country admired for its architecture. In the sixteenth century the exuberant Flemish Renaissance style fascinated the North for a moment. However, the Renaissance and Baroque, together with the subsequent architectural styles of the eighteenth and nineteenth centuries, have always – rightly or wrongly so – been considered more or less vivid quotations in a language that was essentially foreign. The only exception was Art Nouveau when around 1900 Belgian architecture suddenly came to the fore.

The interwar period relied largely on this reputation. Apart from Horta and Van de Velde, Belgium was represented on the international architectural scene by Victor Bourgeois and Huib Hoste. In 1928 they both played a part in the foundation of the 'Congrès Internationaux d'Architecture Moderne', the famous CIAM, at La Sarraz, a château in Switzerland. In his function as chairman of the Belgian section, Bourgeois organized the third CIAM congress in Brussels (1930), centred around 'Rationelle Beahnungsweisen'. He was invited by Mies van der Rohe to design a model house for the Weissenhofsiedlung in Stuttgart in 1927.

Huib Hoste stood in close contact with De Stijl and acted as Le Corbusier's collaborator during the 'Linkeroever' competition in Antwerp in 1933. At the 1932 'International Style' exhibition at the Museum of Modern Art in New York, Belgium was represented by L.-H. De Koninck's Lenglet house. In 1930 Maurice Casteels published *L'Art Moderne Primitif* in Paris and *Die Sachlichkeit in der Modernen Kunst* in Leipzig. It contained a foreword by Henry van de Velde, and provided one of the first general studies on modern architecture in Europe. In his report on ten years of modern architecture, *A Decade of New Architecture* (1951) CIAM secretary Sigfried Giedion mentioned a number of realizations by Belgian CIAM members. Though not among the pioneers, Belgium had taken up its place among the other countries.

Full-blooded chaos

In the period after 1945, which is the subject of this book, the international avant-garde disintegrated, as did their points of contact. The last CIAM congress, held in Otterlo in 1959, was attended by Willy Van Der Meeren and Peter Callebout. Lucien Kroll and André Constant organized an exhibition on Belgian architecture in Barcelona in 1965, but for the rest nothing much happened. If a handful of Belgian architects have commissions abroad and from time to time something is published about them, Belgium's fame in the field of architecture has hardly improved.

As a look at any survey of post-war architecture will show, the names of Belgian architects remain absent. In Dennis Sharp's *A Visual History of Twentieth-Century Architecture* (1972), the writer refers to the Expo'58 world fair in Brussels, but only to the German and Philips pavilions. A single Belgian work, a hangar in Grimbergen dating from 1948 and designed by the engineer Hardy, was taken up in the 'Twentienth Century Engineering' exhibition held at the Museum of Modern Art in New York (1964) and Brussels (1969). Moreover, the New York exhibition 'Transformations in Modern Architecture' (1979) included only the Banque Bruxelles Lambert building in Brussels.

On the other hand, architectural travel guides exclusively dedicated to modern architecture, which started reappearing in the 1960s, could hardly ignore Belgium completely. In 1962 the American architectural tourist E. Kidder Smith wrote in *The New Architecture of Europe:* 'Belgium has produced little of merit, architecturally speaking, since the First World War. With turn-of-the-century pioneers like Baron Horta and Henri van de Velde behind Belgian architectural efforts, this is doubly disturbing. Of all European countries, Belgium is least to be excused for not contributing more to contemporary architecture.' He concludes that there are a few buildings worth a cursory glance, such as André Jacqmain's Foncolin building in Brussels, a block of flats in Brussels by René Stapels and the housing complex 'Champ des Manœuvres' by the Egau group in Liège, but finds the whole 'lamentable'. Indeed, he finds Renaat Braem's Heysel complex 'absolutely frightening'.

A more recent American travel guide, Dennis J. and Elizabeth R. De Witt's *Modern Architecture in Europe* (1987), shows even less interest in Belgium. Yet again the BBL building appears, as well as the 'Mémé' and the Alma metro station in Woluwe-Saint-Lambert.

A friendlier tone perhaps is that of Jan Nairn, who wrote in *The Observer* on 24 September 1967 that 'Belgium, the joker in the European Pack, has managed to create an architecture of such splendid and full-blooded chaos that the visitor suspends all normal jugdment'.

The Belgian solution

The Frenchman Pierre Garcette turns things round when in the same year (1967) he writes in the periodical *Janus 13* that Belgian villa architecture should set the example for French housing policies: 'une solution belge, simple, pratique, économique, humaine,... triomphe du bon sens'. By then, however, we shall already have crossed the Rubicon and have left the closed paradise of architecture far behind.

However, in the 1960s one could even hear expressions of praise among architects for the Belgian indifference. Herman Hertzberger wrote in *Forum* (1970): 'For the moment I still feel that the whole chaos in Belgium is more significant than the chaos over here, which though it has been raked and cleared of so-called weeds, is the same chaos, only it has a layer of varnish through which you have to scratch to get there.'

A quarter of a century on this sort of appreciation has faded away and has made room for a sort of curiosity. In this sense, the evolution of the architectural situation in Belgium is an indicator for the changes in international taste in architecture. Accounts of the present sense of curiosity, which goes together with the encyclopaedic rather than critical character of architectural publications at the moment, make up the contributions on Belgian architecture that have been appearing in foreign periodicals since the 1980s. The culmination of this phenomenon is Marc Dubois' *Belgio*, which was published in Milan in 1993.

Seeing what one sees

This is the present state of things. Among architectural circles, Belgium is virtually unknown. The question, however, is whether this counts as a norm and whether this unfamiliarity implies anything but the quality of the architecture. If we want to study Belgian architecture of the last fifty years, it would be wrong to try and situate it within the existing discourse. It simply would not fit into a conclusive exposé – indeed, the story of architects in itself is anything but coherent.

'Il faut toujours dire ce que l'on voit, surtout il faut toujours, ce qui est plus difficile, voir ce que l'on voit,' Le Corbusier wrote. What matters is not the laying down of norms, but looking at what is going on, at how that piece of land called Belgium has been and is being built on. And then we might see that the lack of embarrassment with which architecture is treated in Belgium is exactly what gives it its significance. Belgian architecture takes up its place at the centre of everyday activity. It does not disappear behind lengthy accounts. It is the commonplace *par excellence*.

Whenever Adolf Loos lashed out at the architects of his day, at Henry van de Velde in particular, his arguments came down to the defence of the commonplace. The best example of this appears in an essay of 1910, 'Architektur': 'May I take you to the banks of a mountain lake? The sky is blue, the water green,

De Haan, residential area, 1994
(Wim Robberechts)
A dream of a place! Every man his own house, all of them equal, all of them nicely spaced on virgin territory, the antithesis of the Liège panorama. This is where the development of individual life can take place, provided the infrastructure of roads and pipes is laid out. Despite the pace of modern culture, this type of house seems to be holding out.

Liège, panorama, 1994
(Bastin/Evrard)
Liège is a model of a city, beautifully located in the valley where the River Meuse and the Ourthe flow together. However, the city also is the model of the tragedy of conscious urban planning that is blind to reality and cannot contain the forces it has unleashed.

and everything bathing in peace and calm. The mountains and clouds are mirrored in the lake, as are the houses, farms, and chapels. There they stand as if untouched by human hands. They are as though they have come directly from God's workplace, just as the mountains and the trees, the clouds and the blue sky. And everything exudes beauty and repose...

There, what was that? Something disturbing the peacefulness. Like a shout for no reason at all. Among the farmers' houses, made not by them but by God, there stands a villa. The work of a good architect or a bad one? I couldn't tell. All I know is that the peace, calm, and beauty have disappeared.

For God knows no good or bad architects. In the presence of his throne all architects are equal.'

Later in his essay Loose rejects the term 'architecture' and proposes 'building' or 'construction' instead. Living has nothing to do with architecture, he writes: 'The house has to please everybody. In contrast to the work of art, which has to please no one. The work of art is a private matter concerning the artist. The house is not.' In Loos's view architecture only applies to monuments and graves. That this distinction was controversial is borne out in Loos's own architecture. He needed this antagonism in order to plot the field of tension between art and life, and resolutely to reject any sort of academic or formal approach. If architecture is in any way connected with art, it is in that it is concerned with the commonplace of life.

Architecture and history

The fact that we are looking at recent architecture confirms the commonplace and lends this volume in the series on Belgian architecture its own specific character. It is about the architecture in which we live. Historical architecture, dealt with in the previous volumes, naturally form a part of this. However, we have become so used to separating it from its present context that we have become unable to recognize its place in it. Historical architecture cannot function as a norm for its contemporary counterpart, because our conception of it often constitutes a fiction in which we project our frustrations. On the other hand, this also holds true for contemporary architecture. It is a mutual relationship.

A concrete example of the relation between historical architecture and the reality of our time, as well as of the unabashed honesty of Belgian architecture, is the lonely spire of the church in Wilmarsdonk, which was appropriated by the Antwerp container port – an extreme, but by no means unique situation. All over the world one can see this sort of dazzling beauty that inspires artists while architects fail to recognize it. Wilmarsdonk's fate also befalls monuments of more recent times. The demolition of the Nautilus hotel in the dock area (1958) is a clear example.

But to experience the drama of contemporary architecture to its full extent, we have to go to Place Saint-Lambert in Liège. What is happening there stretches the imagination. As if in a Greek tragedy, blind fate is relentlessly driving the city to its fall. Resistance would be useless. Though skilled in their field and honest in their intention to bring together a new reality and the existing structures to make the city livable, the architects have unleashed forces they can no longer control. The result is something as yet unnamed. Can this still be called a city? In any case, it is a brutal demonstration of the metamorphosis of cities, except for where they are reduced to touristic communities.

The old texture has remained recognizable and, as is the case for Hôtel Torrentius and Hôtel de Grady near Place Saint-Lambert in Liège, here and there it is even meticulously restored, but on the whole it has been torn to pieces by the network of roads and traffic. The public space has become non-existent, not to mention its lack of coherence.

Not a single city, including Brussels, has seen such a radical confrontation between the existing city and the new reality as Liège has. Nowhere else has the approach to urban development been so thoroughly prepared, though the same tension can be felt everywhere. Not even provincial towns are spared. Ostend, for instance, has been utterly transformed since the Second World War. Only when the process is complete do we notice that the old city has disappeared without a trace, though the original network of streets has by and large been left untouched. In Kortrijk even this network of streets has not remained intact. Kortrijk boasts the first shopping precinct, yet right next to it the Romeinse laan cuts through the city like a strategic highway. Alien, detached ethnologists, if they exist, would have to be called upon to describe the recent evolution of Belgian cities and towns.

The logics of the network

The new landscape is that of the stream of traffic, which does not involve architects. In the book *De beschikbare ruimte* Bart Verschaffel mentions 'the pulverized city' and the logics of the network: 'The word "city" refers, just as the words "fortress" or "cathedral", not only to an architectural type or form of dwelling, but also to a period that lies in the past. Almost every author that has thought about the theme agrees that the word "city" and the image it conjures up no longer suffice to describe or understand the significant developments and transformations that the architectural environment has undergone. Nor can it account for the way in which we live in and with space, even in and with a multitude of spaces at the same time. The "habitat" can no longer indicate the place man takes up in the world. The transformation of the architectural environment and of our experience of space can be understood in the light of the overriding presence of a new type and definition of space: the network.' Indeed, this is the commonplace of contemporary architecture.

The Belgian home

Not only is a new, ethnographical history of the city required, but we are also looking forward to a historical survey of the Belgian home. The row of houses built by the architect M. Poons in Everberg near Brussels in 1981 reflects a naive

Antwerp, Wilmarsdonk, container port, 1994

(Bastin/Evrard)

The forces that make cities burst at the seams also have effects on the periphery. The expansion of Antwerp's port has obliterated entire polder towns, apart from the church tower: a symbol of stability in an ever changing landscape?

Liège, Place Saint-Lambert, 1995

(Bastin/Evrard)

The death of the city can be seen on Place Saint-Lambert in Liège, where in 1970 the execution of the plan by the Equerre group was taken on. It was to transform the 'coincidental nature of the city square into architectural unity'. In fact, the plan went no further than ruining the square. Since 1970 many contradictory plans have come in quick succession, but not one of them has been completed.

ATELIER DE L'ESPACE LÉOPOLD, COLLABORATION BETWEEN ATELIER DE GENVAL, CERAU, VANDEN BOSSCHE, AND C.R.V.

Brussels, *Quartier Léopold*, building site, 1995

(Bastin/Evrard)

As in other cities, Brussels' dilapidated station neighbourhoods have been the scene of building mania. After the *Quartier Nord* and the area around the South station, it is now the turn of the peaceful *Quartier Léopold* around the Luxembourg station, where the controversial European Parliament is being built.

M. Poons and
P. le Maire de Warzée
Everberg, houses, 1981
(Bastin/Evrard)
Back to the Middle Ages? A row of houses
built in 1981, which tries to evoke the
intimate atmosphere of a beguinage or a
city street in the middle of an open field,
reminiscent of the urban area in the
open-air museum of Bokrijk or 'Old
Belgium' at the Expo '58 world fair.
What has become of the link between
architecture and the present?

Guillaume Bijl
Grenoble, Le Magasin, 'Caravan Show', 1989
Besides 'Fami-Home' – the ideal Belgian
home, exhibited on the 1988 Venice
Biennale – Guillaume Bijl's series of
'Transformation-installations' also
includes the 'Caravan Show', which
combines the reality and fiction of
contemporary living. 'Bijl does not
represent reality,' writes Jan Hoet,
'he shows how it (re)presents itself.'

▷   Luc Deleu
**Antwerpen, ICC, 'De laatste steen van België',
1979**
(Bernd Urban/SABAM))
In the courtyard of the 'Internationaal
Cultureel Centrum', the former Royal
Palace, the architect Luc Deleu formally
laid 'the last stone of Belgium' in 1979.
According to Deleu Belgium is completely
filled with buildings. The architect has a
more important calling than building
houses. This he can leave to the people
themselves.

image of the ideal Belgian home, but this would hold true for just about any piece of land cut up for villas or holiday houses. However, the Everberg example evinces a clear and controlled formal intention. It rejects the modernist argument that whoever drives a Porsche has to adapt his house accordingly. Living here affords an escape from the stress of everyday life. There is no continuity, but a rupture. The unity of Versailles, to which Victor Bourgeois still referred, no longer lies within our reach. Why should we not build old-fashioned houses in the era of the high-speed train?

The multiple reality of architecture is hard to discern in architectural periodicals and books. It can be seen in the work of artists and photographers – not of architectural photographers, though – who now, more than ever, have become obsessed by the environment in which we live. They have acquired the role of the alien ethnographer.

Guillaume Bijl's installations show 'fiction as reality', or reality as fiction. 'Bijl does not represent reality,' Jan Hoet writes, 'he shows how it (re)presents itself.' At the 1988 Venice Biennale Bijl reconstructed a 'fermette' (small farmhouse) in the Belgian pavilion, built with sturdy materials, with a lawn and garden sculptures – everything just a little too real. Even more ambiguous is the 'Caravan Show' that he set up in Grenoble in 1989.

An architect who has from the outset of his career instinctively rebelled against the delusion and futility of accepted architectural notions, is Luc Deleu. In 1979 he laid the 'final stone of Belgium' at the 'Internationaal Cultureel Centrum' in Antwerp. Belgium was finished, completely built up.

A personal adventure

The enjoyable part of talking about architecture in Belgium is not its obviousness or its coherence, but rather its sense of adventure and the unexpected ways in which it tries to maintain itself in the face of current developments in the technical and spiritual fields. We are not dealing with a clearly defined period here, as it would be impossible to distinguish strict compartments and clearly defined stylistic periods between 1945 and 1995. Instead we shall divide the period into decades based on uneven numbers so as to reflect the chaotic image of reality as much as possible. Some architects' œuvres span the whole period. We have decided to keep each architect's personal œuvre together, not in order to separate it from its context, but rather to show how they interrelate and are intertwined with each other.

In his lecture entitled 'The Sixties: As They Were', which was taken up in *Making It New* (1994), Henry Geldzahler notes: 'In the final analysis, art isn't about decades and it's not about movements. It's about unique individuals who worked in their own moment, in the context of contemporaneity, and who raided the common tradition in various permutations to create unique works.' In *Atlante dell'architettura italiana del Novecento* Giorgio Ciucci and Francesco Dal Co come to the same conclusion.

Geldzahler gives an account of the New York arts scene during the 1960s and his involvement in it. This account of Belgian architecture after 1945 has also sprung from a personal engagement, which amongst others has led to the publication of two earlier texts, one in 1970, the other in 1980. The first was written for the book *Bouwen in België/Construire en Belgique 1945-1970*, published on the occasion of an exhibition on Belgian architecture commissioned by the National Confederation of the Building Industry, not by some or other organization for architects. The 1980 text was written on request for A+, the periodical published under the auspices of the Belgian Order of Architects. The editors rejected the text, but in 1983 it eventually appeared in the July issue of the Dutch periodical *Wonen/TABK*, the predecessor of *Archis*, under the title 'Bouwen op Belgische gronden'. These texts illustrate how little the problems have changed over the last fifty years, despite the apparent speed of time, fabulous technical developments and the triumph of an architecture of concealment. In fact, we could have copied them unchanged. Perhaps the inertia of architecture should also be called exemplary.

The two texts together form the backbone of the new story. The choice of names and works has not been arbitrary, which does not mean that many of them could not be replaced by others. The history of Belgian architecture during this period still has to be written. We do not intend to provide a complete survey, but to present the reader with a lively chronicle of the attempts to give architecture some sense and splendour in the commonplace of today.

MAURICE HOUYOUX AND JULES GHOBERT
Brussels, Mont des Arts and Royal Library
Albert I, 1949-1964
(Bastin/Evrard)

In 1937 a competition was held for the
construction of the Mont des Arts and the
Royal Library. However, the winning
design by Jules Ghobert and Edward Van
Steenbergen was slightly adapted and
only executed in the 1950s by Maurice
Houyoux, Roland Delers, and Jacques
Bellemans. It is conceived as a central
element of the monumental north-south
axis, a prime example of Belgian 'modern
classicism'.

Chapter 1

1945-1955

Reconstruction and demolition:
the architect's response

Modern Classicism

In the history of architecture, 1945 is not a memorable date. Nor is 1955. Nevertheless, it was during the first ten years following the Second World War that Belgium acquired much of its present appearance. Immediately after the liberation Belgium found itself in a privileged position, economically speaking. The country had emerged from the war relatively undamaged. There was enough money available for large-scale investment and the building sector greatly profited from this dynamism.

Of course, during the war years very little had been built, but architecture had been a constant subject for thought and discussion while plans for the future were being drawn up. All this happened among architects who had already been working in the 1930s and who to some extent were linked to the Modern Movement. The continuity within the process of development is unmistakable.

The central theme of the debate was modern architecture itself and its place in the existing landscape. Not the style or requirements of the individual building, but its contribution to the environment were of interest. As early as the 1930s even some modernists had voiced their doubt as to the possibilities offered by functional architecture, in which form was to be derived from function, and pursued a 'new monumentality' that was to give expression to collective values. In *L'Architecture Moderne en Belgique* (1936) Marcel Schmitz defends the 'modern classicism' of Belgian architecture, in which he saw the balance between the classical idiom and functionalism.

What could be more conducive to monumentality than national or regional consciousness? Indeed, during the war regionalism was the order of the day and references to 'fascist architecture' speak for themselves. The building policies of the totalitarian regimes were in fact not that different from those in other European countries, as Franco Borsi points out in *The Monumental Era. European Architecture and Design. 1929-1939* (1986). For Belgium he refers to the competition held in 1937 concerning the Bibliothèque Royale (Royal Library) on the Boulevard de l'Empereur in Brussels, for which the young Renaat Braem together with Julien Schillemans submitted a design; to the tower of the university library by Henry van de Velde in Ghent; and to the entrance building at the Rémy

production plant by Jean Deligne in Wijgmaal.

Jean Deligne (1890-1985) played an important role in the debate. Educated according to the 'Beaux-Arts' tradition at the Académie in Brussels, he went on to teach at La Cambre, the school of architecture where modernism reigned supreme. During the war he was one of the greatest supporters of regionalism. 'The heritage of a glorious past has been scornfully ignored,' he wrote in 1941.

Other modernists also became involved in the debate. Their mouthpiece was the periodical *Bouwkunst en Wederopbouw* (Construction and Reconstruction), which was published by the Commissioner General's office, in charge of the country's reconstruction during the German occupation. In 1941 Jos Schellekens (1909-1963) wrote in it, under the explicit title 'Nationalisme in de Bouwkunst' (Nationalism in Architecture): 'It is an undeniable fact that a strong national consciousness has grown in all European countries over recent years. This growing national consciousness naturally went hand in hand with the glorification of an earlier cultural heritage... We need not copy what in other countries is considered normal. We must make something that is our own, that reflects our landscape and our people.' The architect, who had built fine modern houses, not least of all his own in Turnhout, concludes: 'We shall again think in a normal way. "Rationalism" wanted to draw all the attention to itself; however, it has shown aesthetic incapability and spiritual imperfection. The younger generation will have nationalist feelings.'

Huib Hoste's (1881-1957) answer to this in the same periodical is sober. Under the title 'Zwicht u van leuzen en slachtwoorden' (Beware of slogans and catch phrases) he wrote: 'National architecture presupposes the existence of architecture; if this is lacking, the whole phrase collapses and boils down to nothing.' Hoste further elaborated on this remark in an account given to the 'Koninklijke Vlaamse Academie' in 1942, published in 1947 under the title *Bouwen op het Platteland* (Building in the Country). In it he quoted Igor Stravinsky: 'Les éléments nationaux tiennent aussi bien chez Pouchkine que chez Glinka et Tchaikovsky une place considérable. Seulement, chez ceux-ci, ils découlent spontanément de leur nature même, alors que chez les autres la tendance nationaliste était un esthétisme doctrinaire qu'ils tenaient à imposer.' In *L'architecte et son espace*

Victor Bourgeois also mentions 'le retour aux sources' with reference to Paul Collaer, who described Stravinsky and Milhaud's innovations as 'retrouver un langage premier'.

When in 1951 Sigfried Giedion, the author of the both authoritative and misleading history of modern architecture entitled *Space, Time and Architecture* (1941), published *A Decade of New Architecture*, he did so to convince himself and the other members of the CIAM that the vitality of modern architecture had come under a worldwide threat from retrograde movements presenting themselves under a multitude of names, ranging from 'regionalism' and 'new empirism' through to 'traditionalism'.

Yet in 1944 he himself had written about 'The Need for a New Monumentality'. In this essay he put it that 'From a human point of view, and from the architectonic view as well, houses and blocks are not isolated units. They are incorporated in urban settlements and these are parts of a greater entity, the city. An architect who is not interested in the whole of planning, from the right height of a kitchen sink to the layout of a region, is not part of the contemporary building scene.'

In this passage Giedion demonstrates the way in which attention has shifted from the style of the individual object, piece of furniture or residential area to its place within the whole and therefore to its inevitable relationship with the local patrimony. However, the modern building or the modern part of a town does not, as a variety of style, fit into the historical environment. They invert the relationship, for as prototypes of the New they make their own demands on the environment.

In 1957, when on the occasion of a further edition of *La Charte d'Athènes*, the CIAM's manifesto of urban development, Le Corbusier looks back on the reconstruction of France, he only discerns opposition to 'the fatal birth of modern architecture': 'Ce fut une marée d'invectives, de reproches, de refus: invectives contre l'art moderne; reproches à ceux qui s'y étaient laissés prendre; refus des solutions techniques qui se proposaient ou s'imposaient, refus d'un système de pensée cohérent: architecture et urbanisme conjugués indissolublement'.

A Belgian version

However, it did not quite come to that in Belgium, where modernism never was doctrinal. In *Modern Belgian Architecture*, published by the Belgian Information Center in New York in 1955, Hugo van Kuyck still sounds hopeful. 'I think that those who believe in renewing the patrimony of our country along progressive lines and with modern means will have a hard fight on their hands, as there is still a latent reaction against all radical thinking... Hopeful signs, however, appear in many quarters. One of them is the keen interest of the architects themselves. The younger generation in Belgium today, abetted by some of their elders, is receptive to newer ideas on a larger scale... These are healthy tokens, and maybe the time is approaching when our men, proud of the traditions of their Flemish and Walloon forefathers, like the great builders of cathedrals and palaces, will plan on a scale which is beyond the

vision of the good bourgeois of today. Maybe our towns of tomorrow, integrated with parks and roads, built with the tremendous technical means now at our disposal, will take an outstanding place in the history of architecture.'

To get a clear impression of the atmosphere at the time, one had better read Victor Bourgeois' *L'architecte et son espace*. Still in 1955, he again took up his career as a modernist. Under this revealing title (The Architect and 'his' Space) he tries to find a way out of the impasse in which modernism and regionalism find themselves: 'L'architecte s'évade des formules même modernes, des conventions plastiques ou industrielles, pour réinventer par la sensibilité et par la réflexion, une nouvelle phase des formes de notre temps'.

The controversy regarding regionalism kept reappearing throughout the post-war period. It even found an international echo in the so-called 'critical regionalism' of the 1980s. Today it has become more pertinent than ever and can be seen as a form of instinctive resistance to the inevitable rationality of modern planning. The reconstruction will evince a compromise between both trends. Regional planning and urban development have expanded enormously, but the ideas formulated by their advocates are but seldom applied.

Although Belgium might be considered one large city, as was already stated at the congress on Garden Cities and Town Planning in London in 1915, a global approach never came about after the war. Inspired by Julien Schillemans's World City, Braem designed his Linear City (1934) that encompassed Belgium in one fell swoop. However noncommittal these ideas may have been in their formulation, they fitted in with notions that would lead to the labour plan ('Plan van de Arbeid') devised by Hendrik de Man. In 1935 this Minister of Public Works projected large-scale infrastructural works, not only to combat unemployment, but also to bring together the various aspects of social, economic, and environmental planning. After the war all this had become taboo, which is not to say that below the surface it did not continue to grow. Amongst many others – such as Deligne, Bourgeois, Henvaux, Demeyere, Soetewey, and the Equerre group – Raphael Verwilghen, in charge of the Architecture and Town PLanning department during the war, played a prominent role.

R. Schuiten
Constructions d'après guerre, 1946
In the 'Cadre de vie' series, dedicated to
the construction of new houses after the
war, the individual house is presented as
an antidote to the 'machine civilization'.
Such a house, possibly prefabricated,
would be 'in contact with the beauty of
nature, which constantly renews itself,
reveals the eternal laws of beauty, and
teaches us a healthy philosophy of life'.

Gordon Bunshaft / SOM
Brussels, Bank Building, 1959
photograph 1970
(Karel Vermeir)
Gordon Bunshaft remarked on his BBL
building in Brussels: 'You make
architecture for a customer and if he asks
a monumental building, you make one...
If you get the opportunity to build near
the Royal Palace and you don't erect a
monument, you are a fool.'

Raphael Verwilghen (1885-1963)

A convinced modernist, Raphael Verwilghen was an engineer-architect who early on became aware of the political and social implications of his profession. In his view architecture was inseparably linked to urban development and planning. He drafted the decree of 25 August 1915, which obliged communes damaged during the First World War to set up a Plan of Reconstruction.

The 1915 decree also formed the basis for the Commissioner General's decree concerning the country's reconstruction dated 12 September 1940. With the exception of a short interruption after the war, it remained unchanged until the 1962 law on urban development and town and country planning came in force. Without getting lost in the legal complications of the texts, it would be interesting to analyse the views that lay at their origin. Verwilghen himself spoke on the subject at the Sint-Lucas institute in Ghent in 1943. 'We are presented here with a fact that is blindingly clear: freedom, one and indivisible, has destroyed authority and at the same time undermined respect for the Spirit and the unity of our nation. This is why urban development, which in itself has a quality of guidance or leadership and therefore requires a clear insight into the problems of communal life and of the authorities in power, has for more than a century been practised in a setting of utter chaos. Gentlemen, I am speaking to you neither as a politician, nor as a moralist, but as a town planner who loves his art.' In another text, the preface to the first issue of *Bouwkunst en Wederopbouw*, Verwilghen writes: 'The image of the beehive, the model for a harmonious society, organized and active, is what we have to bear in mind.'

This notion of town planning led to the absurd institution of 'aesthetic supervision'. This implied the supervision of all architectural projects by a 'professional aesthete'. In fact this supervision was limited to the façade, which prompted Verwilghen to coin the pejorative term 'gevelstedebouw' (urban façade development).

Verwilghen was aware of the increasing gulf between the architect-town planner's vision and reality: 'Indeed, I am sorry to note that, in the absence of specific laws regarding urban development, architects and technicians' designs took on the character of mere dreams. They were mostly beautiful pictures, sometimes rich with suggestions, but increasingly remote from reality... If it is true that it is at the base of the wall that one should judge the bricklayer, then it is equally true that it is in face of the concrete problem that the town planner reveals himself... Sometimes I even have the impression that this gap cannot be bridged, as town planning requires an education that is not only technical, but which adds to this technical perfection a basis of an aesthetic, a philosophical, and a social nature.'

Typical of his school of thought is the development plan he drafted for Antwerp during the war. Ghent, Bruges, and Herentals were likewise submitted to urban development studies. One of the few direct results of the work done by the Commissioner General's office is the construction of the station area in Bruges, finished in 1956, after the station had been demolished by Jozef Schadde in 1948. In 1946 Victor Bourgeois published *Charleroi, terre d'urbanisme,* the result of a study he had been conducting since 1930. During the war Deligne was preparing a plan for the reconstruction of Tournai, though the final project was to be entrusted to Bonduelle. In Liège, which even before the war had been the subject of attempts to find solutions to urban and regional problems, especially by the Equerre group, the population was presented with the 'Plan d'aménagement de l'agglomération liégeoise'. Contests with the same aims were held in other cities.

Verwilghen had predicted what the post-war reaction would be: 'When the war has come to an end, when economic activity re-emerges, without all our provinces being subjected to control, a new upsurge of building mania, which will probably cause enormous, irreparable damage, will engulf our cities and rural areas.' In the whirl of excitement after the liberation, the 1940 decree was abolished. The onset of town planning in Belgium was being ignored by 'the men in London' and almost every prepared plan was rejected. Some of them were reintroduced later on, but only in a fragmented version. Even as early as 2 December 1946, the 1940 text was readopted as a decree. However, it basically remained dead letter, as if neither town planning, nor architecture actually existed.

The Brussels model

It would be impossible to produce an overall view of the Reconstruction of Belgium after the war. There simply was no overall view. Even on this point the Belgian case is far more

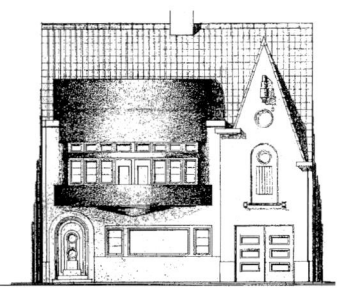

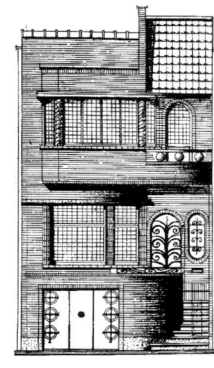
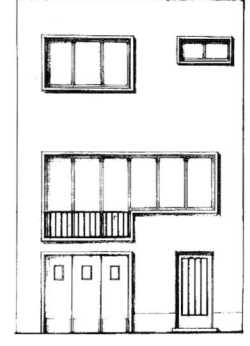

AESTHETIC SUPERVISION
Commissioner General of Reconstruction
Even before the war attempts had been made to gain more control over the aesthetics of construction in Belgium, which led to the law of 20 February 1939 stipulating that nothing could be built without the signature of a qualified architect. During the war aesthetic supervision was carried out by the Commissioner General's office. On the left we can see the plans originally submitted, on the right the corrected versions. This practice has survived until today, though under different names. In other sectors it would be called censorship.

typical than might be suspected, as the earlier quote from Le Corbusier indicates. The reconstruction of a new world allowed latent energy to escape all over, as if the war had broken the dam holding back all pre-war inhibition. Technical developments, the expansion of the city, the demands of industry, and new social amenities pushed architectural concerns to the background. This evolution was illustrated by Sigfried Giedion in *Mechanization Takes Command. A Contribution to Anonymous History* (1948).

In his survey of Belgian architecture in *De Bouwnijverheid* (1966), V.G. Martiny comes to the conclusion that 'it would be needless trouble to try and summarize in chronological order the buildings that have been built in Brussels, Flanders, and Wallonia since 1946: the list would be too long and incomplete for anybody to glean anything from it.' Indeed, architecture cannot be represented by means of statistics.

The post-war approach was clearly demonstrated in Brussels by the completion of the North-South train connection, a large-scale operation, which partly through underground tunnels linked the Gare du Nord and the Gare du Midi via the Gare Centrale. The concept itself dates from the nineteenth century and the works started in 1911 had not been finished by 1945. What did remain were the scars that even today have not completely healed. One of the most densely populated areas of Brussels was razed to the ground.

In 1952 the first trains rolled through the North-South connection. On the same line as the railway tunnel a motorway was constructed, connecting the Eglise de la Chapelle and the Quartier du Nord. The drama of Liège was being re-enacted, albeit as a farce.

One can easily imagine what thought lay behind this monumental axis. Occupied by a number of impressive buildings, it was to determine the new face of Brussels, the modern metropolis, the international traffic junction and centre of communication. Near Victor Horta and Maxime Brunfaut's Central Station, the Sabena air terminal by the very same Brunfaut was put up and some time later Léon Stynen's telex offices.

Further on, towards the North Station, 1948 saw the construction of a new wing to the Belgian National Bank by Marcel Van Goethem (1900-1959). The 1960s brought the large-scale, though never completed national administrative centre by the Alpha group, which included Hugo van Kuyck and Marcel Lambrichs. The axis leads to the misshapen World Trade Center and the waste land of the Quartier du Nord, dominated by the formidable Centre Rogier (1958) by Jacques Cuisinier, described by Bruno De Meulder in *Archis* as 'a rendezvous with the world', a 'city within the city'.

The first phase of the project is still characterized by the construction of the Mont des Arts and the Royal Library after plans by the architects Jules Ghobert (1881-1973), Maurice Houyoux (1903-1960), and Roland Delers (1931-1986). It was the result of a contest held in 1937. The work was started in 1951 despite vigorous protest. The charming garden designed by the French landscape architect Vacherot to fill up the empty spot in

Brussels, Carrefour de l'Europe
photograph 1968

A souvenir: the Carrefour de l'Europe as it remained from the 1960s until the 1990s. It was an improvised car park amid the historically inspired reconstruction of the edges of the city centre and the monumental buildings on the north-south axis: St Michael's cathedral, Léon Stynen's telex building, and Maxime Brunfaut's Sabena terminal.

the Quartier Saint-Roche was replaced by the present-day terraces in 1956. The North-South axis provides a cross section of Belgian architecture and town planning up to the present. Until the 1990s the area opposite the Central Station remained a grubby void. The Carrefour de l'Europe was nothing but a desolate car park.

Still in Brussels in 1945, there was another project by the town planner-king, Leopold II, which had remained unfinished: the national basilica, the Sacré-Cœur in Koekelberg. This was where Leopold II, to crown the broad arterial road, wanted to construct a Belgian Pantheon to provide national heroes with a final resting-place. In the end it became a national sanctuary modelled upon the Sacré-Cœur in Paris.

In 1905 Leopold II lay the first stone. In the interwar period Albert Van huffel drew up new plans, taking into account the existing foundations. The model was awarded the first prize for international architecture at the 'Arts décoratifs et industriels' exhibition in Paris in 1925. The exhibition also included Le Corbusier's 'Pavillon de L'Esprit Nouveau' and Constantin Melnikov's Russian pavilion, whereas the Belgian pavilion was by Victor Horta. Other works featured on the exhibition were the recently finished concrete church in Raincy (near Paris) by Auguste Perret and Huib Hoste's church in Zonnebeke.

Work on the basilica was taken up again by Paul Rome after the war and it was officially consecrated in 1970. The building testifies, as Henry van de Velde put it, to 'a unique style, which bears no name'. This could well be characteristic of the major part of Belgian architecture since the Reconstruction.

The other side of the radical approach in the inner city of Brussels was the systematic demolition of densely populated areas under the guise of redevelopment and improvement. Together with the explosive growth of the urban population this led to a dramatic lack of housing, a phenomenon that also appeared elsewhere in the country. Attempts to counteract this came down to occasional interventions based on the premise that demolition and the building of new housing, in this case high-rise blocks, constituted the most reasonable solution.

Near the North-South railway link, in the working-class area of the Rue Haute where opposition to redevelopment would later be voiced, Charles van Nueten (1899-1989), a lecturer at La Cambre, built an exemplary block of flats in 1950. Here the tragical dilemma of modern architecture had reached a climax. Not only is it exemplary in that the architectural form evinces a high degree of command and that it shows the special care taken over its function as a dwelling, but also in that the concrete reality of living in a building is completely lost.

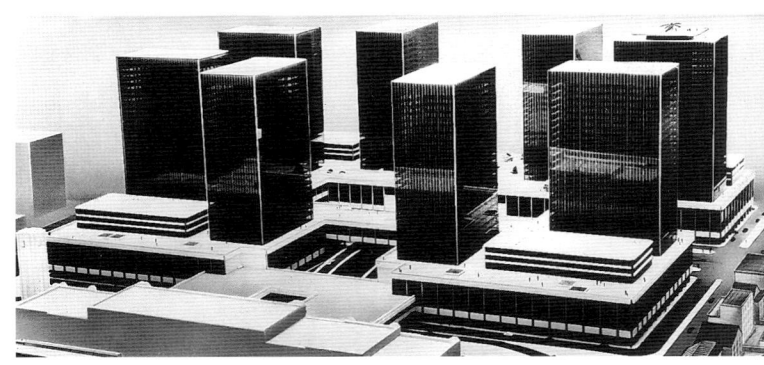

Brussels, World Trade Center, scale model, 1969

Following the north-south axis, the 1960s saw the planning of the immense World Trade Center by Charles De Pauw's Consortium, for which room was already being made. The shining towers, reminiscent of black limousines, were to arise above a network of partly sunk motorways. A number of the towers were built, but the emptly plain is now filled with more elaborate and individualistic architectural objects. The Consortium also worked out plans for World Trade Centers at the Willems docks in Antwerp and the Ilot Saint-Georges in Liège.

ALPHA GROUP, HUGO VAN KUYCK,
MARCEL LAMBRICHS,
AND GEORGES RICQUIER

Administrative Centre, Brussels, 1955

(Bastin/Evrard)

The administrative centre in Avenue Pacheco completes the north-south axis between the new building of the National Bank and the Avenue de la Botanique. It is not intended only as a manifestation of new architecture, but also as a demonstration of the new dimensions of the city of the future. The tower block of the administrative centre echoes Hugo Van Kuyck's PS building at the Porte de Schaerbeek and J. Cuisinier's Centre Rogier.

CHARLES VAN NUETEN
Brussels, housing block, 1950
(Bastin/Evrard)
The building in Rue Haute by Charles Van Nueten fits within the project of the north-south railway link. It was an early attempt at counteracting the lack of housing resulting from mass demolitions in the area by means of high-rise construction. It continues the tradition of social housing in Brussels seen in the work of Emile Hellemans, Léon Govaerts, and Henri Jacobs.

ALBERT VAN HUFFEL
Koekelberg, Sacré Cœur basilica, 1921-1970
(Bastin/Evrard)
While the metamorphosis of the old city into the modern metropolis was rapidly taking place, the construction of the Koekelberg basilica was continued as if nothing was the matter. It had been initiated by King Leopold II, who had laid the first stone in 1905 even before Pieter Langerock's plans for a neo-Gothic cathedral were ready. In 1921 the new design by Albert Van huffel was accepted and fifty years later the completed basilica was consecrated.

High-rise buildings

Just as the flat roof, which had received so much attention in the period between the wars, high-rise buildings became the symbol of modernity to a greater extent than changes brought on by urban development or town planning. In fact, the supposed link between high-rise buildings and urban development is, even in the best of cases, non-existent. High-rise buildings in the first place reflect increasing mastery of new techniques and materials. The completion of Le Corbusier's 'Unité d'habitation' (1952) in Marseilles finally established his reputation.

The battle concerning high-rise buildings as public housing started with the flats in the Luchtbal district in Antwerp, designed by Hugo van Kuyck (1902-1975) just before the war and completed, in a slightly altered version, in 1955. Aligned in order of battle, completely disconnected from the urban context, these block of flats are impressive witnesses to the new age. Partly because of the political factors that determined their allocation the Luchtbal complex became the cause of a fiery conflict between Christian Democrat and Socialist factions. High-rise buildings were supposed to express a free, joyous, socialist lifestyle. Hendrik de Man, one of the pioneers of the socialist movement in Belgium, had already praised high-rise architecture as a sign of cultivation and the rejection of egotism.

This contrast can even be seen in legal texts, for instance in the discussion surrounding garden cities in the 1920s, when the Moyersoen law discouraged 'collective' occupation of garden cities in favour of private home ownership. After the war it was a law drawn up by the Christian Democrat minister De Taeye in 1948, trying to encourage home ownership on as broad a basis as possible, whereas in 1949 the Socialist minister F. Brunfaut promoted collective housing with communal amenities.

The discussion reached its final climax with the construction of the housing complex on the Kiel area in Antwerp by the architects Braem, Maeremans, and Maes. By then the principle of high-rise building had been replaced by the social function of architecture in general and by its ability to contribute to a different form of society. Braem's project uses architecture as an instrument of revolution. Indeed, Braem redefines Le Corbusier's 'architecture or revolution' as 'revolution through architecture'.

It was not only in Antwerp that high-rise areas were created during this period. In Ghent a start was made to develop the area around the Watersportbaan in 1953 in view of the 1955 European rowing championship. In contrast to the Luchtbaan or Kiel districts in Antwerp, several seven- to nineteen-storey blocks of flats, as well as amenities such as shopping centres, schools, and clubhouses were informally scattered over the green. These were designed by a group of architects – including Geo Bontinck (b. 1903), Adrien Bressers (1897-1986), and Fritz Coppieters (b. 1897) – brought together by the housing associations involved. As has happened with most public or semi-public commissions, they show political rather than architectural

Hugo Van Kuyck
Antwerp, Luchtbal, housing complex, 1948-1961
(Frank Philippi)
In the wake of the northern extension of the port in the late 1930s Hugo Van Kuyck was commissioned by 'Onze Woning', a housing association, to design a residential complex with 2000 flats based on the principles set out by the CIAM. However, works were only started in 1948 and the last block of flats was completed in 1961. The photographer Frank Philippi was asked to depict the 'plastic effect' – as Van Kuyck put it – of the architecture.

Géo Bontinck, Adriaan Bressers,
Fritz Coppieters et al.

**Ghent, Watersportbaan, 1953-1965,
renovation Romain Berteloot, 1988**

(Bastin/Evrard)

In the area around the Watersportbaan in Ghent the stark composition of the Luchtbal district in Antwerp is replaced by a less rigid arrangement of tower blocks and discs trailing along the water. The separate elements were created by architects of various schools, appointed by the housing associations taking part in the scheme. The present aspect of the buildings depicted is that of the renovation by Romain Berteloot in 1988.

chracteristics. A number of dilapidated housing blocks were updated to the 'post-modern' era by Romain Berteloot (b. 1946) in the late 1980s. Is this supposed to be the evolution in architecture?

The most ambitious high-rise project is the 'Champ des manœuvres' in Liège by the EGAU group, i.e. Charles Charlier (b. 1916), Hyacinthe Lhoest (b. 1913), and Jules Mozin (b. 1914), carried out between 1951 and 1970. At the same time these architects designed a high-rise complex in Angleur and profited from the Liège tradition started by the Equerre group in 1936 when designing a residential area on the Plateau des Trixhes in Flémalle-Haut.

The 'Champ des manœuvres' complex is beautifully situated on the banks of the River Meuse, 'site pathétique de la région industrielle', but it is also practically isolated by a motorway. Apart from houses it contains a church, a medical centre, a school, playgrounds, and shops. Its homogeneous architecture, which is very fine, is almost pushed into the background. In keeping with the functional approach, everything seems to ensue from the pursuit of ideal circumstances for a self-contained habitat.

However, the question remains whether such an architectural arrangement is compatible with the way people live. The way in which its inhabitants deal with it in any case points to the contrary. The fate of Le Corbusier's 'Unités d'habitation' in Firminy and Briey-le-Fôret which, remaining largely unoccupied, have become totally dilapidated is sufficiently well-known. Are the chaotic developments seen on the left bank of the River Scheldt in Antwerp or the outskirts of Brussels the only alternative? Here, at any rate, there are signs of life, signs of life which are visible in Liège if only through the degeneration of the architecture.

Expansion

Apart from the breakthrough of high-rise construction, the architectural image of the Reconstruction is defined by the enormous expansion of industrial plants and public institutions such as hospitals, town halls, swimming-pools, and churches. In general one cannot speak of architectural ambition – there was no Olivetti in Belgium. In other words, the Belgian authorities stuck to their traditional ways. However, he who wants to see what he sees should beware. The exclusive vision of orthodox modernist architecture has blurred the image, which is why a number of interesting buildings have been excluded from history.

After the war well-known modernists also received public commissions. For instance, in 1947 Edward van Steenbergen was commissioned with a new town hall for Deurne. Braem considered him as belonging to 'a victimized generation'. Architects themselves had evolved in a way comparable to J.J.P. Oud, who had stirred up a storm of indignation among modernists. In the wake of the need for a 'new monumentality' architects had, whether consciously or otherwise, moved away from the radicalism of their pre-war work.

The prime example of the impressive expansion of industry, which knows no lord or master, can be found in Antwerp. Immediately after the liberation Antwerp was well on its way to becoming the largest port in the world. This growth shifted the harbour activities towards the north of the city and required the construction of new docks and industrial areas. All this resulted in a ten-year plan that was adopted by Parliament in 1956.

Before the plan became reality the port had, as Burgomaster Lode Craeybeckx put it, already bitten off quite a chunk of the polders. Polder towns were annexed and disappeared

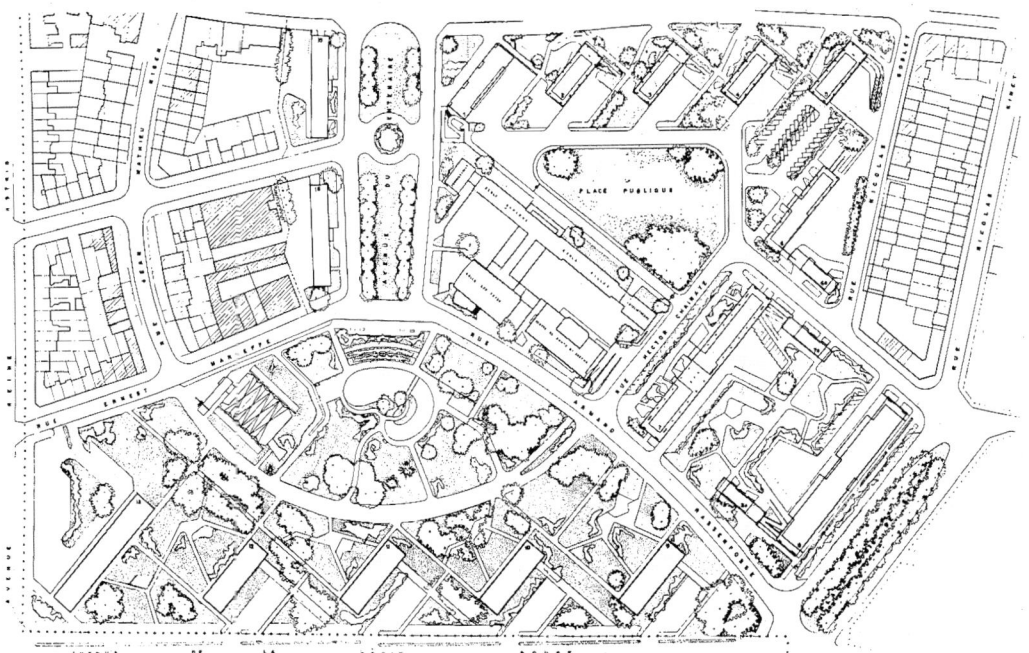

EGAU GROUP, CHARLES CARLÏER,
HYACINTHE LHOEST, AND JULES MOZIN
**Liège, Champs des Manœuvres,
housing complex, 1951-1961**
(Bastin/Evrard)
The most ambitious approach to a compact new residential area in the 1950s is that of the Champ des Manœuvres in Liège. It is beautifully situated on the banks of the River Meuse, from which it is unfortunately cut off by the motorway, and constitutes an attempt at creating a self-contained residential area with all the necessary public amenities.
Its construction involved advanced techniques such as prefabrication and heavy elements.

A circle of 12-storey discs, mainly oriented on an east-west axis, forms a protective belt around a 'place publique' and a park containing public amenities such as a church, shopping arcades, and medical centres.

VINCENT COLS AND JULES DE ROECK
Antwerp, left bank of the River Scheldt ('Linkeroever'), Imalso offices, 1954
(Bastin/Evrard)

The partnership set up by the architects Cols and De Roeck in 1912 carried out a substantial part of the extension of the port in record time. For this they built various industrial buildings, whose divergent specifications they treated with remarkable suppleness. The IMALSO offices (Intercommunale Maatschappij van de Linker Scheldeoever) demonstrates their approach.

HUGO VAN KUYCK
Antwerp, Bell building, 1951-1955, staircase
(Bastin/Evrard)

Not only the harbour in Antwerp knew feverish construction, but the city centre also saw the implantation of new industrial buildings. The Bell Telephone Manufacturing Company employed Hugo Van Kuyck to design a 65-metre tower block with an impressive spiral staircase.

EQUERRE GROUP, PAUL FITCHY, EDGAR KLUTZ, EMILE PARENT, AND ALBERT TIBAUX
Liège, Palais des Congrès, 1958
(aa50, Mil De Kooning)

The congress building is part of the development of the cultural infrastructure that the city of Liège wanted to realize as the completion of its reconstruction after the war. Through its variety of halls and its spacious foyer it can accomodate all sorts of activities, such as congresses, receptions, and exhibitions. A cybernetic column by Nicolas Schöffer stands in front of the building.

Antwerp, Hotel Nautilus, 1959
(Wim Van Nueten)

The Hotel Nautilus (demolished 1995) was completely isolated amidst the new port extensions. It had been built with material recuperated from the Expo '58 world fair in Brussels. It is a good example of the easy 'modernism' of the 1950s. Its belvedere, affording a unique view of the River Scheldt and the port as well as its bars and restaurants, made it a popular outing among the people of Antwerp.

leaving only a few traces, such as the spire of the church in Wilmarsdonk or Oosterweel. The improvised landscape of the port, the enormous chaos in which everybody involved seems to find his way blindly, may count as the model for the whole of the Belgian situation.

Practically monopolizing Antwerp, the firm Vincent Cols & Jules De Roeck – a partnership founded in 1912 for whom Schillemans and Braem also worked – designed a large number of industrial plants in the new area. In less than no time they built various power stations, as well as offices for Esso, General Motors, Ford, and a services centre for Imalso. Cols and De Roeck's almost anonymous work, which can still be enjoyed, may be compared to Bourgeois's factory building in Braine-le-Comte and some plants in the Liège region and the harbour in Ghent.

The centre of Antwerp likewise saw many changes, for instance Hugo van Kuyck's new building for the Bell Telephone Manufacturing C°, whose high bow serves as a point of reference in the city. The concrete spiral staircase in a glass cage behind the tower is an open manifestation of new constructional possibilities and of confidence in the Belgian building sector of the day.

The public amenities were humble compared to industrial investments. More about this will follow in the section on individual architects. Remaining within Antwerp, this is borne out by Paul Smekens' (1890-1983) 'Zeemanshuis', (sailors' house) which was inaugurated in 1956; its contemporary, Marc Appel and Jan Welslau's Veiligheidsinstituut (institute for safety); or the open-air theatre in the Rivierenhof in Deurne by Jos Schellekens.

In a comment entitled 'De overheid bouwt', published in *Bouwen en Wonen* (April 1954), Renaat Braem writes: 'There was a time when every new building put up by the authorities was a new stain on our beautiful country... We are not claiming that now, half a century on, the situation is any better – certainly not if one takes into account the monstrous "Spaarkas" in Brussels, the absurd colonnade of the National Bank, or the exterior wings of the Central Station in the same city. However, a new wind is blowing from the North, full of promise for a new blooming of Flemish architecture in a field where it used to set the tone, i.e. that of building for the community.'

The expansion was approached with even more fervour in Liège, as if they were aware of the fragility of the traditional industries of coal and steel. Even as late as 1967 Jean Lejeune, a local university professor, Alderman in charge of Public Works, and chairman of 'Le Grand Liège', still expatiated on the 'cité ardente' as the 'carrefour de l'Europe' in his book *Liège, de la principauté à la métropole*. This idea of a 'carrefour' (crossroads) was to be taken literally. In keeping with Van Kuyck, his plea also includes the connection of the city to a modern road network. Not a word is breathed about architecture. The new establishments of large companies in vast industrial parks along the River Meuse come down to pure improvisation. Moreover, even if a conscious attempt is made at real architecture, it is all

the sooner consumed by an urge to expand that can hardly keep track of its own evolution. Nor is the urge to expand contained by the boundaries of the city. 'Dans les années qui ont suivi la libération, Liège a d'abord vécu entre ses ponts détruits, ses carrefours dévastés, ses quartiers partiellement ruinés par les bombardements alliés et les fusées allemandes. Quand cette tâche fut quasi achevée, on constata que si la ville du XVIIe siècle n'avait plus convenu au XIXe, cette dernière avait à son tour cessé de répondre à l'évolution en cours et aux exigences prévisibles de l'avenir'. And Lejeune specifies: the streets are no longer suitable for traffic, there are too few parking spaces, the administrative and commercial infrastructures are inappropriate. Proposals for urban motorways, for the redevelopment of Place Saint-Lambert according to the plans by L'Equerre, and for the new Chirou quarter are shamelessly put on the table. 'On pressent les bénéfices que puiserait dans ces connexions exceptionnelles la vie commerciale et artistique du centre urbain et quel serait, du même coup, son rayonnement'. It is in this context that one should see the new Les Guillemins station (1956) by the Egau group, as well as the Palais des Congrès (1958) by the Equerre group in the Parc de la Boverie on the banks of the River Meuse, one of the most remarkable buildings dating from the period.

Restoration

The restoration of monuments and churches destroyed or damaged during the war actually forms a chapter on its own. At the time churches were considered monuments and were therefore within the scope of the commission on monuments and sites, or of whatever was left of it. The relation between modern architecture with its historical surroundings and the demand for architecture with a regional character is acutely pertinent here.

It came to the fore in the debate concerning the layout of the area surrounding the Church of Saint Gudule in Brussels, now Saint Michael's Cathedral. In 1950 Huib Hoste devoted one of his reports to the Royal Flemish Academy to it: 'Sinte Goedele en de Noord-Zuid verbinding' (Saint Gudule and the North-South [railway] link). It became even more poignant in the case of Nivelles, which had suffered greatly from bombardments on 14 May 1940. Victor Bourgeois paid attention to it in the *Cahiers d'Urbanisme* of 1953, under the title 'Destruction et reconstruction de Nivelles'.

The Romanesque abbey church of Saint Gertrude was largely destroyed. It was reconstructed according to so-called 'archaeological' principles by the architects Brigode and Ladrière in two phases: the church itself from 1948 to 1959, the west wing from 1978 to 1984. Jean Pierre Esther remarks in the architectural guide *België/Romaans*: 'The radical interventions – which closely resemble surgical treatment with amputations and prostheses – have on the surface purified the style of the monument to create the impression of a perfect Romanesque building. However, closer study of how the complex has come to its present state damps our enthusiasm. The church in front

**Oostduinkerke, Church of St Nicholas,
1952-1954**

(Bastin/Evrard)

Among the dunes of Oostduinkerke Jean
Gilson built a church as a hommage to
the Belgian brick, with references to the
traditional church architecture of the
interwar period. The other end of the
spectrum is represented by Jozef
Lansoght's 'modernist' coastal church
in Koksijde.

of which we are standing actually is the result of an approach dating from the second half of the twentieth century.'

Esther also reports on the western section: 'As an exception in the history of the conservation of our monuments, the final choice was left to the inhabitants of Nivelles through a referendum held in 1974... In this referendum three separate restoration projects were presented to the population by a specially formed body of internationally recognized historians. The choice consisted of 1.) the reconstruction of the Late Gothic bell cage with a high spire as in 1641; 2.) the transformation of the superstructure without a central tower between the two round corner towers; 3.) a 'Romanesque' solution with an octagonal belfry, inspired by examples from the Rhineland and the architecture of Cluny. It was expected that the people of Nivelles would decide on the first proposal because they were very much attached to the old cityscape with the pointed spire, which stood out in the surrounding landscape. Nevertheless, they chose the third solution, which saw its completion in 1984.' L.H. De Koninck drew up a number of versions for the western section of the church in Nivelles, which were 'devoid of any archaeological concessions'.

The same archaeological reflex can be seen in church architecture during this period. It is one of the few fields where outspoken traditionalism, similar to that of the houses in Everberg, persists. We have already mentioned the basilica in Koekelberg. It was a sign of backwardness in the eyes of the chairman of the 'Prévoyance Sociale'. He regarded the P.S. building by Hugo Van Kuyck (1957) – with the first screen façade in Belgium, built to counterbalance the basilica on the Koekelberg-Porte de Schaerbeek axis – as the symbol of the future.

1954 saw the inauguration of the church of Saint Nicholas by Jean Gilson among the dunes of Oostduinkerke, a 'paroxysm of veneration for the pointed arch'. Braem rounds off his sharp attack against this 'pseudo-pathos' as follows: 'Instead of the lovingly presented, naked truth, here we face a vociferous propaganda machine..., in which we cannot experience mysticism, nor notice anything of the redeeming clarity that should be characteristic of a truly religious building.'

Calculated, skilled, but lifeless traditionalism characterize the work of the Dutch architect Jos Ritzen, an adherent of the Bossche School. Yet in 1930 he made a convincing plea in the publications of the 'Katholieke Vlaamsche Hoogeschooluitbreiding' on behalf of 'inevitably modern architecture'. In 1950 Ritzen took on the construction of the 'Achelse Kluis', a Cistercian abbey, and completed the church of Saint Lutgardis in Tongeren. In 1955 Saint Margaret's church in Knokke was completed. 1956 saw the start of the theological and philosophical college of the Jesuits in Heverlee, an intriguing architectural confession in the midst of the triumphant modernism of the day.

In the debate surrounding modern church building, the discussion about architecture reached its climax half-way through the 1950s. Again it was Le Corbusier who produced the challenge with his Notre-Dame-du-Haut in Ronchamp (1955), in the same way as his 'Unité d'habitation' in Marseilles indicated the breaking-point of high-rise architecture. Reactions to his church in Belgian periodicals ranged from firm rejection to moderate enthusiasm. Braem noted: 'For architects today, Notre-Dame-du-Haut is the touchstone for all the virtues and vices of modern architecture.'

Model housing

The typology of high-rise architecture, the new infrastructure of roads, the growth of building area, industrial expansion, and increasing public amenities may be the most obvious phenomena of post-war architecture, but they are not the most important ones. The general impression remains one determined by the proliferation of private houses as well as by the activities of the 'Nationale Maatschappij voor de Huisvesting' (national housing association) and the 'Maatschappij van de Kleine Landeigendom' (small landowners' association) together with their local subsidiaries.

In 1946 the 'Nationaal Instituut voor de Huisvesting' (national housing institute) in Brussels organized an 'international housing exhibition', an attempt to promote the building of houses using modern technologies, such as prefabrication or modular construction. However, applications of these, e.g. by Willy Van Der Meeren, Walter Bresseleers, or Jean Englebert, were boycotted by the very same institution. Between 1957 and 1984 the institute published its own periodical, *Wonen/Habiter*. The housing associations concentrated mainly upon the realization of smaller residential areas and one-family houses. Their choice of location was determined, as was the case for high-rise and industrial buildings, by the availability of cheap building ground.

In 1953 the 'Société Belge des Urbanistes et Architectes Modernistes' (SBUAM) presented a show house designed by Michel, Brodzki, Bontridder, Palm, and Piryn – a whole mishmash of fundamental modernists. The annual fairs in Ghent and Liège, instituted immediately after the war, also joined in the promotion of 'modern' housing. The list of yearly winners of the Van de Ven Prize gives some indication of what was seen as 'modern' housing. In its report covering 1919-1969 the 'Nationale Maatschappij van de Huisvesting' actually managed to publish an inventory of its building activities without mentioning a single architect's name.

The architect's response

In the early 1950s, the years of reassessment at the first signs of economic stagnation in Belgium, the first voices of protest among architects went up against unchecked building activity. In 1945 *La Maison*, a monthly periodical on architecture, decoration and 'art ménager', was founded under the editorship of Pierre-Louis Flouquet. It was the perfect reflection of what Belgian architecture represented at the time. Nothing was left of the militant pre-war publications such as *Opbouwen, La Cité, 7 Arts,* and *L'Equerre. La Maison* was aimed at the consumer, whom it wanted to familiarize with the maze of architectural ideas.

The only periodical with higher ambitions, but no more than five issues, was *Architectura, Maandblad voor Urbanisatie, Architektuur en Interieur,* which appeared in Ghent in 1948 and included, amongst others, noteworthy contributions by Gaston Eysselinck. This ambition was taken up again by Renaat Braem in 1953, in his *Bouwen en Wonen, Maandblad voor architektuur,*

ALBERT BONTRIDDER,
CONSTANTIN BRODZKI, LÉON PALM, ET AL.
SBUAM show house, 1953
The idea of presenting a show house as a model is typical of the zealous attitude of those modernists who were hoping to introduce their blinded colleagues to real beauty. The model house is a prime example of aesthetic concepts in the 1950s, which were greatly influenced by the design of furniture and other household goods.

stedebouw, woningpolitiek, beeldende kunst, binnenhuiskunst en industriële vormgeving. Braem held out for ten years, then tried again in 1964 with *Plan,* only four issues of which ever appeared. At the same time K.N. Elno and Huib Hoste founded the periodical *Ruimte* in 1953, which lasted for two years.

In 1952 *Architecture* was started up with the aim of rejuvenating modernism. It was initiated by the circle around the school of La Cambre and was designed by Corneille Hannoset. In its editorial it states: 'The *Architecture* 52 periodical has observed: – the lack of doctrine in periodicals on architecture and town planning published in Belgium./ – the lethargy that has set in concerning architecture since the stimulus it received around 1925./ – the ever increasing grip of the authorities on construction and aesthetics./ The *Architecture* 52 periodical has set itself the task:/ – to revive the spirit of inquiry and experimentation among architects and town planners./ – to be more than an anthology./ – to regain the freedom of the architectural concept and expose the paralysing effect of the administration. The ways that we shall try to open up are those pioneered by the CIAM congresses. We know that the Charter of Athens will remain an invaluable guide to us for many years to come.' For a moment it looked as if a real architectural conscience were seeing the light of day in Belgium.

In the play of forces determining our present living environment the architect stays in the background. Indeed, he does not take the Hippocratic oath as doctors do, and yet he feels equally responsible for the well-being of his neighbours. We are not talking about the average career profile of the individual architect here, for since Vitruvius it has been known that the large majority of architects are bunglers. This probably holds true for other professions as well, but in no other profession is the need for self-criticism as inherent as in that of the architect.

The most remarkable fact is that architects continue to work. Indeed, practically everybody doubts their necessity or at the very best simply thinks of them as technically competent. The architect, however, is not satisfied with playing a mere technical role, which he assigns to advisors and other professionals. In his own marginal way, the architect remains committed to what he sees as a better or different world. His specific problem, in contrast to other artists, is that for this he needs the public, whom he despises and who in turn despises him. The architect needs the public in all respects, for it is virtually impossible only to build things for himself.

Architecture needs space. It cannot avoid taking up space and thereby supplanting something else, whether existent or potential. The space in which literature or music exists is endless. One novel does not push aside another. The space in which architecture exists is finite. This is why the architect has no choice but to impose his vision on others in the hope that sooner or later people will recognize and accept it, which seldom happens. It is much more common for a beautiful work to be adapted to suit the owner's own taste and needs in less than no time. Many 'master pieces' from the 1950s have already

been mutilated to the extent that they have become unrecognizable – that is, if they still exist. Our only help in such cases is old photographs.

Many explanations may be found for this age-old conflict, but we cannot escape from the essence of the dilemma: the architect is a troublemaker. This is the rationale of his existence. Modern architects dream of an environment in which everything is organized so harmoniously that its livability can only be guaranteed by authority, as in Plato's ideal state from which all poets are banished, More's Utopia, or the final outcome of De Stijl, a movement in which artists engineered their own superfluity. This holds true for formal architecture and even more so for its so-called non-conformist equivalent. Denis Roche said that 'la poésie est inadmissible. D'ailleurs elle n'existe pas.' Maybe architecture does not really exist either, maybe it all comes down to the apparently indestructible aura, the illusion, the persistent notion that architecture has to exist.

Gaston Eysselinck (1907-1953)

This dilemma of architecture was experienced to the full by Gaston Eysselinck. His project for the post office building in Ostend may be considered typical for the history of architectural practice after the war, 'a tale of hope and drama, both for architecture in general and for Eysselinck personally', as Marc Dubois put it in *De fatale ontgoocheling* (The Fatal Disillusionment) (1986).

Eysselinck was given the commission in 1945. The choice of a 'modernist' indicates the authorities' ambition to put up something that would be more than a banal construction. The first design in 1946 was rejected by the royal commission on monuments and sites. The commission's reputation in the period after 1945 has not always been untainted. They concluded: 'In a word, it looks like an industrial building and appears to be too exclusively functional.' Eysselinck reacted furiously. Indeed, he had designed a building that was functional to the last detail and conceived it according to schedule, but he had also given it, in his own words, 'a distinguished, fatally classical character'. He had taken great pains to elevate the ascetic formal vocabulary of modernism to mature monumentality.

Not only the commission rejected his designs. Jean J. Eggericx, the advising town planner of Ostend and himself an advocate of modernist architecture, who had together with Verwilghen in 1937 built the blocks of flats on Square Meeüs in Brussels – considered precursors of the post office building – was even more strongly opposed to the proposed design: 'J'ai l'impression que la ville d'Ostende sera dotée d'un édifice style ultra-moderne, modèle 1931/1936, aujourd'hui heureusement périmé et dont les matérialisations éphémères ne nous assureront même pas, en fin de compte, l'ultime consolation de laisser derrière elle de belles ruines'.

It was within this negative context that construction was started in 1947. The building was only completed in 1953, after both Eysselinck and his engineer, Mallebrancke, were prohibited by the minister in charge from setting foot on the building site. However, today hardly a trace of Eysselinck's relentless struggle can be seen in the building. Half a century on it remains one of the most distinctive buildings in the history of Belgian architecture. For the city of Ostend it is an 'urban fact', a building able to imbue its surroundings with force and character.

This is all the more so because it is a public building. Eysselinck was aware of the difference between public and private commissions. His building in Ostend demonstrates a kind of belief in the prospects of our time, of which a post office building is an appropriate symbol. 'Eenheid van de wereld door het postverkeer' (world-wide unity through postal traffic) says the title of Cantré's statue above the entrance. Without having recourse to external symbolism, without representing power in some form or other, the building expresses, through its outspoken materiality, a glorious perception of life, both collected and free. Whereas Jean-Louis Barrault blames architects for trying to capture the flexibility of theatre and life in stone, Eysselinck's architecture shows how this antagonism can become fertile.

An important part of the discussion around the post office building concerned the application of monumental art, in particular Jozef Cantré's statue. At the time the application of monumental art was a way to counterbalance leanness in architecture. Eysselinck too believed in the mediatory role that sculpture could play between architecture and the public. In October 1952 the Palais des Beaux-Arts in Brussels even housed an exhibition entitled 'De monumentale kunst in de openbare en industriële gebouwen' (Monumental art in public and industrial buildings).

This 'monumental' art was interpreted as 'mural' art, mostly relief sculpture, which had to enliven the bare surface of the wall. In Ostend Eysselinck wanted to reinvest the sculpture with autonomy by placing it as a free-standing statue above the entrance. In this he was following the example set by Le Corbusier's design for the League of Nations in Geneva (1927) or the design for the Kursaal in Ostend by Léon Stynen (1946). Indeed, he strongly and in the end successfully opposed the authorities' decision not to include the sculpture.

For the cooperative company SEO (Spaarzaamheid, Economie, Oostende – Thrift, Economy, Ostend), Eysselinck designed a large distribution centre with sales offices in 1950. It was situated amidst a block of buildings and formed the connection between Romestraat and Gentstraat. The part in Romestraat currently houses the Provincial Museum of Modern Art. It is a shame that the whole complex, with its inner courtyard, has not been saved. In Belgium this is the earliest example of a museum for contemporary art in an already existing building. Antwerp was soon to follow by Michel Gansard (b. 1950)'s conversion of a concrete warehouse dating from 1922. The Museum of Decorative Arts in Ghent received a partly new building and Koen Van Nieuwenhuyse's dubious plans for establishing the Museum of Contemporary Art in the Casino of Ghent are in the pipeline.

GASTON EYSSELINCK
Ostend, Post Office, 1945-1951
(Bastin/Evrard)
The Post Office shows the ability of modern architecture to create a truly monumental and urban appearance. Its compact volume is impregnated with spaciousness.

The 'dignified, fatally classical character' mentioned by Eysselinck also predominates in the interior. For the exterior he had approached the artist Jozef Cantré, not to decorate the building, but to help communicate the message of the architecture; in the interior he placed two large mosaics by Jo Maes in the entrance hall to demonstrate the function and meaning of the building.

The importance that Eysselinck attached to the coherence of the plastic arts and architecture comes to the fore in this sketch of a section of the Post Office building, which includes a detailed drawing of one of Jo Maes's mosaics, entitled 'Het postverkeer in de toekomst' (Postal traffic in the future).

P T T
PARKING

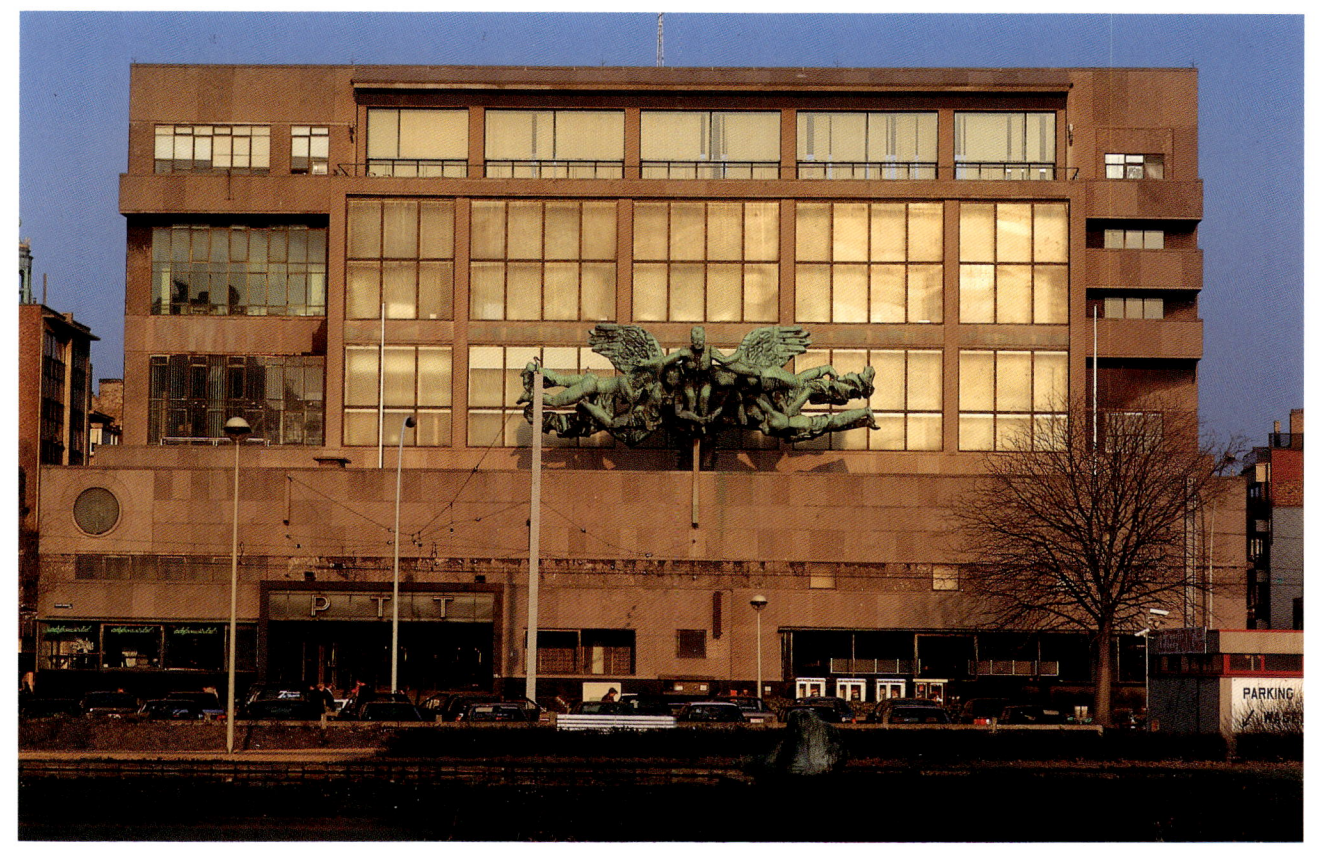

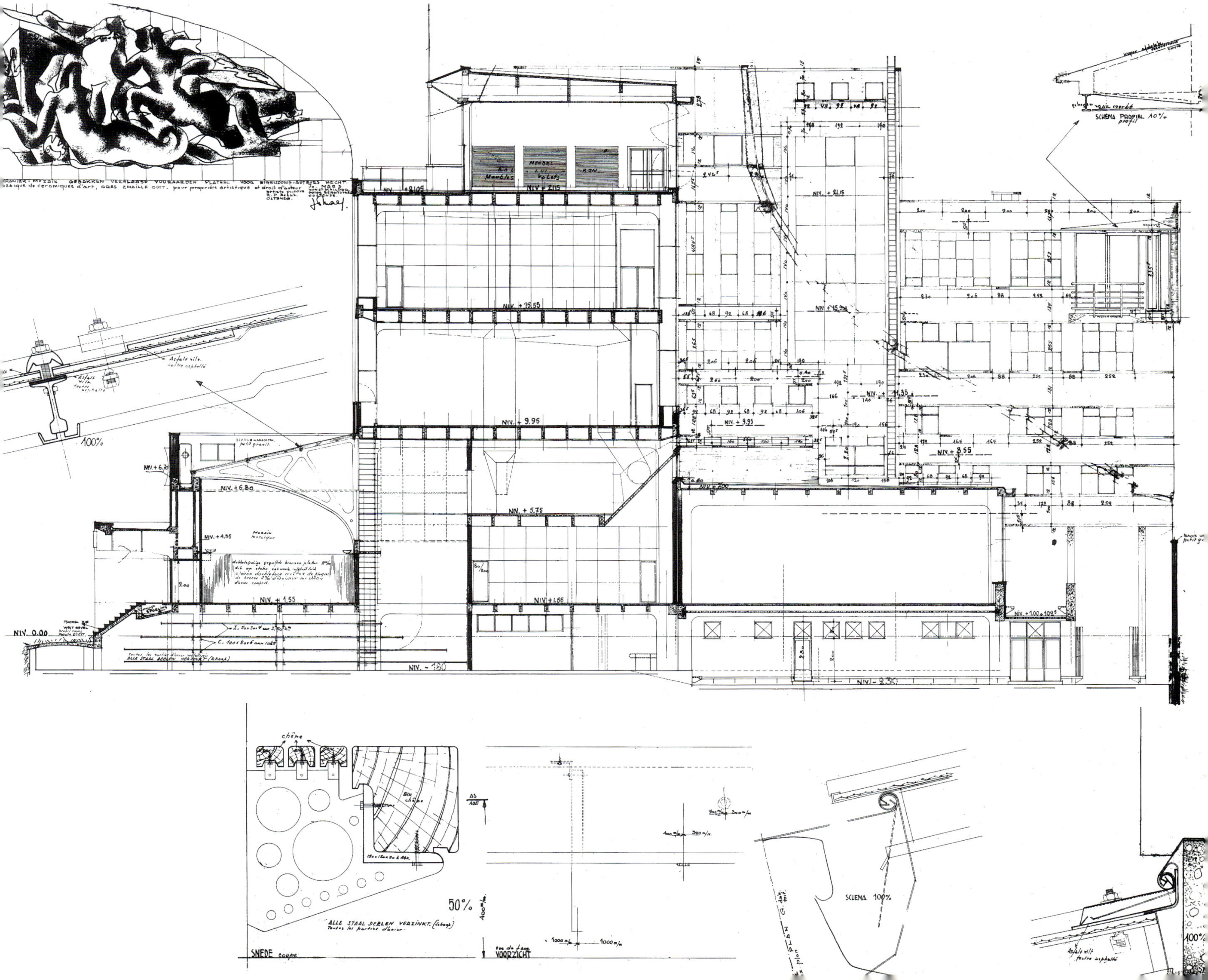
NIV. + 21.05
NIV. + 15.65
NIV. + 9.95
NIV. + 6.80
NIV. + 5.75
NIV. + 1.55
NIV. + 1.65
NIV. 0.00
NIV. + 21.15
NIV. + 15.95
NIV. + 9.95
NIV. + 3.55
SCHEMA PROFIEL 10%
100%
chêne
50%
ALLE STAAL DEELEN VERZINKT. (Schoop)
SNEDE coupe
VOORZICHT
SCHEMA 100%
100%

Apart from their headquarters, Eysselinck designed various branch offices for SEO. These demonstrate how urban and many-coloured his approached to architecture was. It is as if he purposely looked for difficult spots, such as for his own house in Ghent, into which to fit his buildings as flexible bodies. This also largely holds true for the Romestraat building in Ostend, which is a rare example of well-nigh impossible integration of an uncompromising architectural style. It is equally transparent and present through the subtle lines it draws within the space.

The work in Ostend was to be Gaston Eysselinck's last. Embittered by the hopeless struggle against the lack of understanding shown by the authorities, but even more by that of his colleagues, and broken by the sudden death of his friend Georgette Troy, whose headstone in the Ostend cemetery he designed, Eysselinck ended his own life on 6 December 1953.

GASTON EYSSELINCK
Ostend, former SEO building, 1948-1955
(Bastin/Evrard)
The building for the 'Spaarzaamheid, Economie, Oostende' partnership, between Gentstraat and Romestraat, came about in two phases. First a distribution centre with offices and a tea room was put up in Gentstraat, after which the large store in Romestraat was built. It is here that the Provincial Museum for Modern Art is now located.

A photograph of 1955 shows the original façade of the recently completed building in Romestraat. It was constructed according to the golden section, with a movable advertising column that also serves as a platform for window cleaners.

Victor Bourgeois (1897-1962)

In order to recognize the mastery, force, and refinement of Eysselinck's architecture we must remain in Ostend, the city of unfulfilled architectural ambitions, for it is here that Victor Bourgeois' new town hall was constructed on the Leopoldlaan axis on the fringe of the city centre in 1954. Bourgeois is one of the few modernists who realized an impressive œuvre, spread all over Belgium, after the war. Through his role at La Cambre, the school of architecture founded by Henry van de Velde in the La Cambre abbey in 1928, he also had significant influence.

The town hall of Ostend most certainly is not without merit. It is comparable to other buildings of the same period, such as the Palais des Congrès, or the Les Guillemins station in Liège. It distinguishes itself from the 'Feestpaleis', built by Christaens and Viérin on the site of the destroyed town hall on the Wapenplein in Ostend. Yet, it lacks the suppleness and intensity of Eysselinck's œuvre and even of Bourgeois's own pre-war work.

Together with the François Bovesse cultural centre in Namur, which Bourgeois built at the same time as the town hall in Ostend, it appears a bit hackneyed. In *L'architecte et son espace* (1955), Bourgeois unwittingly but pertinently describes the shift that took place here, 'de la justice à l'artifice, du naturel au poncif'.

In one of his last writings, 'Silence et architecture' (1960), he said: 'Nous devons admettre que l'architecture moderne est parfois tombée dans l'artificiel et le formalisme. En effet, tandis qu'en 1914, les architectes d'avant-guerre étaient en retard sur l'évolution des mœurs et de la technique, aujourd'hui au contraire, de hardis confrères prétendent tout inventer et tout devancer. Au lieu de sanctionner et d'exprimer ce qui est, en préfigurant habilement ce qui sera, il coupent tout lien avec les systèmes et les besoins, même évolués, d'aujourd'hui. Le réel se venge.' In fact, the last sentence echoes Le Corbusier's 'Pourtant, la vie sera toujours la plus forte. Il faut la comprendre et ne point marcher contre elle'.

As to the numerous, almost anonymous works that Bourgeois produced after the war, such as the retirement home in Kessel-Lo, the housing estate in Montigny-sur-Sambre, and the 'pouponnière' in the 'Cité de L'Enfance' in Marcinelle, it looks as if he had given up all the formal ambitions of modernism to let only the substance of the work speak for itself.

VICTOR BOURGEOIS
Ostend, Town Hall, 1954,
(Bastin/Evrard)
In contrast to the compact, urban Post Office by Eysselinck, Bourgeois conceived his town hall as a low, elongated complex. At the traffic junction there is a public wing in natural stone, with behind it an office block covered entirely in glass. Bourgeois himself said that 'the town hall is not meant to gather, but to radiate the roads at the traffic junction'. It has to embody open spaces.

VICTOR BOURGEOIS
Marcinelle, Pouponnière, 1955
(Bastin/Evrard)
Bourgeois, who in the 1920s started out with outspoken avant-garde architecture, moved away from the refinement of the 'International Style' in his substantial post-war œuvre. His later works give direct, even brutal expression to the elementary forces inherent in construction. This can be seen in the 'pouponnière', part of the 'Cité de l'Enfance' in Marcinelle.

Léon Stynen (1899-1990)

Ostend yields, apart from the post office building and the town hall, a third example of a public building, the Casino-Kursaal crowning the axis on which the first two are built. Among the modernist architects who started out before the war, it was Léon Stynen who most consistently continued his way afterwards.

The design for the Kursaal in Ostend originated during a very busy period in his career. He was given the commission in 1948 as the prizewinner in a contest in which Jos Smolderen (1889-1973), Maxime Brunfaut (1909), and Joseph Diongre (1878-1963) had also taken part. Just as Eysselinck, Stynen too had to suffer greatly before his design was realized in 1951. Now almost in ruins, there are plans to demolish it. Stynen himself, when he was given the final commission, made a number of counter-proposals as he did not find the location of the building suitable, but to no avail.

Stynen's concept of architecture was not proof against such a struggle. He was a refined aesthete who needed favourable circumstances and, above all, understanding to let his work flourish. The policy in Ostend, or in Belgium as a whole, was aimed at attracting big names, but put no trust in them. The Kursaal in Ostend did not turn out to be what Stynen had imagined and it has greatly suffered from careless use. Stynen already hinted at this in his inaugural speech: 'However, you must realize that this building will neither live, nor have its natural character unless care is taken over the quality of the use that will be made of it.'

The fact that this architecture was not fully developed comes to the fore if one compares it with Léon Stynen's work in Antwerp, even though here too there are variations in quality. 'De Zonnewijzer', a block of flats on the Mechelsesteenweg (1955), near the former Chrysler showroom that he designed in 1947, stands next to the EBES tower block he worked on together with Hugo van Kuyck. 'De Zonnewijzer' shows a rare equilibrium between the conflicts and contradictions of modern architecture. Its architecture is discreetly present, without attempting to comment on a way of life. It provides a spatial framework that only raises it from the commonplace through the reserved refinement of the building itself.

Many of Stynen's buildings in Antwerp remained fragments and the architect dreamt of a coherent whole, a city or at least a district, in which new architecture could irrefutably prove its superior beauty. Stynen passionately started on designs for a new development on the Wezenberg side of Antwerp.

Along the Antwerp ring road he planned a series of six tower blocks that, on a diagonal line to the motorway, would give metre to the passage of traffic and function as a modern town gate emphasizing the presence of the city. Inside the ring road a section was provided for a cultural centre situated in a spacious park. Of this project Stynen coincidentally executed only a few loose fragments, such as the former BP, now the BBL office block in the Rijswijcklaan (1960); the hotel in the

LÉON STYNEN AND PAUL DE MEYER
Antwerp, office block, 1960
(Bastin/Evrard)
As in his designs for railway carriages and mail-boats, Stynen applied industrial aesthetics to buildings. The supporting structure consists of a concrete core with an entablature on which the floors hang. This endows the building with a surprising and transparent lightness. It forms part of a set of three buildings designed by Stynen on the Wezenberg.

LÉON STYNEN AND PAUL DE MEYER
Antwerp, 'Zonnewijzer', block of flats, 1955
(Evrard/Bastin)

The 'Zonnewijzer' block of flats inconspicuously blends into the streetscape. Among Stynen's numerous realizations in Antwerp it is one of the most refined, in which Stynen the aesthete could give himself a free rein in working out both the concept as a whole and the smallest detail. It is an example of cultivated brutalism in which the rough materials used display a high degree of refinement.

LÉON STYNEN
Ostend, Kursaal, 1948-1951
(Bastin/Evrard)

The city authorities of Ostend, who own the Kursaal, have for years been wondering what should become of the building. In the meantime it is being terribly neglected. In fact, it has been an apple of discord from the outset, with Stynen himself unhappy about the result. Nevertheless, the Kursaal constitutes a prime example of the architecture of the reconstruction period, together with the post office and town hall.

LÉON STYNEN AND PAUL DE MEYER
Antwerp, 'deSingel' arts centre, 1959-1988
(Bastin/Evrard)
Originally intended to house the
conservatoire with two concert halls and
spacious foyers, deSingel has grown into
a prominent international arts centre.
The building is dominated by a
monumental concrete disc projecting
above the halls and forms a landmark on
the Antwerp ring road.

G. Legrellelei (1969); and finally, his testament, the Royal Flemish Conservatoire 'deSingel', whose first designs date from
1959. Most of his post-war work came about in collaboration
with Paul De Meyer (b. 1921).

The BP building needs separate mention as it demonstrates an aspect of post-war architecture that has received far
too little attention. It grounds Stynen's aesthetics in the technological evolution that fascinated the architect throughout his
career. He felt challenged by the new possibilities on offer and
wanted to master them through a suitable formal solution that
would subject their brute force to a refined appearance. This is
what he was doing when designing the Ostend mail-boats or
the TEE. His approach evinced openness and, above all, the absolute need for restraint. Stynen did not think in terms of conflict.

There is a striking contrast between the
functional rooms of the conservatoire
and the festive character of deSingel's
complex of halls. Screened from the
street by water, it is composed around a
set of spacious courtyards running
through below the building.

Both inside and out, on the roof and
terraces as well as between and around
the halls, an impressive landscape has
been created for the visitor to roam in.
With its sloping walls and floors the
space between the 'red' and 'blue' halls
make a dramatic impression.

The first designs for 'deSingel' were intended for the protected natural spot that Stynen had included in his development plan for the Wezenberg. Today the building finds itself squeezed in between the traffic on the boulevard and the ring road, with a railway on top of it. This was but one of the reasons why Stynen referred to 'deSingel' as his personal *via dolorosa*. It was a complicated scheme incorporating, apart from the normal facilities required by the conservatoire itself, two large halls that were to be used independently. These have allowed the building to develop into a vital arts centre of international repute at the instigation of Frie Leysen, with the architecture contributing its fair share. Moreover, it was also intended to house the offices and studios of the BRTN, the Flemish public radio.

The building in rough concrete is dominated by a disc with an enormous loophole, a monumental gate, which projects above the halls. Both inside and out, on the roof as well as between the halls, an impressive, accidental landscape has been created. One may see it as Stynen's homage to Le Corbusier. He completed his designs on his journey to Chandigarh, where the town centre was built by Le Corbusier, which left as great an impression on Stynen as the 'Pavillion de l'Esprit Nouveau' in Paris had in 1925. He openly included direct quotations in this generous design, an exception in post-war architecture. In the 1990s one of these quotations, the oval holes in the façade, was humourously reproduced by Stéphane Beel in his design for a door in 'deSingel'. This lovely pastiche clearly shows the extent to which architecture moves within its own scope and tradition and never just comes out of the blue. Stéphane Beel also designed the layout of the exhibition on Léon Stynen held in 'deSingel' in 1990 and demonstrated how a building can be treated as something exciting.

Renaat Braem (b. 1910)

Renaat Braem started out not with buildings, but with spectacular designs. These were not devoid of the influence of his teachers at the Antwerp art academy such as Jos Smolderen and especially Jef Huygh (1885-1946). In his commentary in *Bouwen in België 1945-1970* he notes: 'If "architecture" does not contribute to life, then it is no architecture, but empty fantasy or empty construction,' and further: 'What we have to do is to bring about new lifestyles, creating a new "contenu" by giving it a "contenant" that propels life forward. This would imply that the architect actively intervenes in life and that there is a point to architecture.' This could be the motto at the basis of Braem's diverse, uneven, but always inspired œuvre.

In 1927, at the age of 17, he made a sketch entitled 'Dorpskerkje. Glas en beton' (Village Church. Glass and Concrete), which contains not only the expressionistic élan of his architectural zeal and his future need for monumental commissions, but also some details of his later work. The initial idea and designs for a 'Lijnstad België' (Linear City Belgium) date from 1934. The city lay stretched out over a 100-km line along the Albert canal between Antwerp and Liège and incor-

RENAAT BRAEM
'Dorpskerkje' (village church), 1927
Braem's whole œuvre is prefigured in the sketches he made as a student at the *Academie* in Antwerp. There is a surprising contrast between his use of a diminutive ('dorpskerkje') in the title and the megalomaniac construction that not only demonstrates an expressionist *élan* and Braem's need for monumental design, but also contains details that can be recognized in his later work.

Kraainem, Brauns house, 1948

(Karel Vermeir)

This house in Kraainem can be regarded as Braem's post-war manifesto of a new form of habitation, at the same time bearing in mind that he rejected the one-family home as a superseded and archaic from of architecture. Indeed, the house contains the seeds of the dynamism that Braem was to strive for in his larger projects.

Rather than a static succession of rectangular rooms piled on top of each other, the ground plan shows an organism whose spatial development takes place both horizontally and vertically, and interrelates all the various functions.

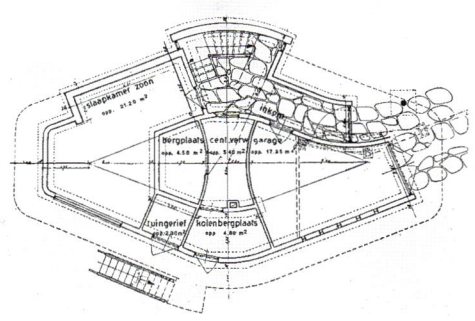

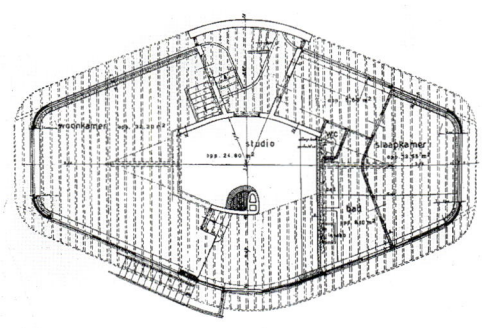

'Dodenstad' (necropolis), drawing 1935

As a part of his linear city – and this is rather unusual in view of the vitalistic approach of modernism – Braem designed a necropolis. Just as the other functions, it is directly accessible from the motorway. The high walls of the collumbarium and their larger-than-life figures function as the formal entrance to the domed hall and crematorium, worked out by Braem in detail.

'Lijnstad' (linear city), drawing 1934

Braem's linear city stretches out over a distance of a hundred kilometres along the Albert canal between Antwerp and Liège. The various elements of living, recreation, and industry are contained beside the streams of traffic in such a way that they do not interfere with one another. The linear city is supposed to enable its inhabitants to live in nature, according to their own nature.

RENAAT BRAEM, R. MAES,
AND V. MAEREMANS

Antwerp, Kiel housing estate, 1951-1958
(Bastin/Evrard)

The organic development of form applied by Braem on a small scale in his house designs reappears in the large residential area on the Kiel. Here the character of the private house is replaced by the affirmation of the collective whole, which is in turn embodied by the sculptures at the entrance as well as by the effect of the connecting elements between he housing blocks.

porated several components, such as habitation, recreation, industry, and traffic in separate zones so that they could communicate without interfering with one another. His sketches of a 'Necropolis' ('Dodenstad') date from 1935. With these drawings he presented himself to Le Corbusier in 1936 and was promptly taken on as an assistant.

Braem was to continue drawing as well as writing throughout his career. We have already mentioned the periodicals that he founded. Though a Marxist who once designed floats for the communist party's march in Antwerp, Braem brought out a pamphlet on Belgium at the Davidsfonds, a Roman Catholic publisher in Leuven, entitled *Het lelijkste land ter wereld* (The Ugliest Country in the World) and subtitled 'Wandelgids in de Belgische jungle, bestemd voor ontwakende slaapwandelaars' (A walker's guide to the Belgian jungle, aimed at awakening sleepwalkers) in 1968. His memoirs, published at Kritak in 1987, received the title *Het schoonste land ter wereld* (The Most Beautiful Country in the World).

In the Brauns house in Kraainem (1950) he brought the first manifestation of what he called a 'liberated lifestyle'. Its emotive form not only differs from his pre-war modernist houses, but also from those he was building on the Schotensesteenweg in Deurne at the same time. Braem enjoys playing various registers at the same time. Just as an eggshell – the ground-plan resembles an egg shape – the shell of the building contains the totality of life in it, which is no longer divided into different compartments, but unfolds with a global dynamism. This signals the end of the traditional Belgian house.

The same thing happened in Braem's project for the Kiel, a residential area for 800 families, the commission for which he shared with V. Maeremans and R. Maes in 1949. In *Bouwen in België 1945-1970* Braem drew a connection between the Brauns house and the Kiel residential complex. This link can be explained as an expression of his pragmatic approach, but the ideology behind this residential area is directly opposed to that of the private house. Such a commission can only be interpreted as an exercise in the use of architectural language, a simple sketch of the form to which the complex whole would have to correspond.

In the first phase, from 1951 to 1954, Braem designed a cluster of high and low blocks of buildings – contrary to the official redevelopment plan that contained a row of buildings such as in the Luchtbal area –, which together constitute a uniform whole similar to that of the Brauns house. The other blocks were added in a later phase, between 1956 and 1958.

The private house did not serve as his point of departure, but collective life and collective amenities in which the individual rather than the closed family played a central role. Braem continually wrestles with these conflicting notions of society and the individual. On the one hand he exlaims in the first issue of *Bouwen en Wonen* that 'Society has to protect itself from the excesses of individuals,' whereas on the other he celebrates the liberated individual who has the right to give his imagination free reign.

RENAAT BRAEM, JUL DE ROOVER,
AND MAXIM WIJNANTS
**Antwerp, 'Politietoren' (police tower),
1952-1967, photograph 1970**
The so-called 'Politietoren' is the only
existing fragment of a large-scale
administrative centre that had to signal
the radical renovation of the inner city of
Antwerp. The powerful architecture of
the tower, with its Gothic-like visible
structure, determines the city's skyline
together with the cathedral and the
'Boerentoren'.

RENAAT BRAEM, R. MAES,
AND V. MAEREMANS
**Antwerp, Kiel housing estate, 1951-1958,
photograph 1970**
(Karel Vermeir)
As in the linear city, the collective
character of the new way of living is
mainly expressed by the communality of
the soil, which is at everybody's disposal.
The housing blocks are placed on pillars
after the example of Le Corbusier's
'unités d'habitation', on which Braem
collaborated during his training period
with Le Corbusier.

He also sees functionalism as a problem. He cannot accept that the Lever building, belonging to a soap manufacturer, looks the same as that of the United Nations. 'The same morphological expression. Something must be wrong, it's architecture in a street without end. Function has to be explored in a way that also takes into account factors of emotion. Let us not amputate our souls! Functionalism has to be developed, the walls of an office block may illuminate? Those of a temple must sing!' And he concludes, in the same issue: 'The greatest problem at the moment is how to develop functionalism further so that it could express positive human values and ideals, as the best architecture in the past managed to do.'

Just as the Brauns house signalled a move away from the traditional house, the Kiel meant a break with the existing pattern of the city with its consecutive streets and squares. Here architecture is used as an instrument to bring to the fore a new way of life. This idea was explicitly promoted by the exhibition of model interiors, 'Het Nieuwe Wonen' (New Lifestyle), which was held in the new complex before its opening in 1953. Contributors were, amongst others, Jul De Roover, Willy Van Der Meeren, Walter Bresseleers, and Emiel Veranneman. The idea of a modern show house and the notion of social furniture were introduced here. They were to lead to the 'Salons voor het moderne sociale meubel' (modern social furniture fair) held in Ghent in 1955 and 1956.

In Antwerp no fewer than sixty thousand visitors showed up. Braem remarks: 'During the exhibition we could indeed see how the powers of judgment of "the man in the street" has been absolutely conditioned by the environment in which he now lives, to the extent that he does not possess the tools to assess the new concepts with which he is confronted without being prepared. So, the most natural reaction is rejection and a lot of goodwill and explanation is needed to conquer this.'

In the same period Braem was also active in the inner city of Antwerp. In 1949 Lode Craeybeckx had conceived a plan to follow the example set by Brussels and Liège, and to build an administrative centre. On Léon Stynen's suggestion Braem, Wijnants, and De Roover were asked to design it. Braem jumped at this opportunity to show how Antwerp too could be transformed into a modern metropolis. Indeed, he was not averse to the demolition of the existing inner city. His first proposal covered the entire area between the Schoenmarkt and Oudaan. Eventually only the block between Everdijstraat and the Oudaan was pulled down, saving Saint Agustin's church by Cobergher as well as the buildings in Kammenstraat. That this implied the disappearance of the much-loved Antwerp shopping arcade, 'La Cité', built by Cluysenaar in 1841 and of the less-loved Van de Ven showroom (1946) by L.H. De Koninck, did not matter.

Braem designed two tower blocks, connected to each other via a low wing on the Everdijstraat side. Of the whole project only one tower block came about between 1957 and 1967, which houses the police. This bare spot in the city centre has remained so, even with its current outline. The building's architecture refers to an approach also seen in the Torre Velasca in Milan by Belgioioso, Peressutti, and Rogers (1958), of which Joost Meeuwissen said that it 'is the most prophetic building of the decade in that it doesn't look like birds or boats, but like a building'.

Braem was commissioned with the design of the Heysel area on the occasion of the Expo'58 world fair, in Belgian terms an exceptional opportunity to work out his ideas regarding a new living environment. It was initiated by Fernand Brunfaut (1886-1972), architect and member of parliament, who lent his name to a law on collective house-building. Braem called it 'the only intelligent initiative related to this world fair'. As usual, he worked within a 'politically correct' team, composed on the bases of political alliance and language, including Victor Coolens (b. 1907), Jean Van Doosselaere (b. 1919), René Panis (1910), the Structures group from Brussels, and L'Equerre from Liège.

Braem wanted to create 'an island with deliberately underlined order and clarity amidst the chaos of arbitrary streets and incoherent buildings in Brussels. This could only be done by means of an orthogonal composition of lines and surfaces worked out to the last detail, which would create the monumentality of the whole. Some might find it too explicit, but it is meant to be a reaction against the apathy generally prevailing in the planning and architecture of the area'.

In the study *René Braem, Architecture,* published by the 'Archives d'Architecture Moderne' in 1983, Francis Strauven concludes: 'But what was constructed clearly demonstrates that architecture can come to nothing, not only through lack of content, but also through the predominance of ideology. Instead of being a basic condition and a source of inspiration for the project, ideology sets itself up as a monomaniacal message that has to be revealed through spectacular architectural rhetoric.'

There are a few more examples of Braem's attempts to carry out his ideas about a new lifestyle, such as Sint-Maartensdal in Leuven (1957-1961) in collaboration with De Mol and Moerkerke; on the Kruiskenlei in Boom (1965-1977); and on the Arenaplein in Deurne-Antwerp (1960-1971). Compared to the Brussels model district they are all of them only fragments. However, they do show Braem's evolution towards ever increasing monumentality in his expression of the architectural form, as if he could only realize his ideas in this hypertrophic way.

The house commissioned by Gerard Alsteens, a.k.a. the cartoonist Gal, in the Labélaan in Overijse (1966), probably most clearly illustrates Braem's last aspirations. It forms part of a series of so-called biomorphic buildings, such as the Middelheim sculpture pavilion, considered 'one of the most successful items in my œuvre' by Braems himself and dismissed as 'absurd, stupid, tasteless architecture' by the Italian artist Luciano Fabro.

The dynamism of the interplay of lines in Gal's house is reminiscent of the Arenaplein in Deurne. The wall sections

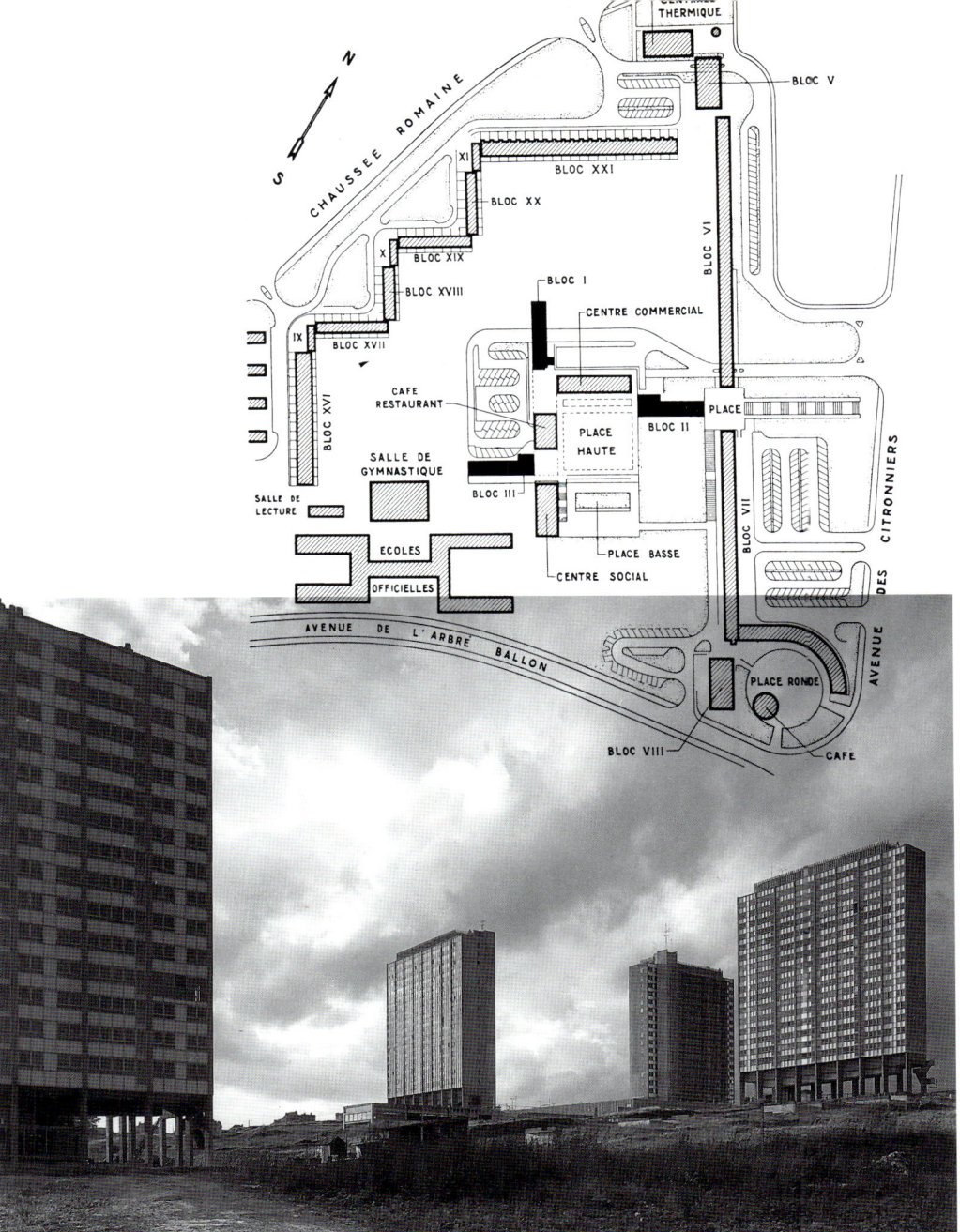

RENAAT BRAEM, VICTOR COOLENS,
JEAN VAN DOOSSELAERE, RENÉ PANIS,
L'EQUERRE, AND STRUCTURES
Brussels, 'Cité modèle', 1956-1969, photograph 1970

    Braem once wrote that the purpose behind the 'Cité modèle', designed on the occasion of the the Expo 58 world fair, was to 'form an island of consciously underlined order and clarity amidst the chaos of randomly laid out streets and, in Brussels especially, remarkably incoherent buildings'. This project too was only partially carried out. Many of the communal facilities that had to make this a model area and soften the stark nature of the whole were left out.

RENAAT BRAEM,
JAN DE MOL, AND MOERKERKE
Leuven, Sint-Maartensdal, housing estate, 1957-1967

(Bastin/Evrard)

    The sharpest contrast between the historical city with its closed development and the open structures of the new city was demonstrated by Braem in Sint-Maartensdal, situated in the centre of Leuven. On the site of a disused barracks he has directed the housing blocks in a forced perspective towards the central tower, whose sculptural crowning dominates the city.

evoke breaking waves, but it is especially the surprising interior which they conceal that is typical. 'The whole', Braem writes in his memoirs, 'opens up towards the light like a shell, around the centre formed by the chimney and the open fireplace.' This is a far cry from the 'modern lifestyle' formulated in the Kiel.

One of Braem's last works is the rector's offices at the Vrije Universiteit Brussel (the Flemish Free University of Brussels), started in 1971 and finished in 1978. The circle is complete. The ground plan describes an ellipse, just as the Brauns house. The murals in the interior are by the hand of Braem himself, just as he had designed the sculptures on the Arenaplein in Deurne himself. The theme of the paintings is the origin and further development of organic life up to the appearance of man and his struggle for harmonious order in society, the struggle for freedom. The rector's offices are designed as a *Gesamtkunstwerk*, not directed to the outside world, but inward, as the secret seat of a new religion that still has to acquire its form. 'We can only give a forward push here and there and, for a happy instant, express something of our hope for better times.'

Renaat Braem
Overijse, house, 1966-1969, photographs 1970
(Karel Vermeir and AAM, J. De Belder)
The house in Overijse belongs to Braem's 'biomorphous' period, during which he interpreted the organic shapes of nature to lend his architecture the dynamic *élan* also seen in his drawings and sculptures. As in the Arena district in Deurne, the wall sections shoot up like waves.

In the interior this sweeping movement changes into a protective gesture, a shell, directed at the regained centre of the house, the fireplace. This is far removed from the dynamic lifestyle seen in the linear city.

RENAAT BRAEM
Boom, housing block, detail, 1972-1977
(Bastin/Evrard)
Just as other projects for a completely
new habitat, the fragments of the
Kruiskenslei residential area in Boom
simply cannot create the desired effect of
a peaceful island of order amidst a
chaotic environment. Perhaps this is why
Braem employs increasingly emphatic
and emotive forms.

RENAAT BRAEM
Deurne, Arenaplein, housing estate, 1960-1965
(Bastin/Evrard)
Braem had great plans for the Arenaplein
area in Deurne/Antwerp.
A string of houses on the edge marked
the boundaries of the area. This was to be
punctuated by four high towers around
the 'Fortje', which would have been
transformed into a cultural centre. The
towers were never built. In later years
Lode Wouters, Fons Mostien, and Boud
Rombouts designed a number of housing
blocks for the Arenaweide, which
remained empty.

RENAAT BRAEM
Brussels, Rector's offices, Vrije Universiteit, 1971-1978
(Bastin/Evrard)
The building containing the rector's offices at the V.U.B. is shaped as an elongated ellipse, which according to Braem is 'the shape which in nature provides the most harmonious solution for the working of the forces of nature'. The building is oriented towards the interior, protecting the core with the murals in which Braem himself depicted his creed of liberated mankind.

Willy Van Der Meeren (b.1923)

Even if Willy Van Der Meeren belongs to a younger generation, his approach can be situated in the 1950s. His work provides much relief in the zealous atmosphere surrounding Braem's architecture. Willy Van Der Meeren is not concerned with architecture, which does not mean that he denies the meaning of form, though on occasion he makes murals or designs for stained-glass windows. In fact, he refers to himself as a 'building designer'. Fascinated as he is by the possibilities of our time, he wants to offer 'as many people as possible' a decent living environment in which their ever changing needs can be satisfied. However, he too is checked by what he calls the superstructure (reminiscent of Marx), the final, inevitably conservative image, which stands in the way when working on the 'infrastructural core' that life in the future guarantees.

Actually Van Der Meeren is no theorist, even though he is present wherever the debate on architecture is being held. He served on the editorial board of *Architecture, Bouwen en Wonen, Plan,* and *Ruimte.* His presence is primarily felt because of the freshness of his approach and his inventive ideas, which reveal the pleasure he takes in building even if the result may not please everybody.

In 1948 he graduated at La Cambre as a student of L.H. De Koninck and V. Bourgeois, after which he went to work as Gaston Eysselinck's assistant. He started out as a furniture designer, which gave him the opportunity to test the lightness of steel constructions. He was also involved in the foundation of 'Formes Nouvelles' and 'Form', two groups that promoted the distribution of modern, so-called better, furniture. His work with a variety of materials, such as metal, wood, and linen according to their own, often unexplored possibilities inspired him without leading him to dogmatic views. His preference for 'base' or 'vulgar' materials sometimes reminds one of Memphis or Alchemia.

A typical work is the studio he built for himself in Sterrebeek (1965). On a soggy meadow, which he could use for free, he stretched a tent over a temporary wooden construction suitable for a latter-day nomad. However, the most remarkable part of the lost construction was this: from the capricious tent shape, which had to be regular in contrast with the light, almost insecure structure it hid, there emanated a sort of mischief, the twinkle in Van Der Meeren's own eyes at the number of taboos he had broken in one go.

The same experimental directness can already be seen in his first house designs, such as the Demeffe flats in Auderghem (1951) or Vanooteghem in Evere (1952). It especially comes to the fore in his devotion to rationalization when building in the social housing sector, more particularly in the so-called CECA house, which he and Léon Palm designed for the European Community of Steel and Coal. It was presented at the 1954 annual fair in Liège for the first time.

Van Der Meeren turned to industrialization and prefabrication not on the ideological ground that they were the means of his day, but simply for the pragmatic reason that they were suitable for better and cheaper housing. He developed a steel structure, which could be prefabricated, just as Prouvé had done. With a minimum of fifty units, such a house would cost BEF 148,000, which even at the time was incredibly little. The interest shown by people in need of housing was great, but so was the oppositon from the National Housing Association. It remained a prototype, which was exhibited as a show house a number of times, and was only constructed in the small 'Vierwindenbinnenhof' settlement in Tervuren, together with the architect's own house.

The houses could be assembled from separate units and in various groups, and their interiors showed great flexibility as well. They were the demonstration of a new way of living, not a plea for formal renewal. Comparison with the 1953 SBUAM house mentioned earlier will be very instructive in this respect. The CECA house is one of the few designs with scope for further development in it. Van Der Meeren himself applied the principle again in a number of housing projects, such as that in the Astridlaan in Kraainem or the retirement home in Evere, both dating from 1957.

While Van Der Meeren was still working on this house, he was commissioned to build a block with 105 flats in Evere for a company called 'Ieder zijn huis' (A House for Everyone), a name he took seriously. Following Le Corbusier's example, he tried to break up the strict barracks-like pattern and conceive the whole as a group of independent houses.

WILLY VAN DER MEEREN
Sterrebeek, studio, 1965
Van Der Meeren's temporary studio in Sterrebeek is the clearest demonstration of his experimental approach. It does not start out from preconceived ideas, but is a pragmatic approach to a concrete problem without avoiding a certain degree of adventure. In it the various constructive functions are separated from one another and allowed to develop independently.

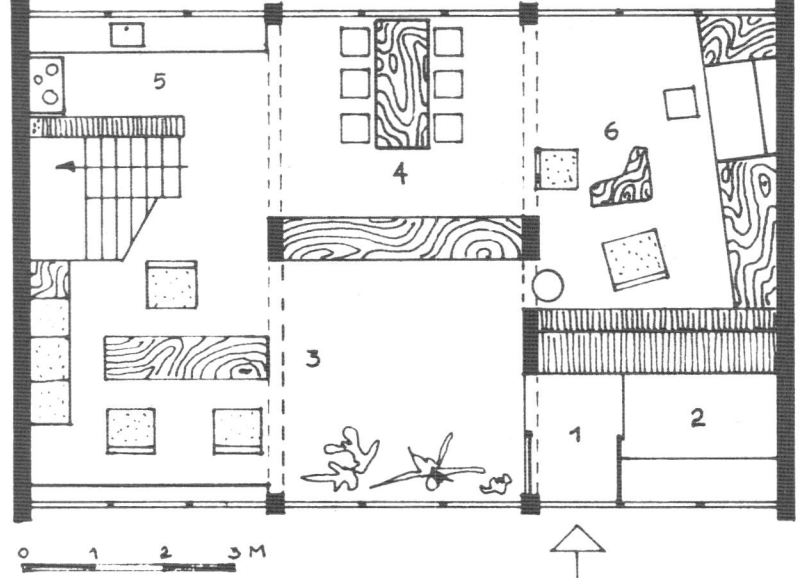

WILLY VAN DER MEEREN
AND LÉON PALM

Liège, annual fair, CECA house, 1954, demolished.

The CECA house, commissioned by the European Coal and Steel Community, took only one month to complete.
In order to provide a comfortable home at an affordable prize to as many people as possible, a high-speed building system was developed through which savings as to time and materials would generally benefit the occupation of the house.

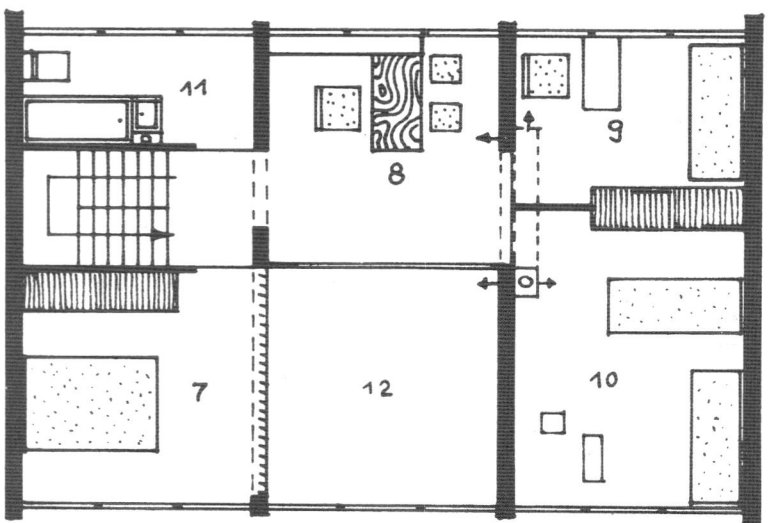

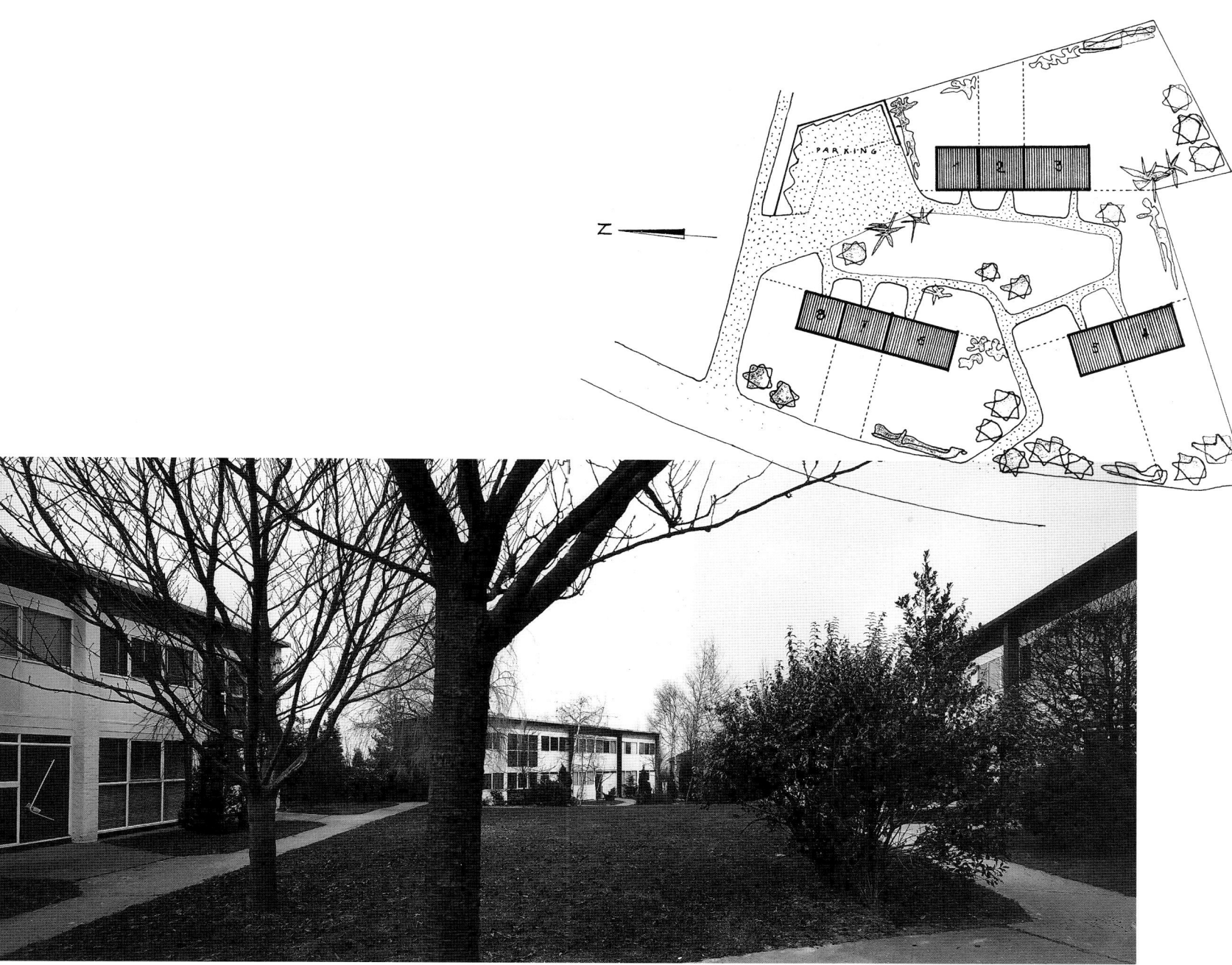

WILLY VAN DER MEEREN
Tervuren, 'Vierwindenbinnenhof', 1954-1956, photograph 1970
(Karel Vermeir)
Prospective home owners showed surprisingly keen interest in the CECA house, but the construction industry and housing associations were against it. The CECA house was only realized in the small 'Vierwindenbinnenhof' settlement. It consists of eight houses, including Van Der Meeren's own, grouped into three blocks.

The car park at the entrance keeps all traffic off the grounds and the communal courtyard is complemented by private gardens.

Yet everything had to be high-rise. As Willy Van Der Meeren admits in conversation with Mil De Kooning, the Socialist burgomaster of Evere Frans Guillaume 'abhorred all those little houses where for every procession candles and crucifixes appear in the windows'. Guillaume had first asked Le Corbusier, but he declined the invitation.

Van Der Meeren had no personal illusions as to the socialist ideals of high-rise construction. Referring to Evere, he wrote towards the end of the 1950s: 'High-rise architecture is – from a human point of view – doomed to fail if it does not actually take into account social life. This does not refer only to common facilities such as a laundry or playgrounds for the children as such, but to a space where the occupant can satisfy his need to meet other people. Think of the promenades under plane-trees in the south of France... In my view it would suffice to transpose this to high-rise architecture to make a great step forward. Despite the spacious walkways and the "three-ply" concept behind the flats in Evere, I have not been a hundred percent successful in this regard.' It never came to an in-depth discussion on the various types of high-rise architecture and Van Der Meeren did not have the opportunity to build on this experience.

Tervuren, 'Vierwindenbinnenhof', 1954-1956, sketch

A colourful evocation of the Utopian dream that this modest ensemble was supposed to reflect. In the distance we can still see the church spire, evidence of a past civilization. The monument of the new civilization is the communications mast in the centre of the square.

In 1967 he built the HBK headquarters in Antwerp, one of his most suited works, a shopping centre in Marke, and in 1971 the halls of residence on the VUB campus in Etterbeek. But as is the case for most of his colleagues, the majority of his works are private houses. In this field his experimental approach has had lasting effects.

One of these houses, designed in 1962 for Maurice Roelants on the Tomberg in Sint-Martens-Lennik, has acquired a wider reputation through its remarkable form and now belongs to the classics of Belgian post-war architecture. Here too, there is no added symbolism. Its shell-like construction heralds the radical break between the protective roof and the shelter below it as seen in the 1965 studio. The architect's point of departure could have been the concrete canopy above the entrance to the block of flats in Evere.

'The location, the view – up to twenty kilometres – and the unity with nature', Van Der Meeren says, 'meant that special attention had to be paid to the occupants' sense of security. An egg-shaped shell offered a lot of solutions. The most sloping shell is directed to the west and creates the impression that the low, fast-moving clouds cannot get hold of the roof. On the other hand one can see these clouds disappear towards the east through the split between the two shells. So, inside one can experience the interplay of the clouds.' 'The house is situated on top of a hill and has a lovely view in all directions. As an onlooker one perceives the house and the landscape as a whole, though from the inside one feels part of the whole.' It is as if the problem of living does not exist.

Together with the contractor and engineer M. Smets (specializing in prefabricated building components) and the engineer A. Mallebrancke a special system of finished floors and façade components was devised. As this saved both time and materials, it meant that the maximum could be invested in the comfort of the housing units.

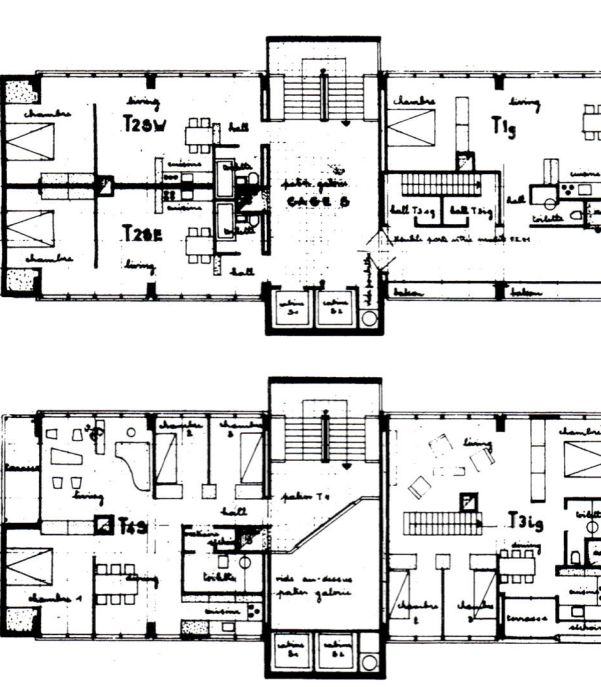

WILLY VAN DER MEEREN
Evere, block of flats, 1954-1960
(Bastin/Evrard)

In the case of this block of flats containing 105 housing units, an unprejudiced approach to the scheme and the application of the most economical – and therefore quickest – methods of construction have led to the remarkably powerful shape that distinguishes it from most other buildings of this kind. The composition is clearly reflected in the differentiated façades.

The interior of the housing unit in the block of flats is closely related to that of the CECA house. Whilst respecting the need for privacy, the focus is on the spatial coherence of the various parts of the house.

Inspired by Le Corbusier's 'Unité d'habitation', Van Der Meeren introduced a three-ply system. From the galleries on the north, between the two vertical staircase wells, the housing units can be accessed on three different levels.

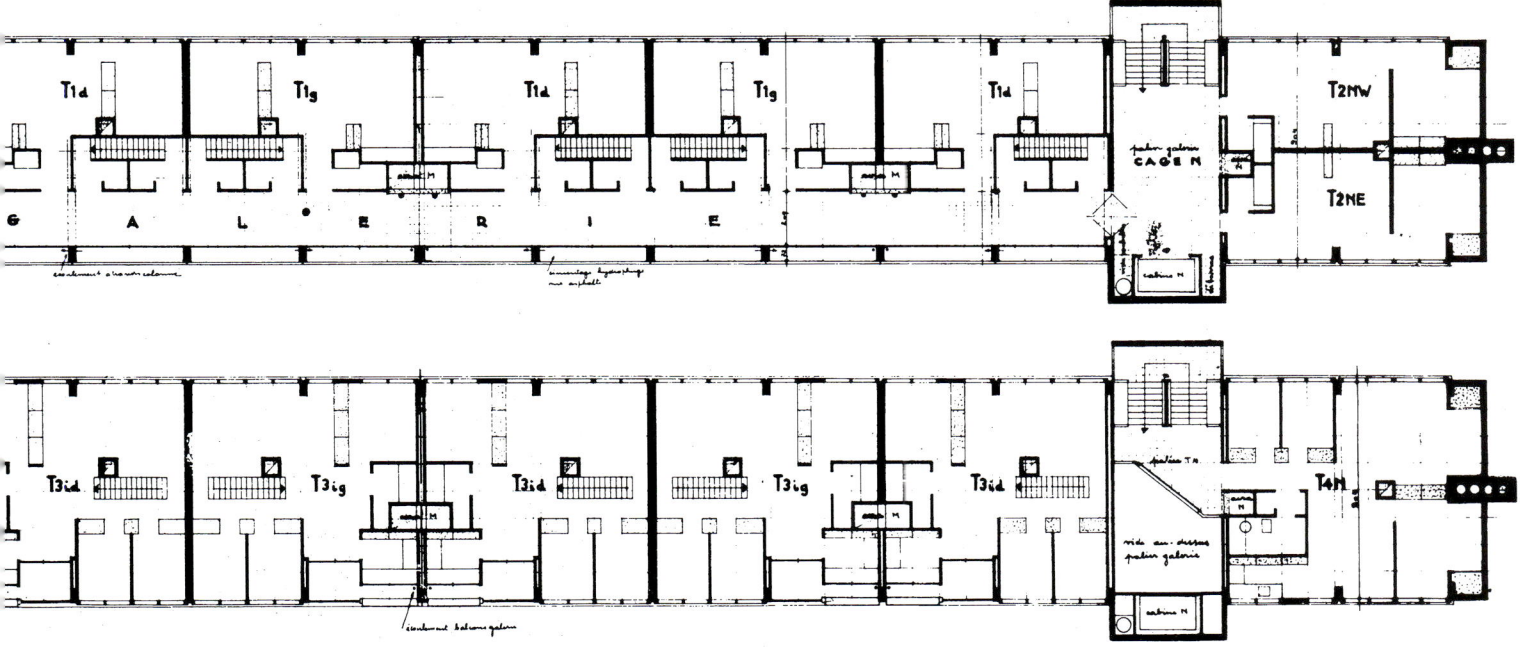

Evere, Clos des Lauriers, residential area,
1957

(Bastin/Evrard)

The principle of the CECA house reappears in this group of fifty houses for the elderly. On the fist floor the houses open up onto galleries. The vaulted stairs are a remarkable feature, reminiscent of the canopy of the block of flats in Evere and the Roelants house.

Sint-Martens-Lennik,
Maurice Roelants house, 1962

(Wim Van Nueten)

'Two roof shells in armoured concrete, cast on a lost form of compost bricks, between which the main reinforcement has been introduced. These stones, as all armoured concrete, remain visible.' This is how Van Der Meeren described the construction. Maurice Roelants continues: 'As to the outward appearance of the house, I wanted to see and feel the roof construction as a homely space and an element full of atmosphere, such as one can still sometimes see in old barns with pointed gables.'

Roger Bastin (1913-1986)

If Willy Van Der Meeren can be called an odd man out in the context of Belgian architecture, then Roger Bastin is its average representative, 'flawless', as Bontridder characterized his work. If such a thing as a Belgian tradition exists, Roger Bastin's œuvre is a case in point.

Bastin was trained at La Cambre in the 1930s under Henry van de Velde and teachers including V. Bourgeois, R. Verwilghen, and J.J. Eggericx. He became an aesthetic advisor to the Commission in charge of the Reconstruction of the province of Namur during the war and in turn trained a number of younger architects, such as Vandenhove and Kroll.

In *Bouwen in België 1945-1970* he summarized the influences he had undergone: his initiation in modern architecture at La Cambre, his introduction to the church architecture of the Rhineland by men such as Rudolf Schwarz, Emil Steffann, and Gottfried Böhm, as well as to the Scandinavian architecture of Gunnar Asplund and Alvar Aalto. 'The general atmosphere after the war', Bastin writes, 'was also largely determined by the obsessive presence of the unapproachable Le Corbusier. All these influences were tempered by my love for rural constructions, their integration within their surroundings, their unity, and their modesty.' And stoically: 'Like all architects I reply with my own means to more or less convenient questions that are formulated in a more or less understandable way by those in a position to build.'

His first effort after the war is characteristic. Together with Jacques Dupuis he completed the church of Saint Alena in Saint-Gilles (Brussels), inspired by Gottfried Böhm. He also designed the 'Port Autonome' at the Quai de Maestricht in Liège, a typical form of the weak-kneed modern regionalism also seen in Edward van Steenbergen's post-war work. There is little in these buildings that point to his later development.

He reached a fine balance in the series of around thirty houses called 'Le Vinâve du Vieux Moulin' and 'Cours Saint-Quirin' in Malmédy (1947), where he had been appointed town planner. They are simple, yet full of character, even surprising because of the curved canopy above the first floor.

The commission for these houses came from ESMA, a company for whom Bastin carried out several other projects. His œuvre is characterized by large commissions. From the ecclesiastic side: the extension of the seminary in Floreffe, the new 'Grand Seminaire' of Namur in Salzinnes, the interracial college of Bujumbura, the Benedictine convent in Rixensart, the 'Civitas Dei' pavilion for the Vatican at the Expo'58 world fair, the pilgrimage centre in Beauraing, and several churches, the best known of which is that of Heer-Agimont (1961). But also from the public authorities: work on the campus in Sart Tilman and Louvain-la-Neuve, the Belgian embassy in Helsinki, the museum in Marimont, and the Museum of Modern Art on the Mont des Arts in Brussels. Bastin remains the most convincing in a few houses from early in his career, for instance the Jadoul house with doctor's surgery in Villance (1954) and his own house in Namur (1959), built in a timeless architectural style

ROGER BASTIN AND JACQUES DUPUIS
Malmedy, Vinave du Vieux Moulin, residential area, 1947

(Bastin/Evrard)

In these houses, built for the employees of an electricity company, there is a beautiful balance between the rural building tradition and the need for innovation.

The small groups of houses are loosely arranged to form a sort of sheltered environment.

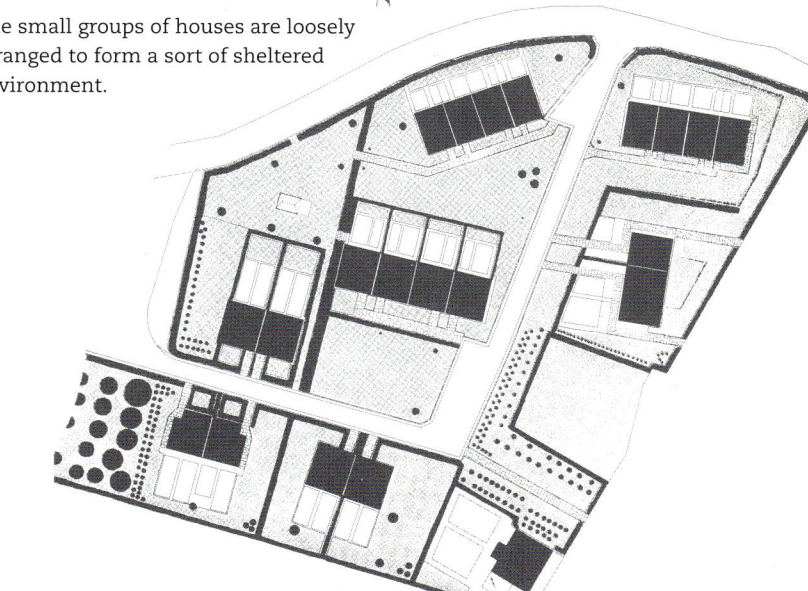

that does not reject modern attainments, but discreetly integrates them with tradition in a modest, yet masterly way.

The seminary in Salzinnes (designed in 1958 and completed in 1967) and the convent in Rixensart (1965-1967) clearly show Le Corbusier's influence, not only in the design and use of materials, but more specifically in his daring approach and their majestic presence. Abbé André Lanotte rightly refers to the 'Grand Seminaire' as 'un fair urbanistique'. All the inconsistencies in the ground plan or weaknesses in the composition disappear behind the imposing gesture with which the architecture dominates the landscape on the banks of the River Sambre.

However, the seminary does not possess the tension present in Le Corbusier's formal vocabulary, which it takes over merely to prove something. Here the idea was to show that religious architecture can be contemporary. Just as in Le Corbusier's convent in La Tourette, the designs for the seminary had been superseded even before the building was in use. The Benedictine convent in Rixensart realizes, on a smaller scale, the same qualities of landscape. Bastin understood the principles of regional architecture; he did not make the building disappear in the landscape, but let the landscape originate from the building.

In 1962 he was commissioned to build the new part of the Museum of Mariemont in association with Charles Gauquié. It is based in the Warocqué château, which was built by Tilman François Suys in 1833 and destroyed by fire in 1960. A fragment of the old castle was integrated with the new architecture, though as a foreign body. There is no trace of the move towards regionalist integration. The new museum develops into a three-dimensional interplay of closed and open, smooth and rough, supporting and floating surfaces, as if it were an immense sculpture.

The construction of the Museum of Modern Art in Brussels was a tragical episode in Bastin's career. What he had expected to be his climax turned out to be a painful compromise. In his report to the Belgian Royal Academy of Fine Arts in 1979 Bastin himself referred to 'Les projets pour le Musée d'Art Moderne à Bruxelles ou l'architecture entravée'. He started in 1967 and together with Leo Beeck developed a project that was officially approved in May 1973. But then all hell broke loose. The

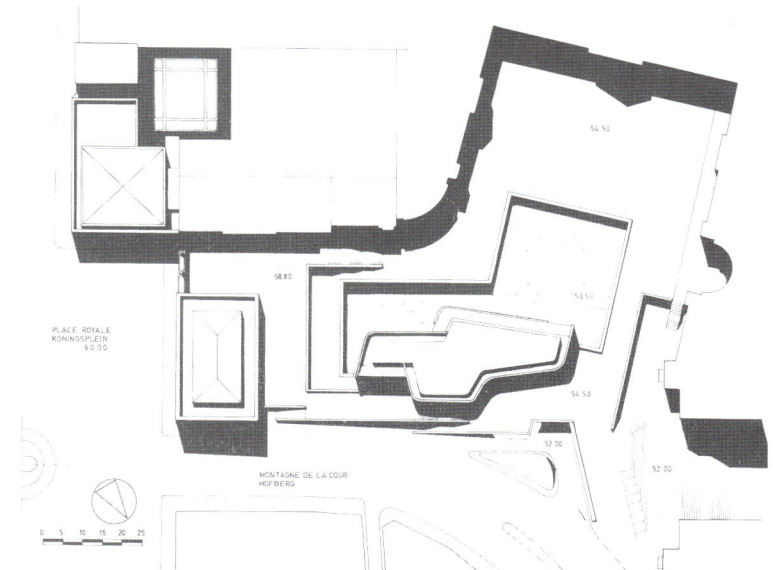

ROGER BASTIN AND LEO BEECK
Brussels, Museum of Modern Art, 1973-1984
(Bastin/Evrard)

Apart from the museums in Buzenol and Deinze, the museum in Mariemont and the Museum of Modern Art in Brussels are the only new museums that have been built in Belgium since 1945. The museum in Brussels caused a storm of protest and drew attention to the problem of new architecture in an old city. In the end it almost completely disappeared under the ground, with a huge light well as its point of focus.

With reference to the museum Bastin spoke of 'confined architecture'. The rejected design 'with its free and twisting shapes, an echo of its surroundings' clearly demonstrates the architect's views on architecture and its potential role in the development of the city today.

ROGER BASTIN AND GUY VAN OOST

Mariemont, museum, 1962-1967

(Bastin/Evrard)

Fragments remaining from the château of
Waroqué (built by Tilman François Suys
in 1833), which burnt down in 1960,
were integrated in an autonomous
composition emphasizing the interplay
between closed and open elements,
smooth and rough materials, supporting
and suspended surfaces, rather than
spatial qualities.

Roger Bastin and Pierre Lamby
Rixensart, convent, 1965-1968
(Bastin/Evrard)
This convent of the Benedictine nuns is a gesture within the landscape in the first place: through its powerful form it defines the features of the environment. The architecture possesses something of the elementary and timeless quality of rural constructions. The living quarters are situated around the cloister and the church. As in Le Corbusier's La Tourette, the conventual cells are on the outside.

main criticism was aimed at the demolition of the block of houses between the Montagne de la Cour and the Rue du Musée. This criticism was not entirely unjustified. The 'free and winding shapes, like an echo of the surroundings', to quote Bastin, were not only devoid of any intrinsic power to set it off against the classical façades of the Montagne de la Cour, but they tore apart the elegant uniformity of the quarter without mercy. Neither the casualness and ease of his own house, nor the visual force of the Mariemont museum is present here. In the end it was determined that the block of houses should be saved and that the whole museum had to be built underground, around a light-well. The museum was inaugurated amidst great festivities on 25 October 1984, after the block of houses had been demolished after all.

Jacques Dupuis (1914-1984)

Jacques Dupuis was one of the most fascinating characters among the group of post-war architects. Although they were long-time partners, he was Roger Bastin's exact opposite. He was an architect in heart and soul, but thought very little of architecture as an end in itself. He did not spend long hours behind the drawing-board, but preferred to travel in order to observe people and mingle with them. He photographed people rather than architecture, which he only did when he had found a noteworthy construction detail.

After he graduated from La Cambre under Eggericx, De Ligne, and Bourgeois in 1938 he designed the grandstand in his native town of Quaregnon together with M. Lhoir and J. Van Laethem. The construction was as elegant as it was daring, which demonstrates the accuracy of his hand. It is the personification of constructive logic.

From 1945 to 1950 he worked in partnership with Roger Bastin and in 1959 with Albert Bontridder. He also collaborated with Simonne Guilissen-Hoa (b. 1916) and designed a number of remarkable works with her, amongst which the kindergarten in Frameries (1953). In it his nonconformist approach, which had already brought him into conflict with Henry van de Velde at La Cambre during his student days, comes to the fore. Here the child's world is included in a 'post-modern' blend of every possible style and form.

In 1947 he designed his first 'liberated' villa, commisioned by P.V. Dupuis in Woluwe-Saint-Pierre, the architecture of which shifts away from orthogonal composition. This denotes the creation of a new type of house that was to become Dupuis's hallmark and whose influence should not be underestimated. The house no longer is a closed volume, but opens up towards the landscape on all sides. The effect is created not so much through the use of open surfaces, but by the accentuation of the directions which these surfaces, whether open or closed, indicate while fanning out from a centre that itself is in constant motion. This dynamic can be clearly seen on the ground plan, but can also be sensed in the interior, which 'contains no more dead corners', as Pierre Puttemans put it.

There is little left of the traditional house and its closedness. As a whole the grounds on which the villa stands form an exclusive living environment. With its specific means the architecture lends it openness and closedness, distance and proximity, height and lowness, colour and rhythm, rest and motion, structure and articulation. It is reminiscent of the décor of a lost or unwritten play, fascinating, mysterious exactly because of its convincing obviousness.

The same holds true for houses built on less suitable grounds, for instance in the city. Here too Dupuis wants to suggest dynamics through ingenious interventions and to escape from the rigidity of architecture. The painter Gaston Bertrand's studio in Uccle (1949) is a good example of this.

However, it was not until the 1950s or early 1960s that his name was finally established on account of a number of large villas, such as the Franeau house in Erbisoeul (1960) and

JACQUES DUPUIS AND
SIMONNE GUILLISSEN-HOA
Frameries, Kindergarten, 1953
(Alexis)

Dupuis's non-conformism, which took no notice of architectural doctrines and did not burden architecture with unattainable ambitions, comes to the fore in the kindergarten he designed together with Simonne Guillissen-Hoa. The world of the child is a welcome opportunity to experience the inventive freedom of architecture in an informal blend of every possible style and form.

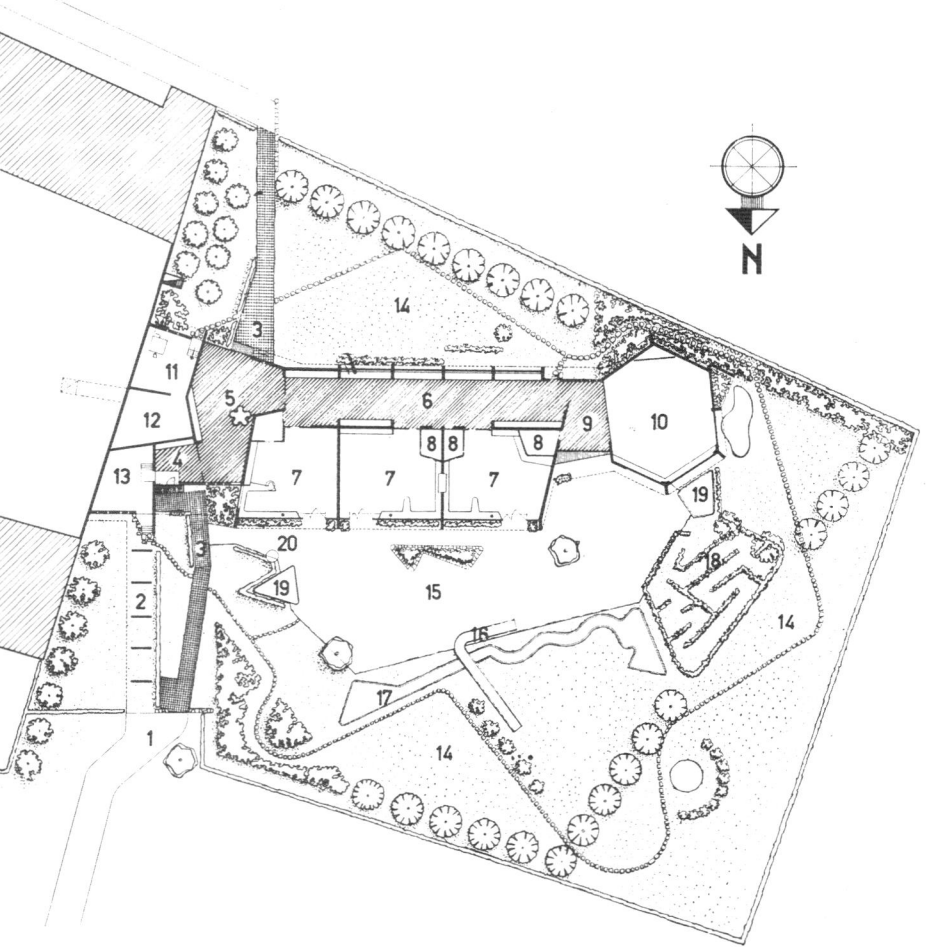

Jacques Dupuis
**Woluwe-Saint-Lambert, Le Parador, house,
1947**

(Bastin/Evrard)
With 'Le Parador' – inn, lodging, an
expressive term indicating the shift away
from the traditional way of living –
Dupuis introduces a liberated form of
habitation in which both traditional and
modern factors have a role to play.

The house is a closed volume no longer,
but opens up to the landscape on all
sides.

The charms of 'middle-class' life are
incorporated in a new form of dynamism.
A great deal of attention is paid to
particular details, which function as focal
points in the flowing space, and to the
preciousness of the materials.

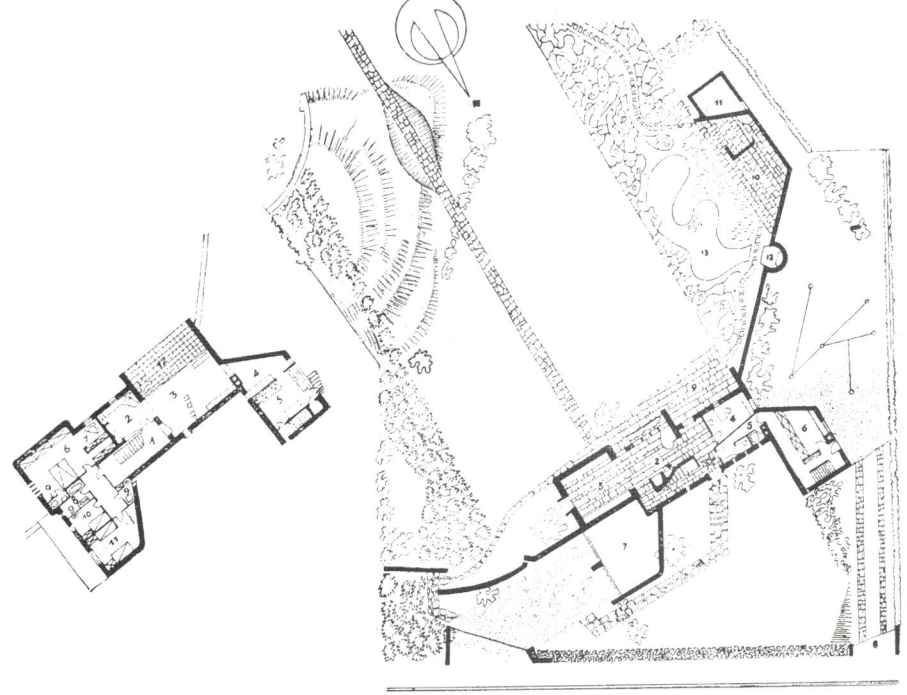

the Vandervaeren house in Herent (1959), both in collaboration with Bontridder. On the villa in Erbisoeul the designers wrote: 'La maison isolée, semblable à l'homme isolé, souffre comme lui du même manque de référence à la vie collective et au monde extérieur. Les servitudes de l'environnement ne jouent pas le rôle négatif, qui leur est attribué généralement. Elles sont en réalité des points d'appui, de référence et de justification de toute composition architecturale. Leur absence oblige l'architecte à créer dans le vide un univers dont le caractère enveloppant devra suppléer au cadre manquant... afin qu'en tout endroit l'architecture soit une présence forte de protection et d'apaisement'.

It would be useless to look for any development in this work. Using the same architectural elements, which are still uninfluenced by the dogmatism of modernism, a new configuration is created each time, adapted to suit the client's wishes and budget as well as the available site. The house is completely detached from the world. Indeed, it forms a world of its own similar to that of the French Baroque château with its gardens, turned inward, depicting a festive moment amidst its labouring environment. Moreover, comparison with the classical château best shows the radical revolution taking place here. The décor is not developed according to a perspective based on a system of straight axes, but reveals a free, almost improvised configuration. It wants to rid the architecture of its compulsiveness, its gravity, a far-off herald of deconstructionism.

The contrast between the liveliness of the theatre and the forced immobility of architecture, to which Jean-Louis Barrault drew attention, here explicitly comes to the fore. However, architecture cannot be improvised; it can only pretend to be. This can create a surpising, though short-lived effect that soon becomes oppressive. The impetus behind much modern work, especially behind that of Dupuis, is reflected here. It is an attempt to lift architecture above its own limitations and, as John Eggericx said about Dupuis's work, practise it as a continuous 'expérimentation sur l'animal humain.'

This approach is almost automatically legitimated in the field of architecture. It is directly opposed to the totalitarian theories of architecture and urban planning of the day and is in keeping with what Jean Dubuffet said about town planning: 'Il faudrait sans doute, dans ces vues d'urbanisme, donner une part très grande au non-délibéré, à l'irrationnel, au chaos. C'est à partir du chaos que la pensée fonctionne; et si on ne lui donne pas à traiter du chaos elle est comme une machine qu'on n'alimente plus'. The question, however, is how directly architecture and urban development should unify with chaos, or whether indeed they should not distance themselves from chaos to make it livable.

JACQUES DUPUIS
Uccle, Bertrand house, 1949
(Karel Vermeir)
The flexible quality of life, which fully occupies the available space of the grounds, is also pursued in less oppulent city houses such as this one, built for the painter Gaston Bertrand. The open space of the interior is alive with tension and the dynamic interplay of its various rooms, whose functions can be changed at any moment.

In Dupuis's work ground plans are better than photographs to illustrate dynamism and relational patterns. They do not simply show the subdivision of a space or a succession of independent rooms, but rather a flexible spatial interplay of related interior and exterior elements.

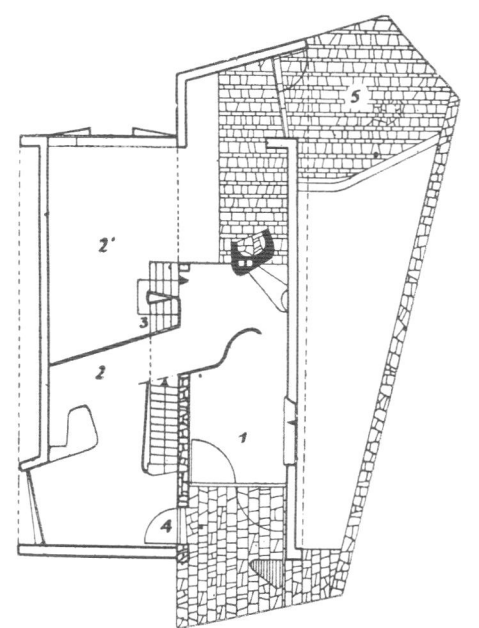
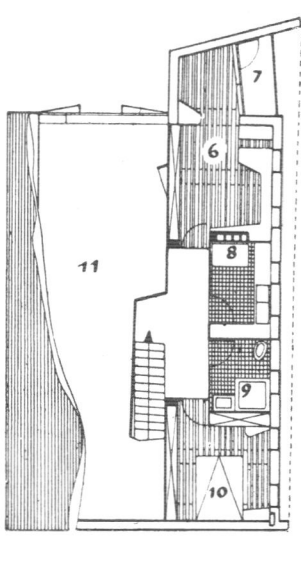

JACQUES DUPUIS AND ALBERT BONTRIDDER
Erbisœul, Franeau house, 1960
(Bastin/Evrard)

The framework with which architecture provides the occupant no longer is a strictly ordered centre of a neatly arranged world, but the coinciding of various fragments in a free and ever-changing configuration.

The absence of a clear frame of reference has forced architects to 'create a universe in the existing empty space, a universe whose all-embracing character has to compensate for the missing framework... so that architecture can have a strong presence and offer peace and protection, no matter where.'

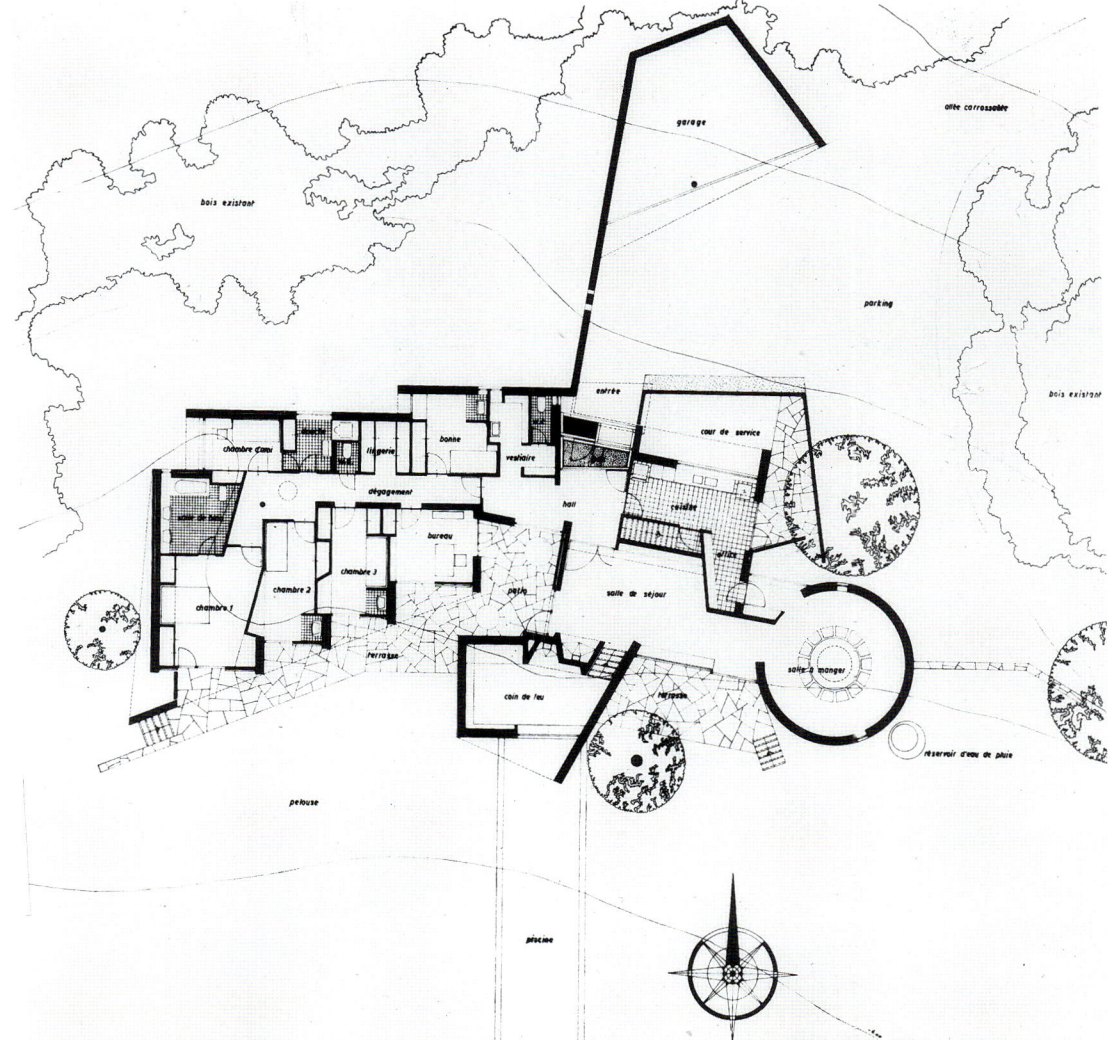

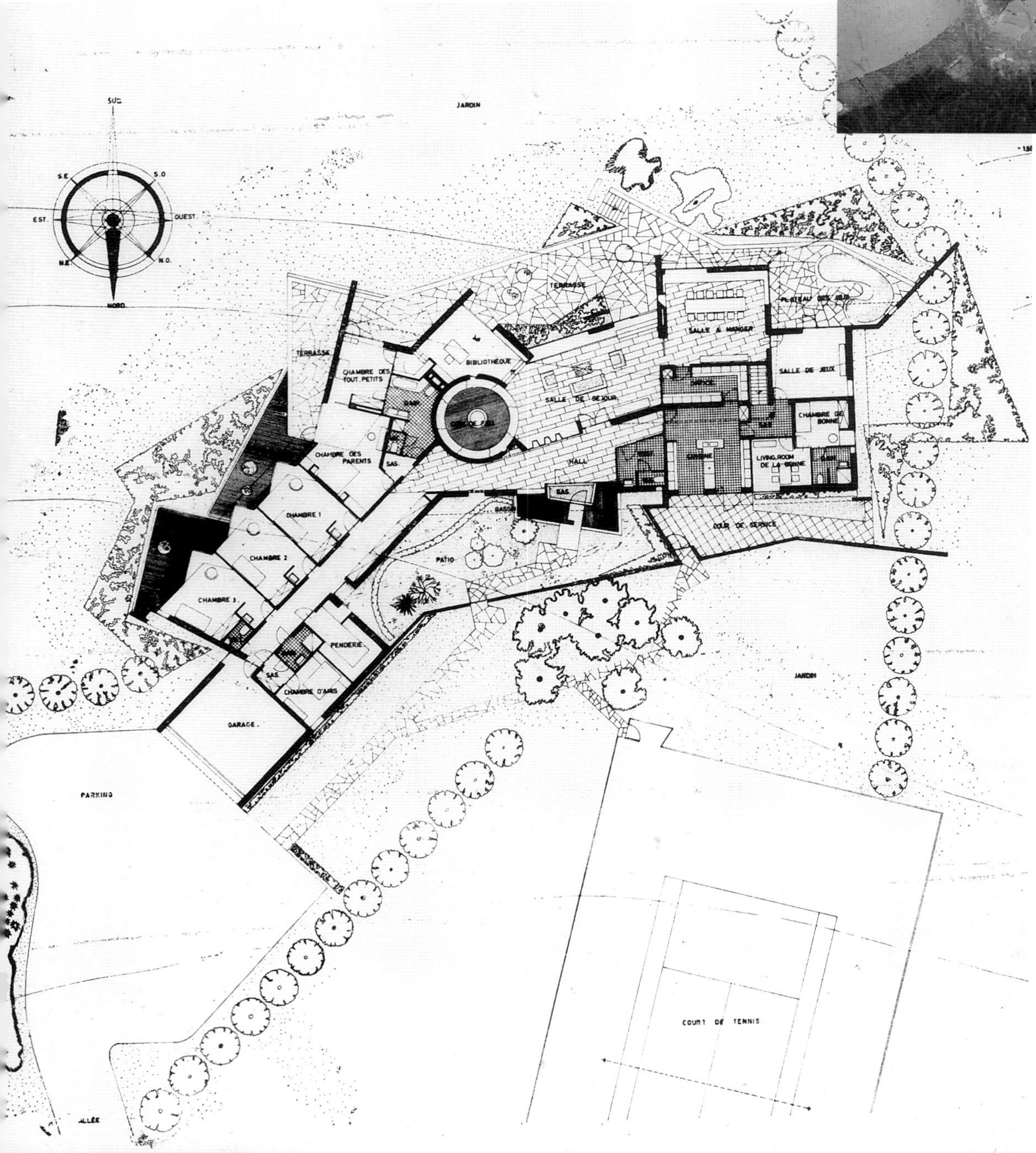

JACQUES DUPUIS AND ALBERT BONTRIDDER
Herent, house, 1959, photograph 1970
(Karel Vermeir)

It would be futile to try and distinguish
an evolution in Dupuis's work.
The same approach may lead to varying
configurations determined by the
surroundings and the means available.
This house on a hill in Herent is different
from one in the middle of the woods, but
their place in nature and their isolation
from the existing living environment
remain identical.

Nature has been given free rein since
1959 and has completely absorbed the
house. It is only on old photographs that
we can still catch a glimpse of it.

Albert Bontridder (b. 1921)

Albert Bontridder, poet and architect, rather more poet than architect, is a case apart. That is why here he enjoys a separate place, away from the rest of his generation. His case is a little like Willy Vand Der Meeren's, but then in the opposite sense: he is no man of deeds, but of reflection. Bontridder has been placed here not only because the major part of his œuvre as an architect was carried out in partnership with Dupuis, but mainly because he as a poet stood closest to Dupuis's approach. 'As both a poet and an architect Bontridder was opposed to the mass production and standardization seen in modern society,' Hugo Bousset once wrote.

He started out as a poet during the war, publishing in French as well as in Dutch. His spiritual fathers were Paul Eluard and Georges Bataille. The titles of his collections are typical of the expressionist pathos of his poetry. One of his later books of poetry, dating from 1979, is entitled *Huizen vieren haat* (Houses celebrating hatred). His collection *Ook de nacht is een zon* (The night too is a sun) (1969), the title of which is derived from Nietzsche, was awarded the Dirk Martens prize in 1979.

It contains the cycle 'Metafysiek van de spiegel' (Metaphysics of the mirror). The eye and the mirror, both important elements in contemporary architecture, are recurring themes in Botridder's writing. In the cycle 'Min is meer' (Less is more), from the same collection, he writes: 'Dwergman-dichter: / saboteur van de sociale herhaling en vermenigvuldiging, / dynamiteur van de eilanden op de bodem van de drooggelegde oceanen, / explorateur naar de bron van de vloed / die opnieuw / – en voorgoed – / over de bezette steden zal stromen. // Enige verdediger van de autonome levenservaring van het individu in de collectiviteit, / eist de dichter / de dienstbaarheid van de gemeenschap / in het teken van de enkeling. // De mindere is de meerdere'.

(Dwarf-man - poet: / saboteur of social repetition and multiplication, / dynamiter of the islands on the bottom of reclaimed oceans, / explorer of the source of the flood / that once more / – and for good – / will stream over the occupied cities. // The only advocate of the autonomous life experience of the individual and the collectivity, / the poet claims / the help of society / in the sign of the individual. // The inferior is the superior.) [reference to the title in the last line impossible to render in trans.]

In 1972 he was awarded the Jan Campert prize for *Zelfverbranding* (Self-cremation), dedicated 'Aan Jan Palach / toorts nummer 1, / ijs in de vlam; / aan Praag in Europa, / aan de schuld in de onschuld, / en bloem in de wroeging.' (To Jan Palach / torch number 1, / ice in the flame; / to Prague in Europe, / to guilt in innocence, / and flower in remorse.) This engagement – several of his poems are reflections on current events – must lie at the basis of his commitment to architecture.

As an architect he designed houses for well-known figures such as L.P. Boon (1952), Marcel Wauters (1960), and Marc Galle (1966). His own house was built in 1959 and received the

In his own house the poet and architect Albert Bontridder, who was Jacques Dupuis's long-time associate, produced his ideal embodiment of the modern house. 'It takes into account human morphology,' as he put it, and 'aims at liberating man from a badly constructed universe.'

Van de Ven prize the following year. Although they are less exuberant, his approach in these houses is close to that of Dupuis.

The cross-fertilization between literature and architecture resulted in numerous essays on the role and character of contemporary architecture and gave rise to the first extensive monography on modern Belgian architecture since 1900. It appeared in 1963 under the title *Hedendaagse bouwkunst in België. Dialoog tussen licht en stilte* (Contemporary Architecture in Belgium. Dialogue between Light and Silence) and was dedicated to 'Mr Léon Stynen, architect, who taught me to hear the dialogue between light and silence'. In 1979, on the occasion of Stynen's 80th birthday, Bontridder dedicated a monography to him, subtitled 'Gevecht met de rede' (The Fight against Reason).

In the conclusion to his survey of Belgian architecture he states: 'Allow me to point out once more that architecture is the basic phenomenon of the civilization in a country or an era, that the name of the architect is a secondary aspect of this problem, which for the sake of ease has been used in this study. Yet architecture cannot be likened to "chevalet" painting. The architect cannot be the sole creator of architecture, to a lesser extent even than the poet is of poems. This is why the architectural patrimony of a country is essentially anonymous. Even the most ingenious work is swallowed up by the order or chaos that the spirit of the time has managed to create in a particular region.'

ALBERT BONTRIDDER
Brussels, Wauters house, 1960
(Karel Vermeir)
Bontridder designed most of his houses for writers and artists, his kindred souls. He built a house for the writer L.P. Boon as well as for the poet and artist Marcel Wauters, who illustrated a number of works by L.P. Boon and Bontridder. Through modest means the architect made careful use of the difference in height of the terrain to invest the house with dynamism.

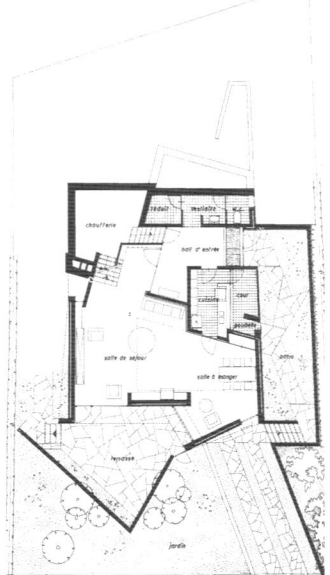

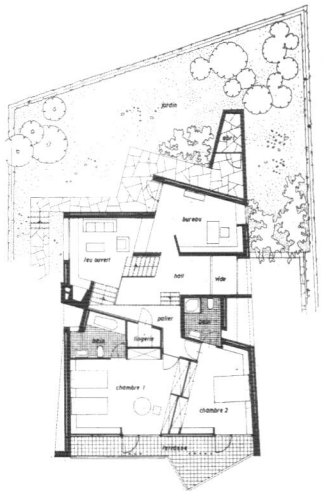

Paul Felix (1913-1981)

Paul Felix approached architecture from a different angle, namely from a Flemish Catholic one. He did not belong to the circle around La Cambre, which dominated the scene in the 1950s and 60s. In a review of Bontridder's book the Dutch architect and critic J.J. Vriend remarks: 'We learn practically nothing about the Flemish; they apparently belong to a different category.'

Trained as an engineer-architect at the university of Leuven at a time when architecture was still considered an inferior subject at university, he tried everything to improve its status in academic circles. As an architect he was a self-made man, who traced his way between the two headstrong groups of 'modernists' from La Cambre and the 'anti-modernists' – for one can hardly call them traditionalists – from the schools of Sint Lucas/Saint Luc.

After his appointment as an associate lecturer in Leuven in 1952 – in 1958 he was to become associate professor – he concentrated not only on introducing a fully fledged architecture department at his own university, but also on rationalizing all the various types of training for architects available in Belgium and tried to have them recognized as university degrees. In this way he wanted to improve the intellectual level as well as the social status of architects. He saw the isolation of architecture and the lack of communication between architects and the public as one of the causes of the poverty of modern architecture. Apart from his lectures at the university he also dedicated himself to architectural science and writing.

In 1954 he compiled an issue of the periodical *West-Vlaanderen* devoted to the development of modern architecture in various countries. In the editorial Paul Felix stressed the current relevance of modern architecture: 'The important image that one has of modern architecture at the present stage is exactly this versatility of forms of expression that moves between two poles: on the one hand rationalism, which wants to express itself through purified forms, and on the other hand a pursuit that through the freedom ensuing from modern techniques leads to plastic interplay.'

PAUL FELIX
Ostend/Mariakerke, Zonnelied, convent, 1957
(Bastin/Evrard and Karel Vermeir)
The Poor Clare convent in Mariakerke, the first building in a new housing development, affords an impression of a complete living community as conceived by the architect. It contains a central communal building, with the rest of the amenities harmonically arranged around it as a sheltered unit. This makes the contrast with the wild expansion of the surrounding residential area all the more poignant.

Here architecture is limited to the soberest means: brick, concrete, and natural pine in a clear construction. However, the church building breaks away from the commonplace not only through its remarkable shape and scale, but also through its decoration. The architect's collaboration with people such as the stained-glass artist Michel Martens and the sculptor Roger Bonduel played a significant role.

At first traditional in its design, Felix's work underwent a sea change in the early 1950s. It is significant that the first example of this, the water tower in Melle (1951), was an industrial building. Modernity was no longer being pursued through the simplification of decorative elements, but in an in-depth analysis of the constructive and programmatic demands. In the same year, together with M. Appel, M. Molleman, and J. Welslau, he entered a design for a competition held by the Ministry of Colonial Affairs in Brussels. It was an undisguised homage to Le Corbusier, similar to the work of Léon Stynen and Claude Laurens at the time.

He established his reputation as an architect in 1954 with the Pius X student hall of residence in the Arenberg Park in Heverlee, which he designed together with his colleague Georges Pepermans. Here Le Corbusier's influence would be hard to discern. Instead there is an uncertain, though refreshing interpretation of the building programme, in a language leaning towards regional architecture. The brick cube of the chapel stands apart in the whole on account of its strong, sober form. Various commissions, especially for individual houses, show the same characteristics. For one of these houses Felix was awarded the Van de Ven prize in 1955.

The block of flats in Ostend he built for himself in 1954 reveals the need for more rigid control over form, which was already alluded to in the Leuven chapel. These characteristics recur in the 1956 plans for the Technisch Instituut and public swimming-pool in Kortrijk, designed in collaboration with Jan Tanghe, Jan De Jaegere, and Christiaan Vander Plaetse.

A synthesis of these almost contradictory trends appears in Paul Felix's best known and most influential work, the 'Zonnelied' Franciscan convent in Ostend (1957). Built on an unspoilt polder plain as the starting point for a new urban development, it creates the impression of a complete community, just as Felix had intended.

Radiating from the central church space, the symbol of the higher values a society strives for, all aspects of human habitation are arranged around courtyards. The formal vocabulary also gives direct expression to the ascetic ideal. The whole is characterized by brick supporting walls and concrete slabs, whereas the interiors are finished with natural pine.

In the early 1960s Felix built a number of churches, including those of the Sint-Xaverius college in Burgerhout, of the 'De Biest' quarter in Waregem, and of the 'Pastoraal en Theologisch Centrum' of the Antwerp dioscese. This last complex (1965) is typical of the large commissions that Felix was to carry out between 1965 and 1975. The architectural form became more anonymous and found its expression mainly through the controlled volumes and the way in which it determines the landscape, an evolution that we also saw in Bastin's work.

In Antwerp the buildings stand somewhat desolate in the surrounding open space. In the training centre in Dworp (1967) they form a compact unit on top of a hill. The university hospital on the Gasthuisberg in Leuven, designed together with Jan Delrue and Jan Tanghe, also evinces an analytical approach to the various sections making up the whole.

The last phase in Felix's development starts with the new public swimming-pool in Ostend (1970). In the provincial library near the beguinage in Hasselt (1974) various trends and elements from his own work find a new balance, especially in the interior. The commission itself, a house for people and books, must have appealed to Felix.

'There is not much point in speaking about the individual evolution of architects,' Felix writes in *Bouwen in België 1945-1970* (1970), 'Architecture always results from the interplay between factors beyond the reach of the individual. We should have known this long ago, but the post-war period has made it clear again: we get a distorted impression of the achitect if we see him as the prophet who is going to teach people how they are supposed to live and expect them to be respectfully obedient.'

PAUL FELIX AND GEORGES PEPERMANS
Heverlee, Pius X, student hall of residence, 1953

(Bastin/Evrard)
This simple hall of residence in the park of Heverlee was a breakthrough not only within the œuvres of these two professors of architecture at the University of Leuven, but for the approach to architecture in general. Architecture was shown not to be an elitist preoccupation, but an everyday need, influencing even the most banal aspects of life. The college chapel, a free-standing brick cube, contains the seeds of the radical innovations in church architecture that were to follow.

PAUL FELIX AND GEORGES NOLENS
Hasselt, Provincial Library, 1973
(Bastin/Evrard)

In his later work Felix presented a mild synthesis of the various trends that have influenced both his own evolution and that of architecture. With the provincial library in Hasselt he returned to a more receptive form, in keeping with the surrounding beguinage.

PAUL FELIX

Dworp, Destelheide, training centre, 1967

(Bastin/Evrard)

The training centre in Dworp is the most balanced of all the larger commissions carried out by Felix in the 1960s. Here his architecture has become more formally explicit and aims at dominating the landscape through the clarity of its shapes.

PAUL FELIX AND GROUP PLANNING
(JAN TANGHE)

Ostend, swimming-pool, 1975-1978

(Bastin/Evrard)

In contrast with the library in Hasselt, which is integrated in its surroundings, the swimming pool in Ostend is intended to accentuate the unusual character of the area. Paul Felix often pointed out that architecture does not concern the architect alone, but should be the interplay of forces beyond the individual.

Peter Callebout (1916-1970)

It is in the work of a gifted artist like Peter Callebout that one has to look to see the real motive of the search that occupied Felix throughout his life. In Peter Callebout's curriculum vitae in *Bouwen in België 1945-1970* (1970), published in the year before his death no mention is made of any writings or works of his. The most important statements made by him have come to us through *Plan 2*, November 1964, on the theme 'Heeft architectuur nog zin? Gewetensonderzoek bij een whisky...' (Does architecture still have a point? Soul-searching over a glass of whisky...). Callebout is embittered: 'Architecture and Town Planning are dirty words,' and 'In my view, "architecture" ought to disappear before there can be a question of architecture again... In fact, we can see present-day architecture as an immense swindle, in the moral sense an organized dirty trick, for we are knowingly supplying inferior goods to our customers.'

Moreover, an architect cannot help supplying inferior goods, partly because he is not *au fait* with his trade, but also because the organization of the building sector is such that he cannot possibly control what happens to his own work. Indeed, there is no other profession where self-criticism is so sharp and where professionals have been complaining about impossible working conditions since the first century BC. Almost an echo of Callebout's comment, Charles Vandenhove claimed: 'There has been no more architecture since we have architects.'

And yet Peter Callebout continued to produce some of the most refined buildings of the post-war period. Callebout was born in London in 1916, the son of an architect, Ernest Callebout. He learnt his profession in his father's office and they collaborated until 1952. It took a Royal Decree to make him register as an architect.

One of his first independent works was a house for the artist Yvonne Gérard in La Plante near Namur in 1951. Using the traditional, rustic materials of the area, he created a building that is remarkable for the precision with which it was situated, both distinguished and exciting, modest and refined.

The same qualities appear in his award-winning design for a wooden holiday home at the 1956 annual fair in Ghent. It is conceived as 'a structure made up of standards and joists forming a basic cell of 12 m². The cells can be connected at will and the walls can be left open or filled in.

This idea was further worked out in his own house, which he built in the Mosweg in Nieuwpoort (1956) as part of a small development with six houses, comparable to the 'Vierwindenbinnenhof' in Tervuren by Willy Van Der Meeren around the same period.

It could hardly have been simpler: a square ground plan containing different service and serving zones, built in the most elementary of construction materials. And yet, as with Gérard's house, this simplicity does not make a miserly impression, but rather emanates richness. Callebout said about the Japanese house: 'Everything is balanced, through simplicity, through the order of it.' The house on the Zeedijk in Zeebrugge (1961), in collaboration with Fernand Sohier, shows the same skill at transfiguring a traditional type from within.

One of his last works was the 'Centrum voor Kunst en Kunstambachten Valerius De Saedeleer' in Etikhove (1968), which has been seriously mutilated. This was his second commission from Elisabeth De Saedeleer, for whom he had designed two semi-detached houses in Nieuwpoort in 1965. In an unpublished thesis submitted at the architecture department of the university in Ghent, *Peter Callebout. Beschouwingen over figuur en werk* (1993), Gert Van Conkelberge describes the arts and crafts centre: 'The building site was located on top of a

PETER CALLEBOUT
Namur, Gérard house, 1951
(Bastin/Evrard)
In the context of Belgian architecture, this small terraced house built for the artist Yvonne Gérard in La Plante (near Namur) is a clear indication of the individualistic position taken in by Callebout's work.
It cannot be classified under abstract categories such as regionalism or modernism; it does not strive for innovation, but depends on the intrinsic quality of the work itself.

slightly sloping hill and at the time was occupied by an old barn. After a number of preliminary designs, in which Callebout tried to realize the scheme in the barn itself, he radically changed his approach. A part of the old barn was retained up to half its height and he incorporated the remains as a terrace wall in his new design, which makes a swooping gesture across the sloping terrain. A Japanese-style walkway with wooden boards, slightly elevated above a bed of cobbles can already be seen from the street and slowly winds along the remaining parts of the old walls towards the entrance of the museum. It can also be used for open-air activities, such as fashion shows and small concerts. Below the wooden volume of the actual exhibition space there is an entrance and the utility rooms, which are partly sunk into the hillside and out of sight... However, it is difficult to describe in words the spatial experience, which is created by minimal means. The long side walls, the floor and ceiling, all three conceived as "loose" elements, and the glazed frontal and rear façades direct the view via sharp perspectives towards the surrounding landscape, transforming the whole into an "open show-box". The lateral windows, at the level of the roof-beams, create ideal natural illumination and emphasize the rhythm created by the beams and columns.'

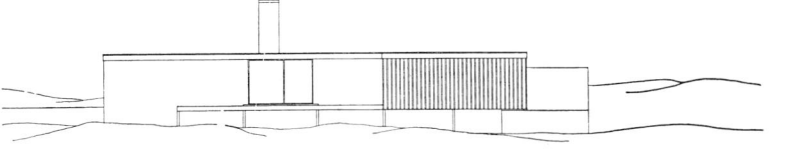

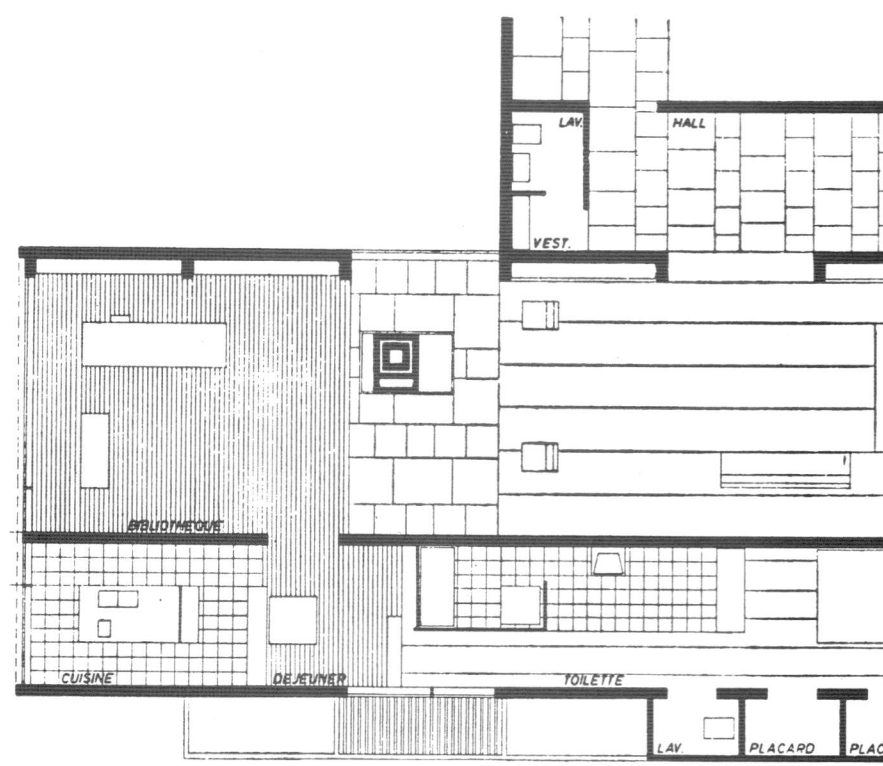

PETER CALLEBOUT
Nieuwpoort, own house, 1956

(Karel Vermeir and Bastin/Evrard)
Callebout's own house, built in a small development on the Mosweg in Nieuwpoort, uses minimal means to create intelligent architectural comfort and luxury. It is through this restraint that the architect shows his mastery.

The interior consists of a single large, clear space which, just as the house itself, is emphatically horizontal. According to Louis Kahn's principle the interior is divided into two strips: one for the service area and technical equipment, the other for the reception and living quarters.

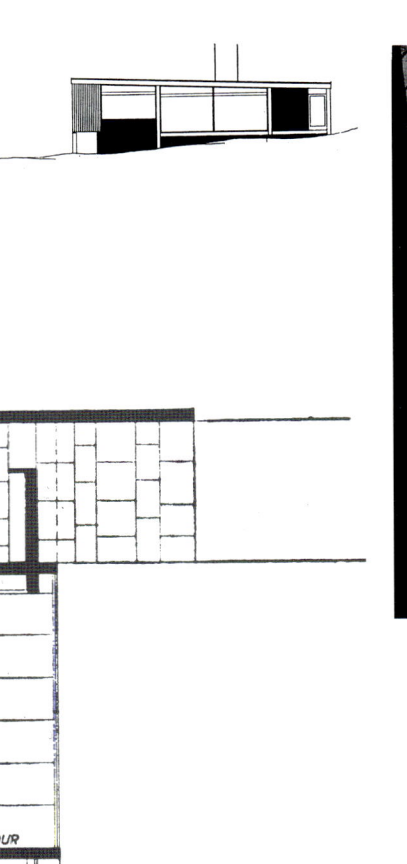

PETER CALLEBOUT AND FERNAND SOHIER
Zeebrugge, house, 1962
(Bastin/Evrard)

Just as the Gérard house from the early
period, this holiday home in Zeebrugge,
built in collaboration with Fernand
Sohier, demonstrates the architect's calm
and peaceful craftsmanship whose
perfection lifts his work from the banal.
In Sohier's view its value lay in the
independence with which it moved away
from the trends and dogmas of the
architectural world.

JOZEF LIETAERT
Heusden, Landuyt house, 1962
(Bastin/Evrard)

Jozef Lietaert cared as little about current
architectural trends as Peter Callebout
did. He did not advocate a new style.
His work refers to the countryside,
not in imitation of the past, but so
as to apply its honest craftsmanship to
contemporary architecture while making
use of new techniques and taking into
account present-day lifestyles.

Jozef Lietaert (1908-1989)

In contrast to Peter Callebout, Jozef Lietaert was never admitted to his colleagues' guild. He too was a self-made man, trained in A. Bresser's studio, and was allowed to practise the profession by Royal Decree. Nor did he consider architecture a matter of words. Only once did he write on it – and rather late, in 1973 – in an article in A+, entitled 'De oude landelijke woning, een niet romantisch meesterwerk' (The old rural homestead, a non-romantic masterpiece). It explains his own approach: 'Our forefathers neither knew, nor recognized any norms for being "rustic". They simply built in the country, though with knowledge of and a sense for proportion and balance.'

It is no coincidence that in 1962 Lietaert collaborated with Nico van der Laan, of the Dutch Bossche School, on the church and Wijnberg presbytery in Wevelgem. However, through its conviction and passion his work breaks away from the all too serene rationality of the Bossche School, the best example of which in Belgium is Dom Hans van der Laan's Roosenberg convent in Waasmunster.

Lietaert's work possesses a surprising materiality within post-war architecture. This already came to the fore in his earlier works, such as the sculptor Vanderkerckhove's studio in Kortrijk (1955), built with concrete slabs. It is remarkable how many artists' studios there are in Lietaert's œuvre, a phenomenon that appears in modern Belgian architecture as a whole.

An impressive example of his approach can be seen in the house and studio he built for Octave Landuyt in Heusden near Ghent (1962). The closed U shape is situated on a somewhat elevated plateau, with the studio contained in the slightly diverging wing. In contrast with the rough brick and massive volume on the outside, the interior walls are smoothly plastered. No direct reference is made to rural architecture, but it has the same power of conviction and formal necessity. As in Peter Callebout's work, one can see the pertness, the wilfulness of this architecture, which takes no notice of the noise around it and maybe therefore demonstrates the typical character of Belgian architecture. Even though the architect may be bound to all sorts of restrictions, it is the way in which he knows to turn these conditions into his own personal work that legitimizes his architecture.

Flea Market

Through the prism of these diverse figures, a few of whom doubted their own personal contribution, some light is shed on the structural shifts facing architects since 1945. The collection of buildings looks like a flea market, and ideed, it is one. This also implies that there are surprising discoveries to be made. Each object stands on its own, one next to the other, a Braem next to a Callebout. However, this does not check structural development, which takes place in all fields of modern life. They cross these fields and erode their borders, sometimes visibly, sometimes almost indiscernibly.

Mobility comes to the fore together with all its opportunities and demands. Leisure activities imply new ways of filling space, both in- and outside of the house. Technological evolution soon led to the post-industrial era and the development of the services sector. The telephone and television have installed themselves in the living-room, the house has become cluttered with electrical household appliances. Demands as to modern conveniences are continually on the increase. The dismantling of the larger cities is unmistakable. Urban culture is no longer limited to the city. The periphery has become an independent concept. A few small exceptions apart, Belgium has not known the same systematic development of satellite cities or extended residential areas as in its neighbouring countries. The private home continues to dominate the architectural patrimony, although it is increasingly taking on the character of the individually-owned flat. Commissions for public buildings are more anonymous. The various regions are becoming more prominent.

All these facts could lead to an anonymous history of architecture, as Siegfried Giedion put it, or as in Gerard Monnier's *L'architecture en France. Une histoire critique 1918-1950. Architecture Culture Modernité*. Yet even Monnier cannot avoid underlining the role of the individual architect in the interpretation and composition of all the developments or indicating his determining influence. Whichever way one looks at it, it is only through personal contributions that new building schemes and new relations can bear on a deeper awareness of life and manifest themselves as 'objets à réaction poétique', in Le Corbusier's words.

JACQUES MOESCHAL
Zellik, Monument, 1963
Sculptors were called upon to underline the motorway culture. In Zellik, at the approach to the first Brussels-Ostend motorway, the architect and sculptor Jacques Moeschal designed a monumental sculpture. He also erected similar constructions at the border crossings to France on the motorways from Mons and Kortrijk.

Chapter 2 # 1955-1965

The last of the modernists:
the guard will not be changed

A landscape of motorways

There is something arbitrary about dividing up historical developments. After all, history does not pay heed to dates. One may justify choosing 1958, the year of the Expo '58 world fair in Brussels, as the end of the first phase of the reconstruction in Belgium. However, there are better reasons for taking 1955 as the starting point of the central phase in post-war architecture, a time when a new generation came to the fore. They remained prominent until the end of the 1980s, a generation who had grown up with modern architecture and also put it behind them, like sons do with their fathers. In this process of emancipation the Expo '58 was little more than a marginal phenomenon.

After 1955 the results of earlier planning became visible, for instance through the incentive of Omer Vanaudenhoeve, Minister of Public Works and Reconstruction from 1954 to 1961. In 1955 the Road Fund was instated and in 1957 a national motorway plan was announced together with the 'Groenplan' (Green Plan), which was to protect the countryside. According to the Minister they went hand in hand, for motorways were to make the landscape more accessible and allow people to discover its beauty. In the same year Vanaudenhove announced a new global law on town planning, which only came into force in 1962.

The new motorways have radically determined the landscape and the lives of its inhabitants, generating their own form of beauty. At the 'Bouwen in België' exhibition (1971) they were given a prominent position. They demonstrate an unintentional beauty that does not present itself as an object, but rather as something to be experienced. The monumental sculpture erected by the architect-sculptor Jacques Moeschal in Zellik (1963) at the slip-road to the first Brussels-Ostend motorway seems to be an archaic relic, lost in the presence of the new spatial reality.

The American John Brinckenhoff Jackson already pointed out the spatial reality of the motorway in the early 1960s. In contrast to Kevin Lynch in *View from the Road* (1964), he does not look from the motorway, but at it. In *A Sense of Place, a Sense of Time* (1994), his lyrical prose evokes the introspective tendency of the lonely driver on those endless motorways, where according to him our sense of place is replaced by a sense of time.

Antwerp, laying out of the ring road
In 1955 Minister Omer Vanaudenhove set up the Road Fund and in 1957, the year before the Expo '58 world exhibition in Brussels, he announced a national motorway plan together with the Green Plan. In later years the laying out of motorways with traffic junctions near larger cities proved to have a lasting influence on the landscape and the role architecture would play in it.

LUCIEN-JACQUES BAUCHER,
JEAN-PIERRE BLONDEL,
AND ODETTE FILIPPONE
Brussels, Expo '58, Marie Thumas pavilion
(Sado)

At the Expo '58 the younger generation of Belgian architects wanted to promote a new architectural style making use of the technical possibilities of light spanning structures and shell roofs. The Marie Thumas pavilion built by Baucher, Blondel, and Fillipone in collaboration with René Sarger, the engineer of the French pavilion, is a prime example of this.

The intensive lighting of the Belgian motorway network reinforces this experience of a world of one's own even more. Victor Bourgeois had already founded a magazine called *Au Volant* (Behind the Steering-Wheel) in 1919 and some time later devoted an essay to 'electrical architecture', which lights up in the dark. In the commentary on his town hall in Ostend he referred to the 'architecture of movement', long before Paul Virilio was to make a dogma of 'dromology'.

The construction of the Belgian motorway network and the extension of the existing roads brought with them the spread of a number of activities beyond the traditional centres, as well as a growth in industrial estates, shopping, residential, and service centres, camping sites, road-houses, discotheques, and cinema complexes. The result was an exodus from the cities and the expansion of the built-up area. Marcel Smets refers to a diffused nebular city. The 1962 law on urban development had little or no influence over these developments and the disputed district development plans, which were a result, only encouraged them further. The 'Structuurplan Vlaanderen' (Flanders Structural Plan), which is being worked out under the direction of Charles Vermeersch and Louis Albrechts, is to take up the thread again.

Expo '58

The Expo '58 world fair held in Brussels from 17 April to 19 October 1958 was one of the new developments that was plugged into the new road network. In contrast to earlier world fairs in Brussels, Liège, Ghent, or Antwerp, the opportunity to improve the city structure was largely ignored in 1958.

This was the first Expo after the war. The preparations started in 1955. The motto, 'Human progress through scientific progress' was symbolized by the construction of the Atomium, an extra large depiction of an invisible iron particle, for which A. Waterkeyn, A. and J. Polak were responsible. The 'Arrow of Civil Construction' by Jacques Moeschal and Jean Van Doosselaere, above a miniature Belgium with a prominent network of motorways, was also supposed to express a sense of trust in the future. The arrow was demolished in 1970.

Conscious town planning was nowhere to be seen at the Expo '58. The emphasis was on architecture, which was expected to be on the point of a breakthrough. However, it only demonstrated its multifariousness. Belgian architects of name were not involved in the overall project, but were engaged for

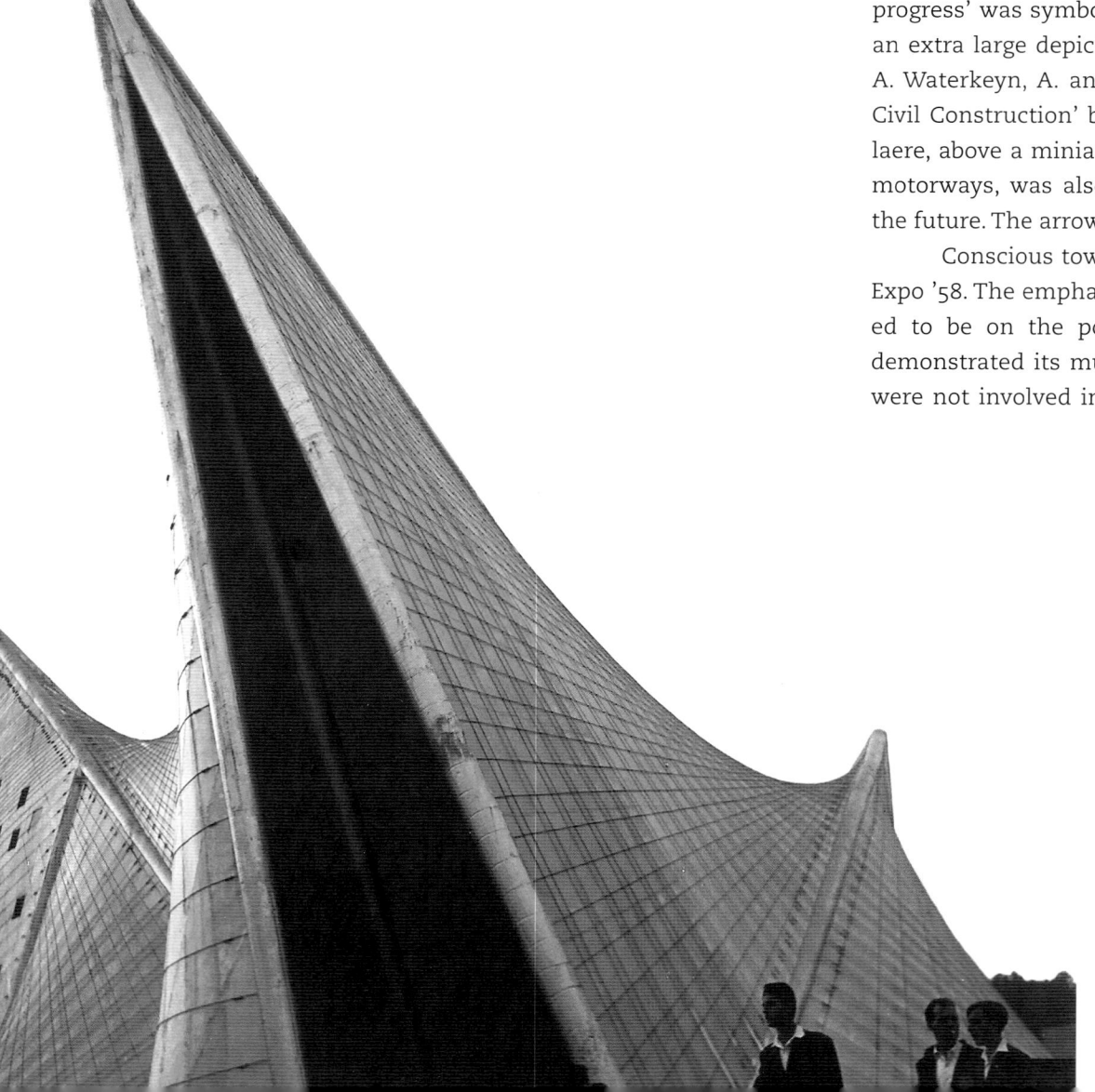

LE CORBUSIER AND XENAKIS
Brussels, Expo '58, Philips pavilion
(Frank Philippi)

The Expo '58 world fair, held in Brussels from 17 April to 19 October 1958, can be considered as one of the developments stuck onto the new road network. Together with the Atomium, Le Corbusier's Philips pavilion symbolized the dawning of a new era.

LUCIEN-JACQUES BAUCHER,
JEAN-PIERRE BLONDEL,
AND ODETTE FILIPPONE

Brussels, Information pavilion Expo '58, demolished 1973

(R. Badjou)

On the occasion of the 1958 world fair in Brussels an information pavilion was erected on Place de Brouckère. Its shell roof was borne by two points of support. Screened by a glass wall, the interior remained completely open.

JACQUES MOESCHAL AND
JEAN VAN DOOSSELAERE

Brussels, Expo '58, Arrow of Civil Construction, demolished 1970

New possibilities were offered by modern building techniques, such as the rapid development of concrete construction to which Prof. Magnel from Ghent had contributed. This was demonstrated by the 'Arrow of Civil Construction' that hung over a miniature model of the Belgian landscape, prominently showing the motorway network.

separate pavilions, such as Bastin for Civitas Dei, Bourgeois for the Eternit tower as well as the Wood and Germinal pavilions, Callebout for the arrangement of the exhibition on fifty years of modern art, Dupuis for the façade decoration of Palace V and the Public Housing pavilion, Wybauw and Thierry for the MBLE pavilion, and Stynen for the Petroleum palace. Stynen was also asked – together with Prof. C. Magnel, a specialist on concrete – to design a 600-metre television tower. His proposal of a 750-metre tower was rejected only when it was realized that such high transmission towers were no longer necessary.

Few of the Expo '58 pavilions actually made architectural history. In Dennis Sharp's collection on 1958, only the German pavilion by Eierman and Ruf, and Le Corbusier's Philips pavilion are included. The fair presented a complete survey of the various approaches to architecture at the time: the 'structuralism' of the Spanish, 'modernism' of the German, 'high tech' of the French, 'post-modernism' of the Italian, and the 'brutalism' of the Dutch pavilion. Only the Philips pavilion, designed by Le Corbusier in collaboration with Xenakis and Edgar Varèse, is impossible to categorize as it presented a *Gesamtkunstwerk* in which the history of mankind was evoked at an incredible pace in a building that looked like a whirlwind.

The Belgians

At the Expo '58 Belgian architecture was suggestively presented: as an ark spanning a few square metres, lost in the commotion of the fair. Josse Franssen (b. 1906), the deserving architect of flat buildings in and around Brussels (such as in Avenue Broqueville and Boulevard Gén. Wahis) was commissioned to represent the architecture of Belgium, but was denied any means for doing so. Architects had to defray the costs of their participation themselves.

Just as the National Housing Association, Franssen also opted for an anonymous presentation at the fair. In a closed square space which, like a cut-off pyramid, tapered upwards, photographs were stuck to the wall in a single continuous collage. In the low entrance to the pyramid the names 'Hankar', 'Horta', and 'van de Velde' were inscribed, with mention of a few of their most prominent works, but without any illustrations. The transition to the naos bore a statement by Le Corbusier: 'Concevoir raisonnablement, c'est nouveau et c'est ancien; cela conduit aux extrêmes, non au juste milieu'. This anonymity may have been a flight of fancy, yet it was characteristic of a certain type of architecture in the 1950s and 60s.

The work presented at the Expo '58 by young Belgian architects was not really typical of their later work, as if the temporary and exceptional nature of the situation encouraged them to experiment. Constantin Brodzki built the Fauna pavilion. The group Baucher, Blondel and Fillipone together with the engineer René Sarger, the designer of the French pavilion, designed the Marie Thumas pavilion, the Information pavilion on Place de Brouckère in Brussels, and the Expo commission's offices, which received the 1958 Van de Ven prize. The group Courtois, Montois, and Moens designed the Transport pavilion,

JEAN-PIERRE BLONDEL AND
ODETTE FILIPPONE
Brussels, Residence 'Les Terrasses', 1967-1969
(Bastin/Evrard)

After their association with Lucien-Jacques Baucher, the architects Blondel and Filippone (husband and wife) distinguished themselves through a whole series of tasteful residences. 'Les Terrasses' is probably the best known and most typical of these. The use of receding and projecting sections created not only comfortable apartments with their own exterior areas, but also a plastic volume.

JOSSE FRANSSEN
Brussels, Expo '58, Modern Belgian Architecture

(Bauters)

At the Expo '58 visitors were made aware of the existence of Belgian architecture through a small exhibition organized by Josse Franssen. It was like entering a shrine: on the inside of the pyramid the walls were covered with anonymous photographs of modernist buildings.

Neder-over-Heembeek, Solvay research centre, 1965

(Bastin/Evrard)

At the Expo '58 the group formed by Courtois, Montois, and Moens attracted attention through the light construction of their Transport pavilion, which was afterwards reconstructed in Liège. After his association with Courtois had come to an end, Montois took on several large orders, such as the Solvay research centre in Neder-over-Heembeek, the Hilton Hotel in Brussels, and the academic hospital in Woluwe-Saint-Lambert.

which was awarded the Reynolds prize by the American Institute of Architects and was later reconstructed in Liège. The Red Cross pavilion was by the hand of Thierry Hoet (b. 1927). In most of these cases the architects applied the new technical possibilities of shell roofs and light spanning structures.

Brodzki's work will be discussed further. That of the other architects (Baucher, Blondel, Fillipone, Montois, and Courtois) is extensive and may count as representative for the mitigated modernism of the 1950s. It provides, especially in and around Brussels, the backdrop against which other works can be seen. From 1953 to 1963 Jean-Pierre Blondel (b. 1924) and his wife, Odette Fillipone (b. 1927), collaborated with Lucien Jacques Baucher (b. 1929). Their most remarkable work constituted a series of tasteful, smart 'résidences'. In 1969 Baucher designed the recreation hall of the Palais des Beaux-Arts in Brussels, where he demonstrated his fondness for open structures. In 1954 he had compiled an issue of *Architecture* on Jean Prouvé in which Van Der Meeren and Palm's CECA house was also included.

Robert Courtois (b. 1922) played, and still plays, a role in social and professional bodies of architects as the organizer of congresses and exhibitions and as the editor in chief of A+. Together with Henri Montois (b. 1920), his long-time associate, and the engineer A. Lipski he had built the De Backer industrial complex in Zaventem (1957), which for quite some time was considered a model for contemporary industrial architecture.

Henri Montois worked on large complexes, such as the Solvay research centre in Neder-over-Heembeek (1965), the Hilton Hotel in Brussels (1967), and the training hospital of the Université Catholique de Louvain in Woluwe-Saint-Lambert (1967).

On the occasion of the 1958 Van de Ven prize, awarded to Baucher's team, Pierre-Louis Flouquet optimistically wrote: 'The new generation can clearly be regarded as the "génération de la relève". They are every bit as good as the previous generation. We can see the same élan, the same passion for formal innovation, the same application of reason, the same social considerations without neglecting the right to beauty. The proposed works show an almost complete disappearance of architects above the age of forty.'

Nuclear town

In the same round of the 1958 Van de Ven prize mention was made of several buildings at the nuclear centre of Mol, just as in the 1957 round. The commission for the nuclear energy research centre, set up in 1952 to study peaceful applications, was awarded to Jacques Wybauw (b. 1925) in 1953, partly in association with Jacques Thiran (b. 1928). Around the central buildings and nuclear reactor a residential area was developed for the staff, to which Pierre Coulon (b. 1921) and André Noterman (b. 1921) made the most striking contribution.

This centre is typical and, to some extent, a model of architecture in those years. It comprises a whole range of buildings, from the nuclear reactor through to one-family homes.

Great care was taken of the layout of the landscape, which was the responsibility of René Pechère (b. 1908), who taught garden and landscape architecture at La Cambre.

The area around Mol was industrial by tradition, with glass, zinc, and dynamite production plants looming as alien monsters among the picturesque villages. The antagonism of the forces that rip the city apart had already manifested itself in this landscape. In *Groenten uit Balen* (1972) and *Aantekeningen van een stambewaarder* (1977) Walter van den Broeck describes the atmosphere. The new nuclear town was implanted in the Achterbos area on the Kempisch canal, where Jacob Smits settled among the moorland farmers to paint his 'Symbool van de Kempen'.

Nothing in the new settlement, apart from the nuclear reactor building itself, refers to its *raison d'être*. Everything evinces a distinguished geniality, a new sort of rural life. Even at the time the centre was considered one of the most important architectural schemes in Belgium. The editorial board of *La Maison* noted in November 1957: 'Le Centre de Mol se présente aujourd'hui comme l'une des réalisations architecturales les plus complètes que l'on puisse voir en Belgique. Il réalise avec une précision et une fermeté qui ne manquent ni d'esprit ni d'élégance, cette variété dans l'unité chère aux esprits classiques.' Wybauw himself commented: 'Les architectes se sont efforcés de réaliser les bâtiments du Centre de Mol dans un esprit d'économie, avec l'unique souci d'être fonctionnel et de répondre de façon réaliste à tous les points du programme. Ils ont voulu que le raisonnement rigoureux préside à chaque décision, afin d'éliminer les tentations d'un formalisme omniprésent, qui, de tous temps, guette l'architecte comme un mauvais génie. Leur effort tendit encore vers la définition d'une

▷ CLAUDE STREBELLE
Liège, Sart Tilman, central boiler house, 1966-1968
(Bastin/Evrard)
In 1960 Claude Strebelle was commissioned to design a new campus for the University of Liège in a stretched out park in Sart Tilman. This marked the beginning of the expansion of Belgian universities and was an ideal opportunity to demonstrate the Walloon identity. Strebelle set the tone in the buildings he designed for the entrance to the grounds.

JACQUES WYBAUW AND JACQUES THIRAN
Mol, nuclear centre, 1953-1964
(R. Lamarque)
The architectural project for the nuclear centre in Mol was quite ambitious. The central buildings and nuclear reactor, as well as the residential part had to be a model of a new, independent settlement. The commission was awarded to Jacques Wybauw and René Pechère carried out the landscaping of the area.

ambiance d'ensemble empreinte de calme, de raison et de sérieux, mais dont l'expression soit néanmoins souriante'. With reference to his Home Vandervelde II in Oostduinkerke (1957) Lucien Engels, his contemporary at La Cambre, speaks of 'une ambiance heureuse'. However, his work is a more brilliant version of modernism that does not try to avoid formalistic exuberance.

Together with the nuclear town we have to mention the initiative set up by the firm Janssen in Beerse, who in 1956 commissioned Paul Meekels (b. 1933) to design an industrial complex comprising laboratories, warehouses, offices, and a caretaker's lodge. Merkels showed that there is a more direct and characteristic solution. The unconstrained form shows architecture in all its stratifications, from efficient construction through to its expressive capacities. Its casualness contrasts with the geniality of the nuclear centre in Mol, the orthodoxy of the De Backer complex by Courtois and Montois, as well as with Engels's cheerful modernism.

Sart Tilman

The new campus for the university of Liège at Sart Tilman was quite an ambitious project. Claude Strebelle (b. 1917) was commissioned to design it in 1960, the start of a period that saw the expansion of Belgian universities. As was the case with Expo '58 and the nuclear centre in Mol, this expansion paid little attention to the role it could have played in the urban context. What occurred in Liège was repeated in Antwerp, Brussels, Kortrijk, and Hasselt. In Leuven and Ghent this trend had less effect, where the the inner city remained the centre of university activities despite the expansion of Leuven into the completely new city of Louvain-la-Neuve.

Sart Tilman never became a real campus. It is nothing more than a loose collection of buildings on a green. Of the 557-hectare domain about 200 hectares have been reserved for building the five faculties on. Strebelle himself prodides an explanation: 'The main connection is horseshoe-shaped and runs over the top of the hill, enclosing a wooded valley which in the overall composition will be a place of peace and quiet. The science faculty is situated in the centre of the grounds... The medical faculty and its hospital have access to the natural sciences, especially the pre-clinical sciences. The hospital is located in the south wing.'

There is a certain amount of centralization around the student restaurant and halls of residence, but an actual community, which is the essence of a campus, would be hard to distinguish. However, if one studies the collection of buildings in the park as one would do at an open-air museum such as Bokrijk, one cannot but admire this architectural display of the work of all well-known Walloon architects of the day. Indeed, this display focusses not only on architecture, but also on the Walloon identity. The list of names is as impressive as the high inspiration to make a clean break with the dullness of ancillary architecture such as that of the nuclear centre in Mol. Claude Strebelle himself set the pace with two buildings at the main

RAYMOND-M. LEMAIRE
Leuven, Groot Begijnhof, restoration,
1964-1971
(Bastin/Evrard)
The Groot Begijnhof in Leuven was saved from total disintegration thanks to the intervention of the art historian Prof. Raymond-M. Lemaire. It was thoroughly renovated and developed into a model urban area combining student accommodation and various cultural institutions related to the university.

In this renovation Lemaire not only promoted the conservation of the architectural heritage, but also pointed out its relevance to the contemporary urban context.

YVES LEPÈRE AND JOSEPH POLET
Louvain-la-Neuve, Station and University Halls, 1976
(Bastin/Evrard)
In contrast to the Sart Tilman campus, where the architects could work independently on separate buildings, the Louvain-la-Neuve project saw everything subjected to a sort of aesthetic supervision that was to ensure the coherence and harmony of the whole. The architects were nevertheless expected to create some measure of variety within this strict framework. Together with André Jacqmain's library, the university halls by Yves Lepère add a monumental accent to the overall composition.

entrance to the grounds, the central command post and the central boiler house, both designed in 1966.

Louvain-la-Neuve

The division of the Catholic University of Leuven in 1968 [into separate Walloon and Flemish institutions -trans.] provided an opportunity to construct an ideal modern city for the Walloon university. Victor Gruen, the American town planner who was also asked to make a proposal for the Meir in Antwerp, submitted a project for a compact city: a flat disc crowned with high-rise tower buildings, as modern architects had always imagined it to be and as can be seen on mediaeval representations of cities. But those days had long gone.

There was widespread protest against Gruen's concept. It was worded by Professor Raymond Lemaire (b. 1921), who from the start had pleaded against a separate campus somewhere in the area. He was in favour of a proper city based on the model of Leuven, where the students could integrate in everyday urban life.

Lemaire, a historian specialized in architecture, had earned his reputation as the restorer of various churches, but especially for his reconversion of the 'Groot Begijnhof' (beguinage) in Leuven. He wanted to turn it into a model quarter containing student housing, cultural amenities, and congress facilities: a comfortable and prestigious meeting-point for the academic community.

Both the 'Groot Begijnhof' in Leuven and Louvain-la-Neuve were based on a brilliant idea: 'a city with human dimensions'. *In concreto,* however, this meant streets and squares without cars, no high-rise buildings, no illuminated advertising, no disturbing materials or constructions, no noise, everything under control; in a word, nothing associated with urban life today. What in Leuven simply fell into his lap, he had to create in Louvain-la-Neuve.

The location was chosen in the valley of the Malaise on the Lauzelle plateau, on the N4 motorway near the E40, in the district of Ottignies. The structure of the new city had to be one with a 'core', as formulated at the 1951 CIAM congress in Hoddesdon: a traffic-free city centre with around it, within a walking distance of six to seven hundred metres, four residential areas. Its size would be 50,000 inhabitants, including 20,000 students.

For the city centre the idea of a concrete plateau was decided on. It would bring together services, roads, car parks, and the train station, with above it a varied pedestrian area with low and medium-high buildings. It was certainly not to be a uniform city. In keeping with the complexity of the European city, a mixed architecture was opted for. The choice of different architects would guarantee the liveliness of the streetscape. However, this was not to go off the rails, so the architecture was subjected to a number of aesthetic regulations pertaining to its height and the materials used. Lemaire, who during the war had been involved in 'aesthetic supervision', reintroduced the system here.

In the first place, this meant control over the streetscape, the city's appearance. Associations with the conservation policy of monuments in historical cities such as Bruges readily come to mind. The question is if one can use appearance to shape a city. The pastiche of a holiday port city, Port-Grimaud in the south of France by the architect Spoerri, has been a success, but it is based on entirely different aims. Spoerri aimed at pleasing, whereas Lemaire wanted to use architecture as a corrective means against bad taste, an aim which inevitably destroys both architecture and the city itself. Louvain-la-Neuve constitutes the inversion of the Port-Grimaud approach, its identity being a lie.

The discusssion about control over form almost inevitably led to conflicts within the responsible Urbanisme/Architecture group. Within this narrow framework Walloon architects, many of whom had also been working in Sart Tilman, were invited. They included Roger Bastin, André Constant, Jean Van Coppenolle, Jean Cosse, Pierre Coulon and André Noterman, Jean Fettweis, Simonne Guillissen, Pierre Humblet, André Jacqmain, Jean Mabardi, Georges Pepermans, Jean Potvin, Roger Thirion, Emile Verhaegen, and Charles Vandenhove. André Jacqmain's proposal of a monumental library on the Place des Sciences was acceptable because of its exceptional building programme and location. However, when Charles Vandenhove pressed on with his project for the modular construction of the science faculty it was rejected as a foreign body and branded 'outrageux'.

The younger architect Yves Lepère (b. 1942), who had trained under Louis Kahn, built the 'university halls', a name that was to evoke the traditions of Leuven. This building, as Francis Strauven put it, 'surmonte la hantise du pittoresque qui tortille la rue des Wallons; à l'endroit où il s'implante, ce cheminement devient rue'. An impressive project is currently in the pipeline for a 'musée du dialogue' by the hand of the Japanese architect Kisho Kurokawa, but it is uncertain whether it will ever be carried out.

RAYMOND-M. LEMAIRE,
JEAN-PIERRE BLONDEL, PIERRE LACONTE,
AND THE GROUP
URBANISME/ARCHITECTURE,
Louvain-la-Neuve, 1969-1979
(Bastin/Evrard)
The beguinage in Leuven served as a
model for the new city designed by
Lemaire and the Urbanisme/Architecture
group to accommodate the university of
Louvain-la-Neuve. It was not conceived
as a separate campus, but as an actual
city on a human scale.

City models

The two, or rather, three development models applied in Sart Tilman and Louvain-la-Neuve embody the both complementary and contradictory trends that were to shape cities in the period after 1955. Sart Tilman represents a shift away from the city's historical growth in favour of new construction on the outskirts. In the two concepts of Louvain-la-Neuve we can see the opposite. On the one hand the city is subjected to an unsparing urge for demolition, on the other hand attempts are made to protect sections of its torn texture, as a comfort in the process of mourning the city.

Making the city centre accessible to traffic and the merciless clearing away of slums after the 1953 law on urban renewal led to many inner cities being taken on. The compact city with its tower-block skyline, as Victor Gruen had intended Louvain-la-Neuve to be, remained a secret ideal in the minds of the authorities and architects.

In Brussels the fever of the world fair reigned supreme. Work on the North-South railway link was making headway. The South Station was demolished in 1954, the North Station in 1956. Instead of the latter the 'Centre Rogier' was erected, an urban landmark between the Koekelberg basilica and the PS building, as the terminus of the North-South link. Next to the South Station the 'Tour du Midi' tower block arose. The small ring road was finished in 1957 and, as a counter-balance, the borders of the 'ilôt sacré', the core of the city of Brussels, were laid down. In 1958 the Tekhné group, after several failed attempts, completed the new structural development plan for Brussels. In 1956 the burgomaster of Anderlecht, J. Bracops, presented his plans for the 'commune d'avant-garde' to the public.

In the same year Stanislas Jasinski (1901-1978), who had trained under Horta and van de Velde and collaborated with G. Brunfaut, started on the construction of a luxurious block of flats: 'Le Grand Large', a tower block that became the model for the new 'résidences', the general outlines of which had been determined in the period between the wars. The 'Résidence Palace' in Brussels (1923) by Michel Polak (1885-1948) was the prime example. They were named according to the flattering manner of villas: 'Résidence Green Dale' or 'Résidence Forestière'. Although a 'résidence' is a high-rise building, it need not manifest itself as such. Early in 1995 the importance of apartment buildings as witnesses to this century was underlined in an exhibition held by the 'Fondation pour l'Architecture' in Brussels.

These 'individual' residences were the opposite of real urban architecture, such as that of the Place du Roi Vainqueur in Etterbeek by Paul Posno, completed in 1958. The square in Etterbeek was the last city square completely surrounded with uniform buildings. It was the result of a competition held by the local authorities in 1936, although its construction only started in 1947 and was completed in the wake of the Expo '58 world fair.

A forgotten form of urban architecture, the nineteenth-century shopping arcade, became fashionable once more during the 1950s. In 1958 Brussels saw the completion of the Galerie Ravenstein, which communicates with the Central Station, after plans by Alexis (1877-1962) and Philippe Dumont (b. 1914), together with Alexis Dumont's Shell building of 1933. In Antwerp the arcade between the Huidevetterstraat and Korte Gasthuisstraat was laid out.

Other cities also knew such silent metamorphoses. In Liège the inner city saw the appearance in quick succession of a number of 'résidences' by Jean Poskin, bearing names such as 'César Franck' and 'Jean Delcourt', as if they were to continue the tradition of nineteenth-century statues. In Ghent the place

Brussels, Carrefour de l'Europe and Philips building, photograph 1970

(Karel Vermeir)
The view from the Carrefour de l'Europe towards the city centre and the Philips building by the Structures group clearly shows the brutality of this sort of intervention as well as the contrast between historically inspired reconstruction and the modern approach.

of the South Station near Albert Park was taken in by Geo Bontinck's EGW building (1955), or at least by one of its wings. A pastiche of the other wing appeared in 1994, by the hand of Dirk Bontinck. Here too the mansions around the park were replaced by 'résidences'. The same happened around the city park in Antwerp. We have already mentioned the situation in Ostend. Indeed, the whole Belgian coast has been blessed with such 'résidences'.

These massive, though incidental interventions make it hard to imagine that in the early 1960s many cities had approved plans to stem reconversion. In Liège reconstruction was mercilessly pursued in a last desperate attempt. The development plan adopted by Antwerp in 1960 was, according to Burgomaster Craeybeckx, supposed to encourage the modernization of the inner city and heal the scars left by the war. It was quietly written off in 1974. The Central Station and Leysstraat narrowly escaped demolition. The nineteenth-century monuments dedicated to famous burghers of Antwerp, such as Van Dyck and Teniers, had to make way for traffic. They were put back towards the end of the 1980s to enliven the renovated shopping precincts.

As late as 1965 the South Station in Antwerp was demolished in view of the motorway that was to join the Meir. For the Cogels-Osy Art Nouveau quarter in Berchem, where the picturesque station was replaced by a pitiful construction, the 'Koninklijke Maatschappij van Bouwmeesters' (royal society of

architects) in Antwerp had their plans ready. In the blank space of the then contemptible, but now much appreciated Cogels-Osy area there was to be a collection of loose blocks around a large shopping centre amidst green fields.

In the early 1960s the block of buildings on the Wapper was pulled down to afford a better view of the new Stadsschouwburg, a theatre designed by Renaat Verbruggen, Marc Appel, and Rie Haan, completed only in 1980. As compensation the Conscienceplein was made free of traffic and a plan to upgrade the city centre was drawn up by the group Cogge, D'Huyvetter, Jagenau, and Toubhans.

The inner city of Antwerp, much damaged by German missiles, was the subject of lengthy and heated discussions. The choice lay between a modern interpretation of the empty or emptied spots, or a form of reconstruction that would be a compromise between old and new. Braem was a champion of the first view and enjoyed the support of Burgomaster Craeybeckx, who was all in favour of a large-scale approach. We have already discussed Braem's administrative centre. Finally the choice fell on a rather meager filling-in of the area around the Vleeshuis, after a project by the architect F. Groothaert, which imitates the rhythm of the lost stepped gables. Its realization may be seen as a turning point, the end of modernism.

A stone's throw from there, in the Huikstraat, Edward Van Steenbergen Jun. (b. 1925) and Frank Commers (b.1944) put up an exemplary ensemble of houses, which did not take the

whole discussion into account, but became a foreign island in the city because of its introverted character. In a later phase, towards the end of the 1980s, these architects reinstated the closed pattern of the streets by building a block of around forty flats.

The great residential development of Antwerp happened, as in other cities, on its outskirts: the Luchtbal and Kiel areas, as well as in Kielpark on the Jan de Voslei, in a complex by the hand of Jos Smolderen (1889-1973) and in the high-rise block of flats by Jul De Roover (b. 1913). In 1961 a start was made on the development of the large-scale Europark on the 'Linkeroever' (left bank of the River Scheldt) after plans by the Brussels-based group of Aelbrecht, Brunswyck, Moureau, and Wathelet, which had been selected through a contest. The results of the international competition for the 'Linkeroever' held in the early 1930s were not taken into account.

The exodus from the city was not restricted to people living there. In Liège not only the university and training hospital were moved to Sart Tilman, but a second hospital was built on the outskirts of the city. In Antwerp Braem, Francken, and Van Riel started on the new Middelheim hospital in 1957, a commission dating from 1946. In Bruges the final plans of the new Sint-Jans hospital were approved in 1962. It was to be located outside the city and was designed by Jozef Lansoght, the architect who also built the churches of O.L.Vrouw-ter-Duinen (Our Lady of the Dunes) in Koksijde and Sint-Jan-de-Doper (St John the Baptist) in Menen.

As in Liège, the inner cities were being reserved for shops and offices. A prime example of this development is the Quartier du Nord near the North Station in Brussels. Here a lively popular quarter was brutally razed to the ground without there even being a guarantee that the megalomaniacal World Trade Center would ever be built. It was the heyday of men like Charlie Depauw and Paul Van den Boeynants. To glean something from the metamorphosis of the city, one should read François Schuiten and Benoît Peeters' *Brüsel,* a comic strip in which these notorious characters also feature.

On the other hand there is resistance against this trend of renovation, often against people's own better judgment, in order to preserve the existing city and urban culture, or rather what is seen as such. As from 1955 there was a growing awareness of the decreasing quality of life as reflected by architecture. Not only was the comfort of a new home beyond the means of a large part of the population despite all sorts of premiums, but it also became clear that such comforts offered no alternative for the social culture that still lived in the remaining or newly formed slums. The architect was at a total loss if he wanted to face up to this situation. The form he could offer had gone up in thin air and he was not equipped to formulate a reply to this new reality which he had just woken up to. He could become a bad plumber or an improvised social worker, but he was all alone with his ideal of architecture that would serve society. No amount of education had prepared him for this, nor could he call upon professional organizations or the public opinion.

PAUL POSNO
Brussels, Place du Roi Vainqueur, 1947-1958
(Bastin/Evrard)

One of the last examples of genuine urban architecture can be seen on Paul Posno's Place du Roi Vainqueur in Etterbeek. It resulted from a contest held in 1936. However, its construction was started after the war and only completed in the wake of the Expo '58 world fair.

RENÉ AERTS, PAUL RAMON, YVAN BLOMME, JEAN PETIT, ADRIAAN BRESSERS, A. VAN ACKER, MARCEL LAMBRICHS, AND JEAN VAN DOOSSELAERE
Brussels, Tour du Midi, 1962-1967
(Bastin/Evrard)

In 1949 A. Payen's *Gare du Midi* (1869) was replaced by a new building designed by Jean Petit together with Adrien and Yvan Blomme. Between 1962 and 1967 the 150-metre-high *Tour du Midi* was erected right next to it. The tower block, an impressive element in the urban landscape, was designed by a whole group of architects and conceals its ingenuity behind a dark glass façade (which at present requires replacement). It is strikingly superior to its chaotic surroundings.

STA JASINSKI
Brussels, Residence 'Le Grand Large', 1956
(Bastin/Evrard)

In 1957 the residence specialist Sta Jasinski noticed that the 'apartment in a collective building' had at last become acceptable to Belgians. His luxurious block of flats 'Le Grand Large' serves as an ideal example of various similar buildings throughout Belgian cities.

Brussels, Quartier du Nord,

(Bastin/Evrard)

The drastic changes brought about in the cities did not spring from a particular view concerning their development, but are the result of the impulsive promotion of interests. The Expo '58 world fair provided Brussels with a perfect excuse to step up urban redevelopment regardless of its social repercussions. The *Quartier du Nord* has become the symbol of marginalization.

◁   JOSSE FRANSSEN
Brussels, Residence 'Josaphat', 1957

(Bastin/Evrard)

The idea of a 'residence' usually boiled down to a arbitrary collection of apartments whose shape and size were determined by the available terrain instead of an inner logic. Nevertheless, with his keen sense of form Josse Franssen tried to transform this vagueness into a recognizable object with its own identity.

Lucien Kroll (b. 1927)

Lucien Kroll can be seen as the main protagonist in this tragicomedy. Obsessed as he is with architecture and its form in particular, he wants to bring it to obvious expression beyond the limits of its possibilities. It takes a large dose of imagination to go on pursuing the myth of participatory architecture for as many years as Kroll has, but then architects have seldom lacked this sort of imagination.

Starting out in partnership with Charles Vandenhove, he collaborated with Vandenhove on a number of fine houses, which sometimes also incorporated new techniques, as in the two semi-detached houses in Waterloo (1956). However, in those early days Kroll was mainly busy with the presentation and promotion of Belgian design. He was a founding member of the Design Center in Brussels in 1956, organized the 'Salon de l'Esthétique industrielle' of 1956 on the occasion of the annual fair in Liège, and was responsible for the layout of the 'Signe d'or industriel' exhibition of 1959. He also promoted Belgian design abroad, for instance on the XIth Milan Triennale in 1957, or the 1962 annual fair in Helsinki.

His interest in modern techniques has remained constant. Apart from several articles with titles such as 'Demain l'industrie dominera l'architecture' (Tomorrow's architecture will be dominated by industry) (1965) or 'L'informatique contre l'architecture' (Information science against architecture) (1968), this interest resulted in *Composants. Faut-il industrialiser l'archi-*

tecture? of 1983. This did not stop him from defending an unorthodox figure such as Antonio Gaudi. In a 'Tribune libre' in *La Maison* he interpreted the architect's work as a liberation of the constructive imagination.

Kroll wanted to use the means offered by his profession to come to a less rigid, more natural form of architecture adapted to the occupant. In a presentation of his most recent work in *L'architettura*, May 1994, he retrospectively summarizes his approach: 'Que cherchons-nous? Fatigués des architectures héroïques? Même pas: toute architecture est miraculeuse, même la plus commerciale. L'ambition: retisser un quartier ordinaire, banal, continu, 'composé' de tout ce qui est nécessaire à la survie urbaine, pour lui garder son désordre organique et

LUCIEN DEVESTEL
Brussels, Berlaymont building, 1963-1969
(Bastin/Evrard)
In Brussels not only the areas around the major stations have seen the construction of massive buildings, but other parts of the city have likewise been razed to the ground to make way for new building complexes. In 1963, after the European Community had made their headquarters in Brussels (1958), Lucien Devestel started the construction of the cross-shaped Berlaymont building.

pour qu'il se transforme de l'intérieur. Lui assurer tout ce qui conditionne sa communauté, son réseau de relations, donc exactement l'inverse de la charte d'Athènes. Il ne faut rien séparer, ni les fatigués des énergiques, les dormeurs des actifs, les pauvres des riches, les noirs des jaunes, les épiciers des juges et des curés, etc. Un paysage? Tout compliquer pour arriver à perdre la maîtrise de ce paysage? Et retrouver une forme de ville contemporaine et locale tout autant qu'éternelle et universelle. Est-ce moderne? Non! Quelle importance?'

The dream of a universal paradise, the biblical playing of the lion with the lamb: how can architecture make this come true? This is the fatal illusion. Kroll does exactly the same as Lemaire in Louvain-la-Neuve in that he proposes a sort of anti-formalism that is at least as formal. He justifies his authoritarian intervention in *Bouwen in België 1945-1970* as follows: 'The collective creativity we are hoping for will not come about spontaneously: it cannot but be the result of a lengthy process of practice, research, the contemplation of examples, study, and education.'

In one of his first independent projects he demonstrates how it has to be done. In a condominium (1961) in which he too owned a flat, he goes very far in renouncing architecture, which here becomes the ascetic framework that refers to introspective life and experience. The 't Holleken church in Linkebeek (1961) is also characterized by this remarkable asceticism. If his recent works evince some qualities, these lie in the simplicity and directness that occasionally appear from behind the ludicrous formal repertoire, which is supposed to reflect the inhabitants' spontaneity, but in fact signals contempt for it.

Kroll soon moved away from this minimalism. In 1963 he designed an ecumenical centre for the abbey of Chevetogne, where he avoided an orthogonal pattern in favour of organic forms, which were to mirror the flexible configuration of a living group. The flexible form of the ground plan was given shape through the same sober means as in the previous work.

Kroll made use of the commission for the medical campus of the Université Catholique de Louvain (1963), known as 'La Mémé' and situated in Woluwe-Saint-Lambert (Brussels) to wage a veritable architectural battle, a feat that brought him national as well as international fame and provided a gripping image of the chaos in Belgian architecture. The protest by students and people living in the area against the master plan drawn up by Henri Montois according to accepted modernist principles, was the ideal occasion to propose a new one: planned chaos with shapeless buildings that were to contain student accommodation, a cafeteria, a school and other public amenities, and the Alma underground station.

Compared to the boring and rigid appearance of Louvain-la-Neuve, that of Woluwe is unexpectedly lively. However, it is only an appearance, a manifesto, which does not have much to do with the reality of living and building as such. Apart from the choice of the architect, participation in the form of this architecture is largely fictitious and, just as the architecture itself, a myth. Whether this architecture is more democrat-

FRANS GROOTHAERT
Antwerp, Vleeshuis area, 1974-1981
(Bastin/Evrard)
In Antwerp hesitation between radical renovation of the inner city and its conservation has led to a fairly historical cityscape. After quite a struggle the Vleeshuis area, which had been redeveloped after the war, was filled in with fake architecture in 1974.

ic, spontaneous, or freer remains an open question. As a suggestion of improvisation and a procedural composition it retains a rigid appearance.

The simulated anarchy of 'La Mémé' ignores the experiments in popular housing that Kroll carried out early in his career for a mission in Rwanda, in which not the result, but the constructional process and contribution of the inhabitants were taken as the point of departure. In Woluwe and in consecutive works, we face the perfect simulacrum of architecture trying to be something it neither is, nor ever can be. The untenability of the so-called 'Sar' principle laid down by John Habraken in *De dragers en de mensen* during the early 1960s, which distinguishes between the bearing, permanent structure and its temporary, varying filling, is demonstrated here while the dangerous political hypothesis on which it is based is revealed. The contribution of the individual occupant is limited to his own small domain, subjected to the authority of the planned infrastructure. Kroll's version may be fun, but only in the touristic sense in which a walk through the remodelled Bruges or Disneyland can be relaxing.

In his later career, when he was mainly working abroad, Kroll continued to apply this formula for success. Towards the end of the 1980s he built the retirement home 'De Duinpieper' in Ostend, in which there is no sign of respect for the tastes of its inhabitants, but only of his own pleasure in playing with forms. Yet there is enough of the architect in him to keep even this unlikely mix under control.

Charles Vandenhove (b. 1927)

After the termination of his association with Lucien Kroll in 1957 Charles Vandenhove followed a direction that led him away from the polemical position held by his erstwhile partner. Few people have been such strong advocates of the personal engagement of the architectural œuvre. However, this obstinate attitude has produced an almost timeless architectural style, architecture without the architect. It brings to life the ideals preached by Kroll even better than his own simulated freedom does.

Charles Vandenhove's own house, which he designed in 1961, is a clear indication of the consistency of his approach. It is situated on a piece of ground that was considered unfit for building on and flanks the hills enclosing Liège. By means of brick wall sections, which have been left unfinished both in- and outside, and a series of stairs the walk is calculated to lead through a suite of rooms, the interior and exterior combining to form a single whole. This architecture is reminiscent of a ruin in which one can settle down. It is independent, and opens up possibilities without prescribing anything. The process of building remains present in every fragment, retaining its regularity, its controlled, though unconquered gravity.

The house follows the development of Vandenhove's œuvre. In 1974, when he was working on the glass hall of the training hospital in Sart Tilman, he placed a glass tent on a metal structure above the dark crypt. Fifteen years later he added yet another extension to the house, a zinc barrel vault on the other side, just as those he used in the 1980s. Such adaptations can also be seen in several of his other buildings.

CHARLES VANDENHOVE

Liège, Inichar, offices and laboratories, 1960-1965

(Bastin/Evrard)

After his association with Lucien Kroll, Charles Vandenhove started out in Liège with a series of impressive buildings, showing his conscious approach to architecture. The headquarters of the 'Institut National de l'Industrie Charbonnière', commissioned in 1960, was the first of these. He used prefab elements combined with brick façades to create powerful volumes endowing the area with a stately, open structure.

◁ In all his buildings an important role is given to the monumental stairs constructed of prefab elements.

Campus Sart Tilman, Institute of physical training, 1963-1968

(Karel Vermeir)

Commissioned by the university of Liège, Charles Vandenhove designed various buildings in the 1960s, ranging from laboratories to the Brull hall of residence on the banks of the River Meuse.
He continued the series with a book repository on the Sart Tilman campus, followed by the institute of physical training with its characteristic closed concrete façades and the enormous roofs of the five sports halls.

CHARLES VANDENHOVE

Olne, house, 1967-1969

(Bastin/Evrard)

We can distinguish a number of typological approaches in Vandenhove's œuvre. One of these, prominently featuring a pavilion roof, can be seen in a house in Olne of 1967. It reappears in a metal version in the Standard sports hall in Sart Tilman.

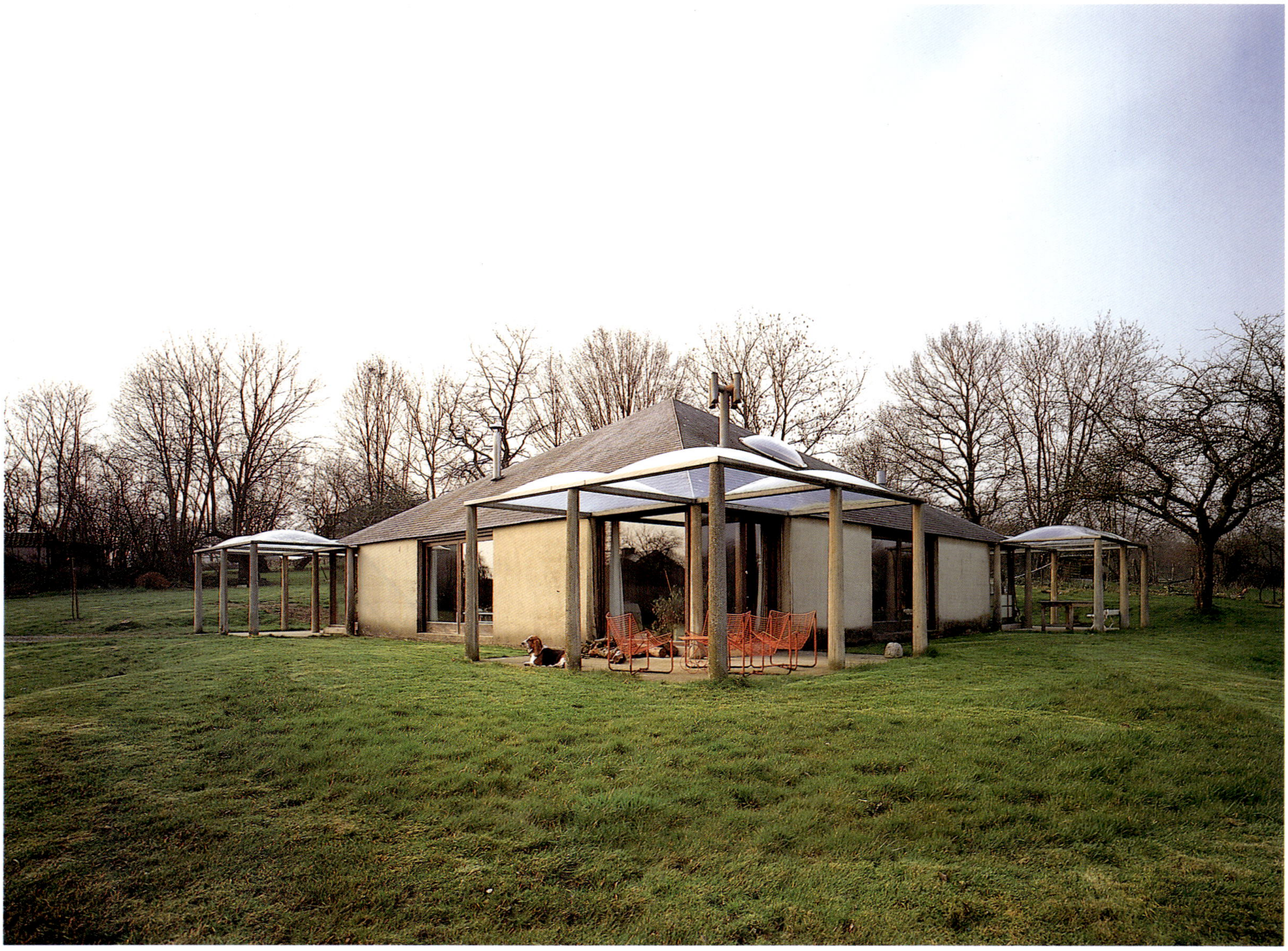

Saint-André, house, 1969-1970

The house in Saint-André is of the same type as that in Esneux, but very different as to material and construction. It also distinguishes itself through the fact that it is symetrically disposed below the metal saddle roof and placed on a plinth containing the garage and utility rooms. There are two small apartments situated on either side of an open space.

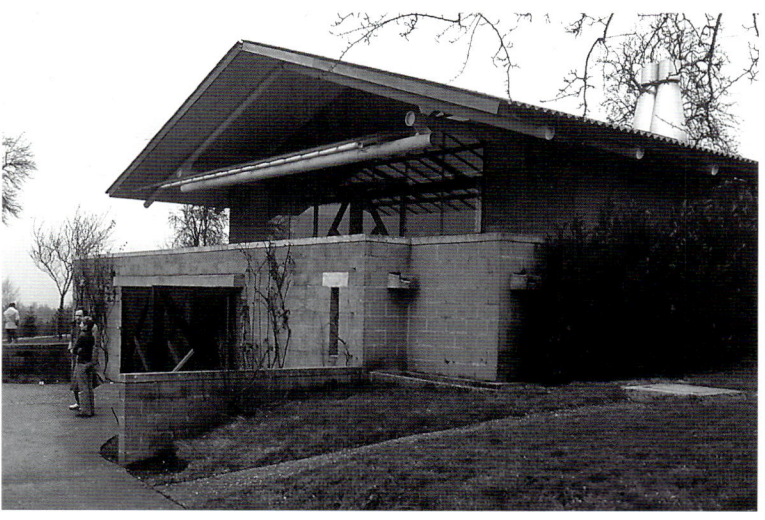

Soumagne, house, 1983

(Bastin/Evrard)

This transformation of a farm near the River Meuse shows the same blend of old and new elements in Vandenhove's work. The existing structure was meticulously restored so that the wealth of new elements that were added does not detract from its force, but rather contributes to it.

CHARLES VANDENHOVE
Woluwe-Saint-Lambert, market-place, 1989-1991
(Bastin/Evrard)
Vandenhove designed a closed square with a gallery around it in the centre of Woluwe-Saint-Lambert. It was an attempt at reinstating the tradition of monumental urban architecture, but was only carried out in part.

Esneux, house with annexe, scale model, 1974-1994
(Kim Zwarts)
The house in Esneux is composed of an elongated volume below a pitched roof. It was built in 1974, but in 1994 an annexe was added in the form of a closed square volume. Just as in Vandenhove's own house, the contrast here serves to highlight the individual character of each element despite their being so closely interrelated.

Liège, Hors-Château, renovation and new elements, 1978

(Bastin/Evrard)

The renovation of the Hors-Château area became the prototype of numerous housing complexes that Vandenhove was to build later, in the Netherlands especially. On one side of a closed courtyard the houses in the traditional style of the Meuse area were renovated, on the other he built new houses dominated by a block of flats. The monument on the square is by Anne and Patrick Poirier.

CHARLES VANDENHOVE
Liège, own house, 1961-1963
(Bastin/Evrard)

The construction and continuous
transformation of his own house,
situated against a steep hill on the
outskirts of the city, give a clear
impression of the evolution of
Vandenhove's work. Originally designed
in 1961, a metal construction was placed
on the brick plinth and filled in with
glass. In later years a metal barrel
vaulting was added at the other end.

The ethereal interior below the metal
supporting structure, originally
completely covered in glass, perfectly
blends with the rest of the house even
though they sharply contrast. The sense
of unity lies in the architect's approach
rather than in his use of materials or in
the style.

In 1960 he was commissioned to build the headquarters of Inichar, the national institute of the coal industry, in Liège. Clearly outlined volumes, accompanied by walkways and stairs, determine its open configuration in which the contrast between open lateral façades and prefabricated concrete elements with their quick rhythm and closed brick façades play an important role. Nothing is left to chance, and yet there is nothing compulsive about it. It is as if it could have been different, without losing its specific character. One of the most remarkable details, if one can speak of details in this case, is the spiral stairs made of prefab elements, which can be seen as a summary of his whole approach. They also played a prominent role in Vandenhove's later work. Indeed, staircases functioned as a privileged symbol in many post-war buildings.

Also in 1960 Vandenhove was commissioned with the 'Centre Hospitalier Universitaire', the training hospital of the university of Liège on the Sart Tilman campus. He continued working on it up to the end of the 1980s and it has already been classified as a listed building. In order to satisfy the specifications set out in the building programme Vandenhove developed a system of prefabricated elements similar to that seen in the Inichar and other projects. This system enabled him to deal with the frequent changes imposed on the scheme over the years. Whereas at Inichar the façade surfaces – their openness and closedness – were significant, here the transparent structure is developed as the central idea. The building is finished, so to speak, when the structure is complete.

One of the most remarkable facts regarding the way it is finished and the effect it creates is – apart from the sumptuous details – the collaboration with contemporary artists, a constant in Vandenhove's work, to which it is both complement and confrontation. In the rooms and passages Vandenhove provided enamelled aluminium panels for which designs were made by various artists, such as Daniel Buren, Olivier Debré, Jean-Charles Blais, Sol LeWitt, Jacques Charlier, Jo Delahaut, Niele Toroni, Marthe Wéry, Claude Viallat, and Léon Wuidar. The constructional system of the hospital is also applied in Vandenhove's plans for a private clinic in Verviers as well as in the research and training laboratories of Louvain-la-Neuve, which have been referred to, and in the projects he submitted for the competitions for the Centre Pompidou in Paris and the Free University in Brussels.

While the work on the *opus magnum* of the hospital was under way Vandenhove built, also on the Sart Tilman campus, an imposing institute for physical education, a collection of five halls for the various sports as well as facilities for education and administration. Vandenhove had already built a book depot on Sart Tilman. The campus shows the different stages of his development and the way they interlink. Near the campus Vandenhove also built a sports complex for Club Standard, the whole of which is housed under one large metal roof. Afterwards an indoors tennis court was added, which, just as in his own home, emphasizes the continuity and evolution of the work.

CHARLES VANDENHOVE
Liège, Sart Tilman campus, 'Centre Hospitalier Universitaire', 1962-1986
(Bastin/Evrard)
The university hospital on the Sart Tilman campus is Vandenhove's *opus magnum*. It took a quarter of a century to build and was listed soon after it had been completed. This is very fortunate, as the present administration do not appear to appreciate it.

Vandenhove developed a system using prefab elements in order to meet the requirements of the complex building specifications in a flexible way. Originally this system incorporated six separate blocks that were arranged around a central core containing the the impressive glass entrance hall.

Besides these large projects, all of them carried out from his small offices, there are several private houses. At the same time as his own house Vandenhove built the Repriels house (1962) in Plainevaux near Liège. At a stone's throw from there the Thonon house was built in 1978. The Schoffeniels house (1967) in Olne is surprising in that it incorporates all functions below a single pyramidal roof in a way similar to that of the Club Standard sports complex. The canopies on the corners show how existing standard elements can create a poetic whole. The Dufays house in Saint-André near Liège also looks into new possibilities offered by constructional methods and formal control.

1978 opened a new chapter with the restoration and renovation of the Hôtel Torrentius and of the Hors-Château area in central Liège. He transformed the Hôtel Torrentius, built by Lambert Lombard in 1565, into his own house. Hors-Château was undergoing urban redevelopment to renew the dilapidated central area by building social housing and renovating a number of houses in the local Meuse style. Characteristically, Vandenhove interpreted this new commission as a prototype of what he sees as urban life. By placing the houses around a courtyard he interiorized urban life and created transitions from the public street to the private interior zone.

The entrance to the courtyard is formed by a portico with Ionic columns on one side and on the other by a sort of propylaeum with columns. On the square there is a monument by Anne and Patrick Poirier, which gave the square its name (Place de Tikal) and a lonely tree. There is a channel conducting water from the fountain towards the other side of the square. Vandenhove was to follow this type in all his commissions for

CHARLES VANDENHOVE
Liège, Hôtel Torrentius, renovation 1979 and Hôtel de Grady, renovation 1993
(Bastin/Evrard)
The renovation of Hôtel Torrentius, built by Lambert Lombard in 1565, signalled a new phase in Vandenhove's œuvre. Here the continuity with the architectural traditions of the Meuse area became explicit; Vandenhove successfully blended his earlier formal patterns with the Renaissance architecture of the building. The 'hôtel' with its courtyard could be considered a model of urban housing.

As in most of his works, Vandenhove collaborated with other artists when renovating Hôtel Torrentius. The decoration of the large hall on the ground floor, which still contains some original frescos, was entrusted to the French painter Olivier Debré.

social housing. The fountains he designed may serve as the architect's signature to his work.

This approach resulted in a number of realizations, such as the 'Maison Blanche' reception centre in Esneux (1980), the Delforge house in Namur, and the conversion of a farm in Ayeneux, both in 1983. The real breakthrough came in 1985 after the exhibitions of his œuvre at the 'Institut Français d'Architecture' in Paris and the 'Ludwigstiftung' in Aachen and, in 1986, in the stock exchange of Berlage in Amsterdam. These exhibitions led to a wide range of commissions in Paris, but especially in the Netherlands, with housing complexes in The Hague, Amsterdam, Maastricht, Breda, and Wageningen. As with Kroll, Vandenhove's most important work of the last decades is to be found abroad. In Belgium he designed a town square with surrounding buildings in Woluwe-Saint-Lambert (1984), only a part of which has been carried out, and the remarkable pavilion in the Middelheim sculpture park in Antwerp.

CHARLES VANDENHOVE
Antwerp, Middelheim park, pavilion, 1984, sketch

The colonnade pavilion in the Middelheim park may be considered a perfect example of Vandenhove's approach to architecture. It is a trademark that is present in all his other buildings, that lends them their force through its relentless tectonics, tangible mass, and geometrical composition. The pediment was finally placed at some distance from the pavilion itself.

Brussels, Théâtre de la Monnaie, Salon Royal,
1986

(Bastin/Evrard)
In 1984 the transformation of the
Monnaie theatre was entrusted to Urbat,
the firm formed by Jacques Aron, Frédéric
De Becker, and Pierre Puttemans.
Vandenhove was commissioned with the
arrangement of the royal saloon and the
renovation of the entrance. For the
entrance he invited Sam Francis to paint
the ceiling and Sol LeWitt for the floor
design. For the saloon he collaborated
with Daniel Buren and Giulio Paolini.

◁
Esneux, Maison Blanche, reception centre,
1980

(Bastin/Evrard)
The earliest example of Vandenhove's
new approach, in which decoration
acquires a distinctive place within the
constructional composition, can be seen
in the reception centre for children in
Esneux. The strict symetrical
composition is even more strongly
emphasized by the small differences
between the front and rear façades.

André Jacqmain (b. 1921)

'Dagobert was a famous ruler who, just as many others at the time of the Pepinides, left the mania to act the boss to his clerks and devoted himself to the sweeter side of things.' This is the final sentence of André Jacqmain's contribution to *Bouwen in België 1945-1970*. It bore the title 'Omtrent het formalisme der architectuur in België, van bij de Pepiniden tot op onze dagen' (On the formalism of architecture in Belgium, from the Pepinides to our day). The sentence is typical of him. Architecture has to produce beauty and has to please: 'We who live in Belgium are in love with the things of the earth.'

Jacqmain's work flourishes in an atmosphere of enthusiasm and friendship. As he puts it himself, his work 'originated from friendship and only exists for friends'. 'I have spent my life piling brick on stone. And I think that it is only to this extent that I have really lived, for it was a way in which I could withdraw from a society for which I feel very little love.'

His reflections on his own work, *Over architectuur. André Jacqmain en het Atelier de Genval* (ed. Pierre Looze, 1988), open as follows: 'Not a single stone vault possesses any spatial value, or is able to acquire even passing significance, without it referring to the vault of heaven. A stone floor can only testify to human presence if its connection with the sand of the shore, the mull of the earth, or the rough unevenness of the rock is felt and fully appreciated. Not a single column, erected by human hands to defy the clouds, can fulfil this challenge unless its vertical line is connected to the line the sun draws in the sky between sunrise and the evening when, at noon, it casts its shortest shadow on the ground. Indeed, it is not without reason that man blesses the earth by leaving on it a trace of his presence. In architecture he finds his best weapon and his most beautiful seal. Vaults, floors, and columns are the actual witnesses to his thoughts and his desire to defy the indifference of heaven.'

'In my view architecture is only created when man understands the vital necessity of embodying his aspirations in stone. When he kneels in prayer below the vault. He has to live amidst his works of art, for his consciousness derives from his sculptures and columns. Moreover, I feel that without images and idols, that is, without references to the immobile, it is virtually impossible to know what life is.'

Jacqmain no doubt is the most versatile designer of his generation. Maybe it has something to do with the fact that he trained at the Brussels Académie under Henry Lacoste, who taught him 'to make shameless use of all images that come to us from outside'. Although he is older than Willy Van der Meeren, he should be situated in the same period. Indeed, his work has little to do with the problems of reconstruction, urban redevelopment, or architecture 'for as many people as possible'. His architecture is only concerned with architecture itself. He plays with form and meaning, just as his friends, the painters and sculptors.

His first work, the house of the painter Carlo de Brouckère in Torhout (1950), on an old farmyard, comes as a complete

ANDRÉ JACQMAIN
Torhout, house, 1950
(Gilles Ehrmann)

André Jacqmain's earliest work, the painter Carlo de Brouckère's house in Torhout in the courtyard of an old farm, came as a complete surprise. It pokes fun at the dogmatic approach and consequently emanates a great sense of freedom. It perfectly blends with its surroundings without sacrificing any of its refinement in the use made of materials.

surprise. It pokes fun at every form of dogmatic approach. It perfectly fits into the rural surroundings, even though it is incredibly refined at the same time. The house and studio for the sculptor Olivier Strebelle (1955) is very similar.

One of his most unusual works is the Urvater museum-house in Rhode-Saint-Genèse (1960). Jacqmain personally describes it as 'Mexican'. Its history is is one of tragedy. It held its original function, a shrine for the Urvater collection with works by mainly Magritte, Ernst, and Matta for two years. Now all that remains is a ruin – the walls still stand, with emptiness between them.

The same holds true for the 'unfinished' Laval house (1968) in Bercuit, Grez-Doiceau. It is all that is left of a large-scale project for a golf-course and residential area. Jacqmain comments: 'The house was drawn as the ground plan of an ancient city, built, burnt to the ground, and reconstructed several times... The walls separate. The walls reunite. A plant. Nothing in it is straight. The use of a plumb-line is forbidden: the bricklayers are forced to build manually, weighing every stone in their hands. The eye of the architect and the pleasure of the one who builds the house together form a certain exactingness.' One would be forgiven for thinking that this is Kroll speaking.

The 'Pangolin' house, the scaly anteater, built for Pierre d'Ieteren in Knokke-Zoute (1966) hides – below the enormous scale of the roof with its reference to the standard villa in Knokke, to which Dupuis' 'Zeeëgel' also contributed – an unexpectedly large and white interior that is reminiscent of the inside of an animal, a womb. In the meantime Jacqmain also built the Goldschmidt-Clermont house (1966) in Uccle, clear and square.

Jacqmain distinguishes between the different periods in his career according to the materials he used. He speaks of a brick period, a concrete period, and a stone period. This division is not very strict, but it does demonstrate his attention to the formal and expressive potential of the material. The brick period is characterized by the Urvater house. For the refined Foncolin office building (1957) in Brussels, which he designed together with Jules Wabbes, a self-bearing concrete façade was incorporated, in which concrete was used as a precious material. Here concrete is assigned a completely different task from that in larger commissions such as the Sart Tilman campus and Louvain-la-Neuve.

In Sart Tilman Jacqmain built the cafeteria and student halls of residence (1967) and later, in 1981, the faculty of law in collaboration with Claude Strebelle and Daniel Boden. In the cafeteria rough concrete was used not as a structural element, but as a protective wall around a hidden interior which, with its brick walls and skimming light, makes a magical impression. One enters as if in a mysterious limbo, gets carried along the half-lit stairs, until one reaches the bright sanctuary above, a belvedere giving out onto the beautiful landscape. The happenings in the self-service student restaurant itself result in a heavy anticlimax.

André Jacqmain
Knokke-Het Zoute, 'Le Pangolin', villa, 1968
(Fabien de Cugnac)
Just as in Torhout Jacqmain had paid tribute to the surroundings, he here manipulates the architectural type of the luxurious villa so that it loses its banality and becomes a pure, evasive dream. With its enormous roof, the villa seems to be appropriately named.

Le Pangolin's interior is the antithesis of the Urvater house's. Both are equally exceptional. Le Pangolin is completely closed up, introverted, a cosy refuge. There are no sharp contrasts, but everything flows together in even curves.

Andé Jacqmain
Uccle, villa, 1966
(Gilles Ehrmann)
The Goldschmidt house is clear and
square, an almost classical context that
becomes surrealistic through Jacqmains
having himself and his friends portraited
in it.

The residences, the four hundred rooms of which are housed in three 'castles', form a whole with the cafeteria, and were supposed to form the basis of an actual student city for which Jacqmain had drawn up plans in 1962, but which were never realized. Jacqmain comments: 'Now I can feel the extent to which architecture has since the 1960s had to hold back its voice and how fast it has degenerated. Today everybody thinks that architecture is a matter of participation. Everyone gets his share, and everyone gets the short end. In the end nobody gets his due. I have just seen the photographer Gilles Ehrmann back in Paris. He, who is concerned with images, shared my impression. To him secrecy seems essential. The secret of fabrication. You should not share it with the crowd. You have to be alone behind the black cloth, with your eye against the lens. With the most persistent egotism, expressing your own vision of the world in a personal image. This is the most beautiful of all.'

In Louvain-la-Neuve Jacqmain's work also holds a central position with the library on the Place des Sciences, realized between 1972 and 1975. Dictated by the grid of the car park below it, this building consists of series of thin concrete discs, a system that Jacqmain also applied in his pavilion for the world fair in Osaka. These discs can be cut out as one pleases. It is not the structure that dominates, but the interplay between stairs and figures aggressively deteriorating it, as if here Jacqmain were rebelling against the simplism, dishonesty, and cosiness that lie at the basis of this new city.

A work in which natural stone plays an important role is the Glaverbel building in Boitsfort (1967) built in collaboration with Braem, Guilissen, and Mulpas. The idea of a closed ring was Braem's. The effect of the rings in rough natural stone from Hainaut, however, bears Jacqmain's signature. In 1967 Jacqmain set up the 'Atelier de l'Architecture de Genval', which increasingly directed his career. 'I no longer feel as if I am standing beside or above the atelier (studio),' he states.

The Atelier's work comes down to a large-scale operation of luxurious urban redevelopment on different sites in Brussels, the architecture of which they themselves describe as 'a kaleidoscopic mix of styles'. One cannot help associating this with Philip Johnson's cynicism. 'The idea is to organize derivation and to sell its result,' Jacqmain says. The operation started out with the 'Stephany Area' at the top of Avenue Louise, which covers the block between the avenue and the Chaussée de Charleroi. However, the 'Espace Nord' with the new building of the Flemish Community and the '151 Boulevard Emile Jacqmain' tower block together form an 'aesthetic complex' in progress. The Markies building (1988), next to St Michael's cathedral in Brussels – on the North-South railway link, adjacent to the 'Chancellerie' and 'Bois Sauvage' – is the least refined. Jacqmain's defence: 'And if one day we are logical, does that mean that we also have to be so the next?'

Rhode-Saint-Genèse, Urvater house and museum, 1960

(Henry Kessels and Arno Hammacher)
The house that Jacqmain built for the Urvater art collection is most unusual. Jacqmain, who often refers to 'the images that come to us from elsewhere', calls it 'Mexican'. The loose wall sections in concrete and brick form an adventurous track in the surrounding woods.

The transition from the exterior to the interior is a gradual process. At first there is nothing but a floor, but then the house becomes more and more dense, without ever closing up completely.
The ground plans give a clear impression of the architctural progression through the house with all its closed and open elements. They look like a survey of a prehistoric ruin, a fragment of an endless Mexican palace.

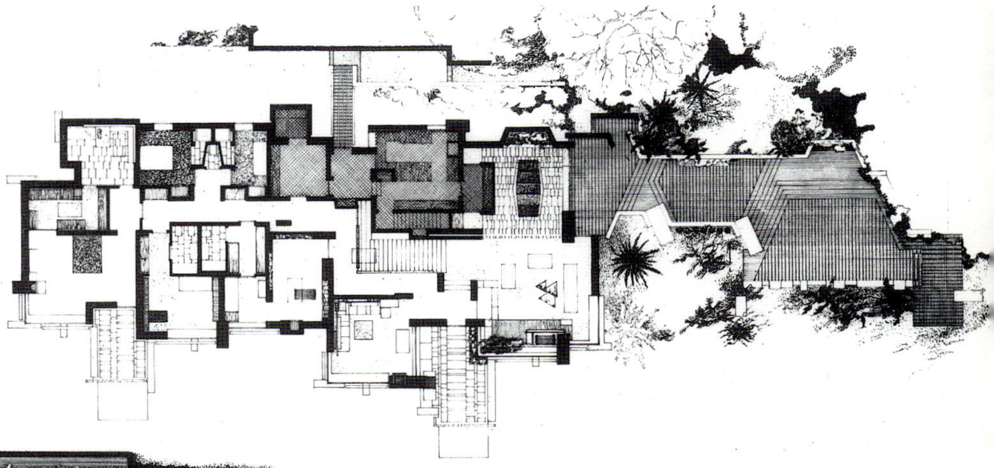

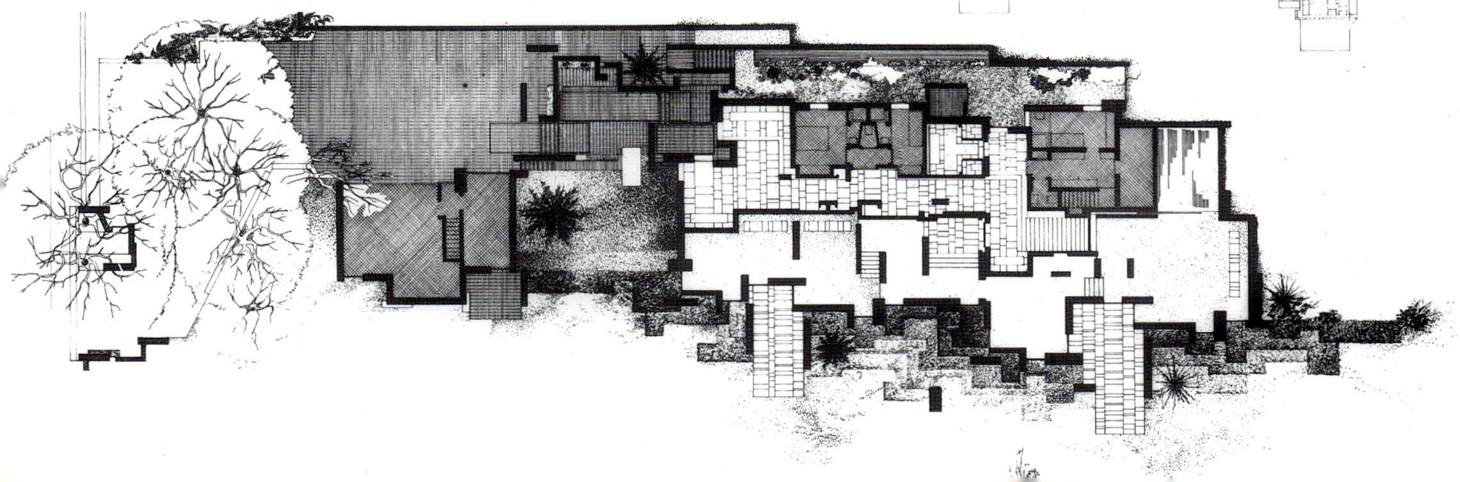

ANDRÉ JACQMAIN
Liège, Sart Tilman campus, cafeteria, 1962
(Bastin/Evrard and Henry Kessels)
In 1962 Jacqmain designed a whole
campus, a student city, for Sart Tilman.
However, only a few fragments were
carried out. The impressive cafeteria was
built in 1967. It is reminiscent of a high
fortress, the concrete functioning as a
structural element rather than as a
protective wall. The architect has also
used the different levels of the terrain to
great advantage. The mysterious interior,
which is dominated by dark brick,
sharply contrasts with the exterior, the
skimming light creating a magical
atmosphere. The visitor is drawn
upwards to the belvedere, which affords a
view of the beautiful landscape garden.

Louvain-la-Neuve, science library, 1970
(Bastin/Evrard)
Dictated by the grid of a car park, the
structure of the library consists of a
series of thin concrete discs, a system
which Jacqmain also applied in the
Belgian pavilion at the Osaka world
exhibition. However, this rigid structure
only forms the starting point from which
the freedom of the interior develops into
a labyrinthine landscape.

Just as the cafeteria and student halls of
residence in Sart Tilman, the science
library in Louvain-la-Neuve forms the
visual focus of the new city through its
striking appearance. It disrupts the
simple model of harmony and
emphasizes the individual character of
the building.

ANDRÉ JACQMAIN, RENAAT BRAEM,
PIERRE GUILLISSEN, AND VICTOR MULPAS
Brussels, Glaverbel offices, 1963
(Bastin/Evrard)

The collaboration between Braem and
Jacqmain led to the combination of the
pure concept of the circle and the
material quality of the finishing, which at
the same time charges and erodes it.
Beautifully situated in a park on the
Chaussée de La Hulpe among a number
of prestigious office blocks, it
demonstrates the high notions of
architecture created, Jacqmain says,
'when man sees the vital necessity of
giving shape to his aspirations in stone.'

ANDRÉ JACQMAIN
Bercuit, villa, 1968
(Bastin/Evrard)

The Laval house is all that remains of an elaborate project for a golf-course and residential area. It forms an agglomeration of rooms that seem to have been brought together by coincidence and to offer one another protection in the middle of the woods. The inspiring role given to the material, the original secret of stone, is shown here in all openness.

'The house was drawn as a plan of an ancient city,' Jacqmain says, 'built,

burnt down reconstructed several times. The walls disappeared and then reunited again. A plant. Nothing is straight. It is forbidden to use a plumb line: the bricklayers have to build manually, weighing each stone in their hands.'

Brussels, 'Markies' building, 1985

(Bastin/Evrard and Airprint)

In 1967 Jacqmain set up the Atelier d'Architecture de Genval, with which he has since increasingly identified himself. Their work mainly consists in large-scale operations involving urban renewal in different parts of Brussels. The architect's role is reduced to that of an aesthetic adviser.

The building clearly refers to the nearby Saint Michael's cathedral and is an attempt at restoring the urban block. The 'Markies' building is part of a wider urban renewal project by the Atelier de Genval, which includes 'Bois Sauvage' behind the choir of Saint Michael's, the restorations and new buildings around Jacques Wirtz's garden, and the multifunctional 'Chancellerie'.

Brussels, Wilchers complex, 1993

(Fabien de Cugnac)

The Wilchers complex with its two courtyards forms part of the 'Stephanie area'. It comprises a luxurious hotel, flats, offices, shops, and a car park. It also incorporates buildings by Paul Saintenoy and Henri Beyaert. In fact, the sumptuous luxury of the complex only adds to the dilemma of urban development and architecture in the Brussels region.

Brussels, 'Espace Nord', started 1990

(Airprint)

The metamorphosis of the city towards the end of the 1980s is most strikingly illustrated by the *Quartier du Nord*, which for years resembled an abandoned battlefield and then rapidly started reviving the visions of a real City dating from the 1960s. The Atelier de Genval provided 'aesthetic advice' for the 'Nord Building' (1) and '151 Boulevard Emile Jacqmain' (2). 'North Gate' (3) is currently under construction. 'Phoenix' (4) is still in the design phase.

Brussels, 'Stephanie Area', 1983-1993

(Marc Detiffe)

The double complex on Place Stephanie, where the Avenue Louise begins, is the most striking example of the Atelier de Genval's new approach. Both blocks together form a monumental entrance intended to reinstate the nineteenth-century avenue.

CONSTANTIN BRODZKI
Brussels, Design Centre, 1963

Just as many young people, Brodzki was fascinated by design as the ideal way to integrate new technological developments into contemporary culture. He designed the interiors of the Film Museum and Galerie d'Aujourd'hui in Brussels and was involved in many initiatives aimed at promoting design in Belgium. The most important of these was the Design Centre, which no longer exists, in Galerie Ravenstein.

Buzenol, Gallo-Roman museum, 1959-1960
(Henry Kessels)

All the characteristics of Brodzki's work are uniquely combined in this small museum in Buzenol, which is in a rather neglected state at the moment. The museum, intended for Gallo-Roman finds from the area, is innovatively embedded in the hillside. Visitors descend to the archaeological site via open stairs.

The receding and projecting sections of the façade creates an interior that alternatingly opens onto the wooded hillside and creates a closed space in which precious series of objects can stand out. As in numerous other cases, Brodzki collaborated with the graphic artist Corneille Hannoset on the interior design.

Linkebeek, villa, 1957

The exacting precision combined with
surprising innovation that Brodzki
showed in these interiors reappears in
his houses. While making use of the
different levels of the terrain, Brodzki
built an animated space according to a
consistent logic and a pure sense of
plastic proportion.

Constantin Brodzki (b. 1924)

The three celebrities, Kroll, Vandenhove, and Jacqmain, dominated the scene from 1955 to 1965 and even during the following decades, but this is not to say that they were the only interesting figures. One such is Constantin Brodzki, fascinated by the possibilities which modern techniques afford architecture and art. Together with Jacqmain he was the only Belgian to be included in the series on post-war architecture in *Zodiac*, published by Olivetti and the Palais des Beaux-Arts in Brussels. We have already mentioned his pavilion at the Expo '58 world fair.

His first works consisted of distinguished interiors, such as that of Galerie d'Aujourd'hui (1956) and the Film Museum (1956) in the Palais des Beaux Arts, as well as the Design Centre (1963) in Galerie Ravenstein in Brussels. The weekend house in Uccle and the Villa in Linkebeek may count as typical examples of his exceptional brand of 'modernist' architecture. In both cases playing with the irregularity of the terrain, Brodzki constructs a strict, yet animated space through his extremely accurate treatment of line and surface. In Uccle the carport is situated on the roof, with a flight of stairs leading down to the living area, which in turn communicates with the garden. The villa in Linkebeek is divided into three floors in the central part, with two wings housing the bed- and living-room areas.

Today his most remarkable building is in a dilapidated state. It is the Gallo-Roman Museum in Buzenol (1958), the interior of which he arranged in collaboration with the graphic de-

CONSTANTIN BRODZKI
Brussels, Expo '58, Fauna pavilion
With his pavilion for the fauna of the Congo at the Expo '58 world fair, Brodzki established his reputation as one of the most promising architects of his generation. Not only did he apply new techniques such as the light wooden dome placed on a concrete fence, but he also showed how new techniques and materials could be brought to perfectly controlled expression.

CONSTANTIN BRODZKI AND
MARCEL LAMBRICHS
Brussels, CBR offices,
(Bastin/Evrard)
Constantin Brodzki and Marcel Lambrich's CBR building with its decorative façade made of prefab elements belongs to the collection of office blocks situated on the Chaussée de La Hulpe. Other examples are André Jacqmain and Renaat Braem's Glaverbel building, as well as René Stapels and Pierre Dufau's Royal Belge.

signer Corneille Hannoset, just as that of the Film Museum. In order to reduce its impact on the landscape the museum is sunken into the hill in a way comparable to the weekend house in Uccle. A long open staircase leads down to it. Only one of its façades, with a jagged profile, is visible. The white closed sides face south, whereas the glass sides allow the northern light to enter. Here architecture hardly exists, and yet it predominates. It increases the presence of the landscape and the history it conceals.

His later œuvre shifts away from this beautiful austerity and is to some extent determined by his work for the CBR concrete company. He built their headquarters in Watermael-Boitsfort, right opposite the Glaverbel building, as well as several of their branch offices, amongst others in Lier. Here he used prefabricated concrete bearing elements, following their successful application in the Banque Bruxelles Lambert building in Brussels, designed by the American architect Bunshaft (SOM). This building dazzled his Belgian counterparts, who even awarded him the SBUAM prize.

Among the many applications, which increasingly demonstrated the limitations of the decorative system, the most interesting is that in a park in La Hulpe, which now houses the Swift headquarters. Its counterbalance is the Bofill building, to which Brodzki contributed.

CONSTANTIN BRODZKI
La Hulpe, Gulliver I, office block, 1967
Brodzki's later œuvre is characterized by the systematic application of prefab elements, mainly in buildings commissioned by CBR. One of his most interesting buildings, partly because of its location in a beautiful park, is the former CBR headquarters in La Hulpe, which now houses the SWIFT offices. Towards the end of the 1980s Ricardo Bofill and Brodzki collaborated on Gulliver II, situated in the same park.

JEAN COSSE

Waterloo, villa, 1965

(Bastin/Evrard)

Jean Cosse started out with the design of a model farm for the national small landowners' association. Indeed, the country house was to become his trademark. A typical example, which was also applied by other architects, can be seen in the villa in Waterloo. Shielded from the road, the house opens up towards the landscape.

Ottignies, Saint-André de Clerlande, convent, 1970

(Bastin/Evrard)

The convent and hospice in Ottignies, a typical work from Cosse's later period, was built with the growing student population of Louvain-la-Neuve in mind. Cosse commented on it: 'Simply being there, as if the walls had grown among the trees, being there without any trouble, obvious and yet creating its own space.'

Waterloo, Saint Paul's church, 1968

(Bastin/Evrard)

The sacred dimension of the house is expressed in this church, which is actually conceived as a large house. The church seen as a house was in keeping with the liturgical reforms of the Second Vatican Council. Cosse was to build several churches in later years. These became increasingly monumental, an evolution that can also be seen in his houses.

Jean Cosse (b. 1931)

The home, the detached private house, occupies a privileged position in Belgian architecture, even an exclusive one for many architects. Jean Cosse regards the house as the centre in which life originates and flourishes. 'Le merveilleux d'une maison', says Antoine de Saint-Exupéry, 'n'est pas qu'elle vous abrite ou vous réchauffe (...) mais bien qu'elle ait lentement déposé en nous ses provisions de douceur. Qu'elle forme dans le fond du cœur ce massif obscur dont naissent, comme des eaux de sources, les songes'. This is the detached house on the country which, in Cosse's own words, 'is rooted in the deep sediment from which it originated'. Even in his larger commissions Cosse has tried, though not always with success, to retain the scale of the house.

After graduating from Ecole Saint-Luc in Tournai in 1954, his first work (1958) was a prototype country house commissioned by the national small landowners' association. In the next year he built his own house, which embodies the intimate poetry of the habitat. In *Des maisons pour vivre,* dedicated to Cosse's work, Frédéric Debuyst refers to Gaston Bachelard's *Poétique de l'espace.*

The Toussaint house in Waterloo (1965) can be regarded as the final expression of this form of dwelling. Screened from the country lane by two rows of trees, the house affords a view of the undulating landscape stretching out before it. The architecture is restricted to the simplest of means. It poses no problems, but goes without saying. Cosse has consistently applied this idiom, even if in his later work it becomes more complicated and is enriched with new forms, such as the round window, bow shape, and cut roof surfaces.

When he receives the commission to build a church, his sacral approach finds its ideal expression. The church is the perfect house. This is demonstrated in the church of St Paul in Waterloo (1958). Its exterior cannot be distinguished from that of a large house in that it has the same shape of roof, the same materials, the same scale, and the same intimacy. In the Saint-André de Clerlande convent in Ottignies (1970) near Louvain-la-Neuve, house and church have literally fused. 'Etre là naturellement', says Cosse, 'comme si les murs avaient poussé entre les arbres, être là sans heurts, avec évidence, et pourtant créer un lieu spécifique'.

Lucien Engels (b. 1928)

'Lucien Engels likes strong buildings.' This is the opening sentence of the monography by Mil De Kooning in his collection *Vlees en beton*, dedicated to Engels in 1955. 'His architecture is light or robust – at its best it is both at the same time –, but it is always self-conscious and forcefully present, controlled.'

After completing his studies at La Cambre under Victor Bourgeois in 1950, he started out as Roger De Winter's associate. Together they built a number of terraced houses in Vilvoorde in the early 1950s, which emanate a sense of calm dignity in this crushed industrial town on the outskirts of Brussels. In these houses a self-conscious, though flexible brand of modernism has acquired a natural status.

When Lucien Engels started his own firm in 1954 he broke away from this obviousness and turned to an architectural style that is more forceful in its affirmation. In the Lambiotte house in Waterloo (1954) this pursuit is convincingly given expression. L.-H. De Koninck had called him 'un sauvage' while he was still at La Cambre. Indeed, the Lambiotte house does not follow accepted patterns. It stands in direct contrast with Cosse's approach. No matter how strongly conscious, it remains elusive. It breaks away in all directions and exudes a vitality that is seldom seen in works of this decade. All the ingredients of his later work are present, the water, the railings, the materiality, the ingenuity of the ground plan, but especially the necessity to let the building exist independently as architecture.

In the same year he designed the Home Van der Velde II in Oostduinkerke. This was the beginning of his career as the house architect of the Mutualités Socialistes. For them he also designed the medical centre in Menen (1959), the César De Paepe polyclinic in central Brussels (1961), and an office block for the Federation Brabant in Brussels (1973). All these buildings possess the same single-mindedness as the Home Van der Velde, though without its delightful enthusiasm. It shows dynamism not only in the configuration of three Y-shaped buildings, but especially in the interior and in the sturdy furniture he designed for it. In Waterloo Engels had collaborated with Paul Bury, here with the artists Rik Poot and Jan Cox. In St Lambert's church in Muizen he involved Rik Poot and René Guiette. However, in this work the symbolic expectations of the task seem to have been too much for him.

His work reached a state of equilibrium in his own house in Elewijt (1958), which is at the same time typical of and exceptional in the architectural panorama of the day. Engels himself states that his house 'was undoubtedly influenced by the way in which, in the 1950s, in the United States especially, the Japanese lifestyle was taken up in Western habits'. The closed, elongated northern façade leaves almost no suspicion of the scene behind it, the open interior floating above water, creating its own biotope.

Lucien Engels's œuvre is representative of an extremely gifted generation of architects who at times produced wonderful work. It also distinguishes itself from them, partly through its impertinence, but mostly through the irresistible urge that seems to have led to its creation. We are less interested in what is representative, but rather in everything that bears the hallmark of its own uniqueness.

LUCIEN ENGELS
Elewijt, own house, 1958
(Wim Van Nueten)

Engels's own house takes up a privileged position in his extensive œuvre. It gave him the opportunity to create his own biotope without interference and to devote himself to his esoteric painting in privacy. Behind a closed wall with only a few openings a different world is created in which architecture and nature flow into each other.

Oostduinkerke, Home Vandervelde II, 1954-1957

(Wim Van Nueten)

After carrying out the extension of the Vandervelde retirement home (Gaston Brunfaut, 1934-1939) in Oostduinkerke together with Roger De Winter, Lucien Engels built the large Home Vandervelde II complex between 1954 and 1957. It consists of three Y-shaped blocks, which combine to form a striking configuration. Engels humorously referred to his own architecture as 'tolerantly functional'.

Waterloo, house, 1954

Lucien Engels's work is more representative of 1950s modernism than that of many of his colleagues, but it also distinguishes itself because of his individual approach. Engels conceived the Lambiotte house in Waterloo not only as a living-machine, but also as an intriguing sculptural object. The design for the painted decoration of the garage door is by the hand of Pol Bury.

Georges Baines (b. 1925)

In the geography of Belgian architecture of the day, Georges Baines filled an exceptional position. He did not belong to the group that trained in Brussels, or at La Cambre especially. He studied with Léon Stynen in Antwerp, before the latter went over to La Cambre, and worked for his firm. Baines severely felt the isolation and the lack of tradition confronting the Belgian architect. In *Bouwen in België 1945-1970* he wrote: 'There can be no doubt that architecture as an active component in the creation of a better society has come to nothing in Belgium. The causes for this state of affairs must be sought in the period immediately following the war, when a number of the best architects of a mature generation did not succeed in achieving what one might have expected from them. For everything we lacked a catalyst, a master, who could have guided our thoughts, such as the Smithsons in England or Bakema in the Netherlands. Van de Velde had grown old and was living abroad, De Koninck's work was too humble... and Braem's all too personal work did not contain the transforming influence to show the young generation new directions. As there was no fertile contact with our elders and no group aiming at the exchange of ideas that could be taken seriously... each of us withdrew into his own little world.' In a text entitled 'Un idéal progressiste: critiques et expériences personnelles', which appeared in the first issue of *Les Cahiers de La Cambre* (1984), he deals with the subject at some length.

Whether this analysis is the correct interpretation is not for us to decide now. In any case it reflects the sense of impotence with which an architect such as Georges Baines approached his profession. Throughout his years of lectureship at the Henry van de Velde Instituut in Antwerp, the former Hoger Architectuur Instituut, he tried to correct this situation as much as possible, though without apparent success.

His work bears the stamp of this isolation. It does not have iconoclastic ambition, but intimately wants to make refined objects with the pure means of architecture. Baines insists that the modernist movement, to which he wants to belong, did not constitute a break in architectural evolution, but a return to the essence of architecture, which in the first place relates to space and form.

In 1952 he built his first houses. They are remarkable because of their distinction and thoroughness – Pierre Puttemans speaks of a 'perfection raffinée'. However, this perfection never becomes poor or dry, but shows the traces of the battle with shapeless matter. By degrees Baines developed towards stricter geometry, which reflects his admiration for constructivist art, especially for Max Bill and Georges Van Tongerloo. The house with studio for Vic Gentils in Wijnegem is a good example of the first approach, a house in the Oosterveldlaan in Wilrijk of the second.

The most complete expression of Baines's approach can be seen in Galerie Ronny Van de Velde in Antwerp (1988). It may be compared with Gerrit Rietveld's 'Zonnehof' centre in the Sonsbeekpark near Arnhem in order to recognize both the similarities and the distance between their œuvres. In the colourful mixture of Antwerp's South district, right opposite the massive labour courts, the façade of the art gallery appears as a conscious composition, a homage to the neoplasticism of De Stijl and constructivism. Material and colour contribute to making the façade an even surface in which the architecture of the interior mirrors itself. Light predominates in the interior and modulates the architecture in soft transitions.

This empty space wants to make room for art. However, its emptiness is carried to a point where questions arise as to its viability. One may put it that architecture is made to disappear, be used, and merge into life like the architecture of a Max Bill in Ulm. This architecture, however, is so emphatically present through its conscious reticence that it drives back life and art. Modern art requires characteristic architecture with which it can be confronted and thereby be taken up into life. This is one of the reasons why constant attempts are made to allow the work of art to escape from specially prepared and tailored spaces.

The force contained in one of Baines's last works best indicates the limitations of his earlier work. In 1987 he completed the restoration of the house designed by Le Corbusier for the Antwerp painter René Guiette in 1926. Next to it he built an extension for the new owner of the Guiette house, which at the same time shows respect for the existing, but also the intrinsic substance of the New much more strongly than the Galerie Van de Velde.

Paul Neefs (b. 1933)

For Paul Neefs isolation, which made Baines suffer, was a natural condition. He did not seek tradition in a common creed such as modernism, but oriented himself on actual works of the great modern masters as well as on the architecture of the past. 'Without making any detours,' as Mil De Kooning says in his monography on Paul Neefs, he 'has from the outset never regarded the autonomy of architecture as anything but obvious.' This has not always favoured his position as an architect, but has endowed his work with a radical nature. Even his designs for social housing are characterized by this.

This radicalism has also ensured that his work has stood the test of time. It formally distinguishes itself from the smoothness of the so-called Turnhout School, which was prominent for some time and in which Braem discerned a specific local character. It probably finds its most profound expression in Neefs's work, in its resistance to this specific character.

Neefs's concern with form is turned inwards. The form is not imposed, but grows from the work itself as a silent, though irresistible force. The writer Leo Pleysier, who commissioned a house from Neefs, could therefore characterize his work as 'unemphatic'. A rare testimony: 'Pretending it isn't there, the ugliness that has started its final siege... Pretending nothing's the matter, yes, that is better. Don't look around too much, for otherwise I won't be able to write about what I like in Paul Neefs's work. I'd better stay inside. At home. In home. There I can. There I can more or less find my words. / I've got four ready. Words, I mean. Four core words that are left after twenty years of everyday involvement with this architecture. I'll put them in a row: coherence, transparence, lightness, un-emphaticness./ All four of these are words (characteristics) that virtually surge to the fore in the case of an œuvre such as Paul Neefs's; the only difficulty was to realize which of the four words is the most significant to me. / After twenty years I am pretty sure I finally know: the last one.'

The Pleysier house, built in 1970 and enlarged in 1976, is a typical example of his work, precisely because the exigency of an autonomous form can impress so 'unemphatically' when one realizes and experiences it. The ground plan of the house

of 1970, with its oblique side, was almost literally duplicated in 1976, but not the section.

His own house (1963) is remarkable for its systematic application of the hexa-/dodecagon, fitted into the square shape of the grounds. The location is very important in Neefs's eyes. It is the starting point for a geometry that remains connected to experience. The Thomas house in Vosselaar (1973) is yet another example of the interplay between the ground plan and section, between straight and curved lines, between open and closed volumes. The same approach constantly leads to new configurations.

As with a number of architects of his generation, Paul Neefs's career ended in a rather abrupt, tragic way during the recession of the 1970s.

Vosselaar, house, 1973
(Evard/Bastin)
Paul Neefs's geometrical approach did not lead to uniform results. His is a geometry linked to experience, which belongs to the nature of things. The final result springs from the interaction between form, construction, specifications, and the surroundings.

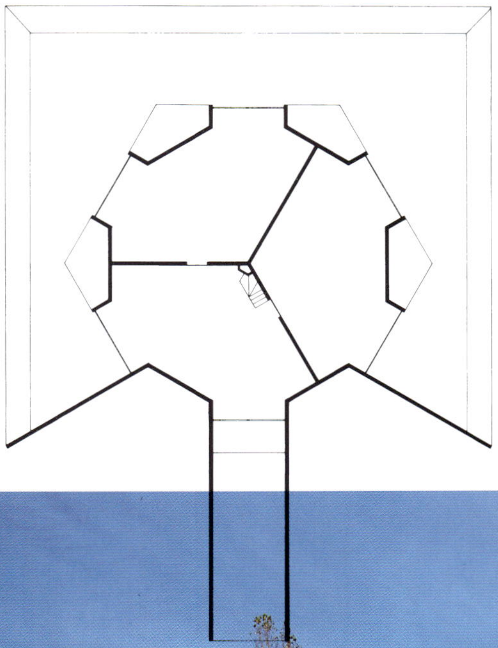

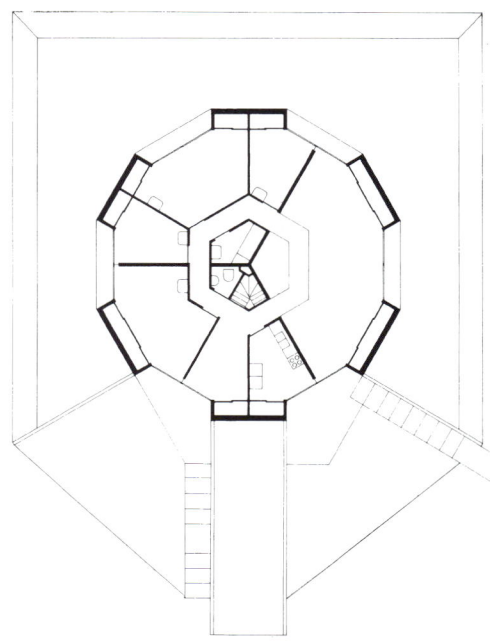

PAUL NEEFS

Oud-Turnhout, own house, 1965

(Bastin/Evrard)

The architect's own house serves as a statement of his principles. The pure geometry of the polygonal shape interacts with the squareness of the terrain. The clear façade with its open and closed elements in both the ground and the first floor further accentuates the geometry of the whole.

Neefs did not treat the ground plan as an abstract idea, but as a perfect aspect of the concept as a whole and of its materialization.

Marc Dessauvage (1931-1984)

Marc Dessauvage, who graduated from the Sint-Lucasinstituut in Ghent, had to struggle against the ideas of the milieu in which he had been trained. The problem with the Sint-Lucas milieu, which opposed the modernist school of La Cambre, was that they wanted to run with the hare and hunt with the hounds. Founded as an institution of the Gothic Revival by Baron Joseph de Béthune, it did not succeed in realizing the movement's basic principles to the extent where they could remain relevant to their own time, which was the case with Granpré Molière in the Netherlands and Rudolf Schwarz in Germany. The vital traditionalism, which could have been a check on and an antidote to short-sighted modernism, was therefore negated.

Immediately after the war, in the years of Reconstruction, things were not so clear. After 1955, however, areas were more clearly demarcated and the Sint-Lucas doctrine increasingly lost its credibility. The periodical *Schets,* published by the Sint-Lucasinstituut in Ghent between 1947 and 1958, chronicles this decline. The title is telling: architecture is relegated to being a 'sketch', an impression. Architects coming from Sint-Lucas could draw! Meanwhile the numerous advertisements in the journal did give some impression of the building activities that graduates from the various Sint-Lucas institutes were involved in.

Marc Dessauvage started his career in 1958, in an architectural competition for the new church in Mortsel organized by Pro Arte Christiana in Leuven. His design was awarded the prize by an international jury comprising Rudolf Schwarz, Hermann Baur, Xavier Arsène-Henry, and Michel Marot. The second and third prizes were shared by other ex-students of Sint-Lucas, Jean Van den Bogaerde and Jos Van Driessche, who got the commission, as well as Arthur Degeyter and Henri Scherpereel. Other prizewinners were Meekels, Michiels and Michielsen with a second prize, Frans Smets with a third prize, and Christiaan Vander Plaetse and Walter Steenhoudt, who received special mention. These names are interesting because they give some insight into the Flemish architectural landscape towards the end of the 1950s.

Marc Dessauvage's project was obviously superior to the other entries. The building with its convincing allure was put up in glass and steel, which threw not only the tradition of church architecture into confusion, but the whole architectural approach of the day. The same can be said of the impressive design of 1959 for the Jesuit retreat in Godsheide near Hasselt.

The project for the competion was adapted for St Joseph's chapel in Willebroek (1962) and worked out in brick and concrete. The roof is supported by concrete pillars whose wings emphasize the rhythm of the contour and the light, with below it glass-and-brick walls demarcating the space. The ground plan does not follow the flowing lines of the competition project, but an angular geometric design. However, the new work retained the openness, lightness, and dynamism of the original. The same year brought about the St Aldegondis church

MARC DESSAUVAGE
Aarschot, Saint Roche memorial, 1963-1965
(Xavier Botte)
In memory of a number of people executed by firing-squad during the last war, Dessauvage transformed the Church of Saint Roche into a crypt embedded in a sloping terrain. The severe square space is dominated by the light falling in from above.

Willebroek, Saint Joseph's chapel, 1962-1964, photograph 1970
(Karel Vermeir)
Marc Dessauvage transformed his prizewinning design for a church into a chapel in Willebroek. The steel was replaced by concrete and bricks, but the dynamism of the original was retained. The chapel heralded a number of impressive church buildings by Dessauvage, especially in the diocese of Mechelen. These ranged from simple village churches to urban complexes.

in Ezemaal near Tienen and St Carolus in Holsbeek near Leuven. In Ezemaal the curved wall delineates the space by embracing it, in Holsbeek the central point is in the roof construction. Yet every time the essence lies in assigning the strict, constructional means a place that is not automatically filled, but waiting for something to happen.

This approach reaches its classical form in the St Roch memorial in Aarschot (1963). The square of the ground plan is determined by the roof construction, just as at St Joseph's chapel. The light from above gives the space a closed atmosphere. Instead of an open spot, there is a crypt. Yet what counts here is the intrinsic coherence of the receptive spatial construction. Architecture does not pose Marc Dessauvage any problems that have to be solved, but is a virtue that can be practised with more or less naturalness, casualness, or ingenuity.

Dessauvage built several more churches over the next ten years, but it would be wrong to brand him as a builder only of churches. His churches are no different from his other buildings. What interested him was architecture, a sort of architecture which, as he put it, expresses dignity, the dignity of a good work. His larger works also demonstrated this essential requirement. In the Magnificat monastery in Westmalle (1966) near St Paul's church (of a few years earlier) he tried, as in his churches and houses, to make the force of architecture serve a new type of collective building in which the individual is not subordinate, but where the collective originates from individual contribution. In the retreat in Godsheide of the same year he applied the same type with individual cells forming the border between the exterior and interior.

In the building of the arts faculty in the centre of Leuven (1969) and the Pauwels hotel in Knokke (1973) – one of his last achievements – this structuralist approach can still be seen. His own house, which he built in 1978 after a design of 1972, in the woods of Loppem, he returns to a more closed form. He himself named it 'Palladio'. The strictly symmetrical ground plan, the same as that of Palladio's Villa Rotonda, is organized around a central open space, with the various living-areas of the house, or rather the places where they might be situated, spread over two floors.

Loppem, own house, 1972-1980

(Filip Tas)

Marc Dessauvage's pursuit of perfect balance between the architectural form and its typological adaption finally resulted in his returning to the principles of classical order. The prototype of this, his own house, bears the name 'Palladio', after the architect of the Villa Rotunda in Vicenza. Perfectly symetrical, the ground plan organizes the potential living quarters around a central open space.

Pellenberg, house, 1965-1967

(Bastin/Evrard)

Marc Dessauvage's greatest breakthrough in the field of church architecture lies in lifting the boundaries surrounding this type of architecture. Whether a church, a convent, or a house, it did not really matter. In each case he focused on the architecture itself, which was to lend the project its dignity. The house built for Professor Ludo Verbeeck in Pellenberg may be regarded as the prototype of numerous original houses by Marc Dessauvage.

Marc Dessauvage
Westmalle, Saint Paul's church, 1964-1967
(Bastin/Evrard)
Even if the form and, consequently, play of light are more complex – for instance in Saint Paul's church in Westmalle – his architectural style remains clear and simple. In the middle of the woods the church fills a clearly defined place without isolating it. The architecture does not draw atttention to its form. It creates a space that does not fill itself, but rather seems to be waiting for something to happen, for some sort of presence.

Westmalle, 'Magnificat', monastery, 1966-1970
(Bastin/Evrard)
Near Saint Paul's church there is the 'Magnificat' monastery. This unusual building is the result of the desire to bring out the individual existence of monastic life within a closed community. The broad curve of the upwardly receding cells determines the communal space in a natural way.

Leuven, Arts Faculty, 1969-1972

(Bastin/Evrard)

The building of the arts faculty in Leuven was part of a larger complex, which also included a church and a number of lecture halls. This design, which blends into the surrounding townscape, was a reaction to Peter Callebout's proposal for a tower block that would have stuck out in the city.

Juliaan Lampens (b. 1926)

Juliaan Lampens graduated, just as Marc Dessauvage and Paul Neefs, from Sint-Lucas in Ghent. Dessauvage rebelled against the reduction of architecture to the swift line. Lampens, on the contrary, exalted it. When Paul Vermeulen remarks that Lampens's work has mostly been neglected because it takes no notice of the crisis in modern architecture, he is only partly right. The real explanation of this lack of interest lies in its impressive simplicity of form.

His architecture is most remarkable as sketches. 'The graphic language is the architect's mother tongue,' Juliaan Lampens writes, 'In [this language] he has to say everything he wants to say... His sketch is the graphic embodiment of the architectural quality from which the architectural character can be derived. No dream that cannot be dreamt, no architecture that cannot be sketched, no sketch that cannot be built.'

This literally comes true in the pilgrimage church Onze-Lieve-Vrouw-van-Kerselare (Our Lady of Kerselare) in Edelare (1961), which Lampens designed together with Rutger Langaskens: one upward line that sticks out above the horizon like the bow of a sunken ship. This church, which is nothing more than a concrete roof below which the interior is led to flow away, can be compared to the cut-off pyramid of St Rita's church in Harelbeke by Léon Stynen, built at the same time. It is quite the opposite of Dessauvage's churches.

In some of Lampens's houses architecture appears as a pathetic gesture. A typical example is the Van Wassennhove house in Sint-Martens-Latem (1974), a closed bunker, where on the inside, in the architect's own words, 'a sense of landscape is created through which the house is not limited to functions, but is extended to habitation.'

Jan Tanghe (b. 1929)

Jan Tanghe completes this list of architects not so much because of his work, but rather because of his presence on the architectural scene. His work shows chameleonic diversity. This can be partly explained by the fact that he often collaborated with others, especially Paul Felix, but in the first place flows from his approach to architecture, which sees the architectural object as a means rather than an end, and does not seem to assign the architectural form as such any autonomous power of expression.

In *Bouwen in België 1945-1970* he says: 'After all, architecture can not be an end in itself, but only a means to stimulating life within the complex social structure.' That the potential stimulus of this means could lie in its intrinsic quality is not taken into account. This is all the more remarkable as Tanghe has always acted as as the advocate of good architecture and has always been trying to promote its quality by improving the social conditions influencing its practice.

In 1966, for instance, he took the initiative to found a partnership of town planners, architects, and engineers. It was called 'Planning' and was most unusual for Belgium at the time, even banned by the order of architects. In its manifesto it says that architecture has to be situated as 'as a link within the spatial, urban development environment' and that its study ought to be multidisciplinary.

However, these noble intentions did not lead to much, which is hardly surprising. The group resembled a sponge that soaked up all influences possible without transforming them in the way the Atelier de Genval did. The whole development of architectural trends can be read from these works, which though demonstrating professionalism, possess no intrinsic power. Apart from Tanghe's own house, the best work is the Provinciaal Instituut voor Hoger Onderwijs in Ghent (1967), in collaboration with Francis Serck, to which a section was added in 1987. Nevertheless, the same period saw the surprising appearance of a house in Marke, houses in Gits and a social housing complex in Ostend, each in a different style, with the emphasis on the word 'style'. Even if this were deliberate eclecticism, one looses track amidst such a mutlifarious collection.

His later work also evolved with the times. The renovation of the Oude Burg in Bruges for the service centre 'De Gilde' may be valuable in that it is conservation, but the new architecture lacks character, is trendy and aims at easy appeal. It is contemporaneous to the renovation and restoration of Hors-Château in Liège by Vandenhove. An ultimate development can be seen in the renovation and enlargement in 1985 of the Concert Noble, built by Beyaert in 1873, and the foot-bridge across the Rue Belliard in Brussels (1988), with sculptures by Jean-Paul Laenen.

GROUP PLANNING AND FRANCIS SERCK
Ghent, 'Provinciaal Instituut voor Hoger Onderwijs', 1967-1978/1981-1984
(Bastin/Evrard)

Jan Tanghe's importance in the field of post-war architecture lies in his personal commitment rather than in his work as an architect. The most significant of the works he built for the Planning group was the 'Provinciaal Instituut voor Hoger Onderwijs' in Ghent. It was constructed in two phases. The new complex has all the functions arranged in staged layers around a covered courtyard, which functions as a busy meeting place.

René Greisch (b. 1929)

Finally, we must mention René Greisch, an engineer-architect worthy of his double title. After graduating from the university of Liège in 1951, he started an independent firm as an engineering consultant in 1959. He had already collaborated with several architects on the occasion of the Expo '58 world fair in Brussels and soon became known among them for the suppleness and inventiveness with which he approached architectural design. One may safely say that the landscape of Belgian architecture would have looked completely different without Greisch.

This certainly holds true for his own personal work and in the first place for the numerous bridges he has designed. They have been honoured with various prizes, most recently in 1994 with Maastricht's Ailbertusprijs. 'Greisch's bridges are what bridges ought to be,' Paul Vermeulen writes, 'events on a route, junctions of tension, where we are struck at the same time by size of the obstacle and its flawless grace, in a word, the dignity with which human ingenuity has taken on the obstacle... In these bridges no interpretation has been added to the structural demands, no comment, no reference, no conceptual or plastic analogy with, for example, the skeletons of fauna and flora, which is the case with Calatrava... There is no sign of the author and there can be no doubt that it is precisely this absence that makes us experience Greisch's bridges as "collective projects". As they did not originate from a subjectively willed form, they are objective, confident of form, empty and receptive for meaning: perfect anchorage for our collective memory.'

The names of the bridges would fill a long list. The best known ones are those across the River Meuse and the Albert canal in Ben-Ahin, Wandre, Lanaye, and Hermalle. Not only do they show a sophisticated solution to the complex requirements of construction and landscape, but they also have a fascinating history. The 138-metre main span of the Hermalle bridge, for instance, was constructed on the banks of the Albert canal and then transported a kilometre on a lifter and trailer. Similar trouble was taken over the bridge of Ben-Ahin: the roadway which, so as not to inconvenience the traffic, had been constructed on the banks of the River Meuse, was swung across the river on a pylon. In Wandre the roadway was shifted under the pylon and across the Meuse. One of the last designs was the cable bridge across the River Leie at the lawcourts in Kortrijk.

RENÉ GREISCH
Wandre, bridge, 1987-1990
(Bastin/Evrard)
Apart from his contribution as an adviser to and collaborator of numerous well-known architects, René Greisch established a reputation through a number of bridges, each and every one of which has become a landmark in the contemporary landscape.

JEAN VAN DEN BOGAERDE
Sint-Martens-Latem, own house, 1966
The success of his own house has remained unique in Jean Van den Bogaerde's œuvre. The inventiveness and freedom expressed in it was never repeated. The application of standard elements did not lead to boring uniformity, but to a lively combination relieving architecture of its heaviness.

A quiet death

This period added a few names to those already seen, but there are many more worthy of mention. Some of them appear in *Bouwen in België 1945-1970*: Jean Barthelemy (b. 1932), who, after a remarkable start, devoted himself to education at the university of Mons; Walter Bresseleers (b. 1927), who in 1963 designed an elegant office block in the Frankrijklei, in 1968 a towerblock on the Noorderlaan in Antwerp, and in 1969 the IBM Center in Diegem; the duo Leo De Vos (b. 1920) and Jacques Kint (b. 1923), who in 1963 designed a rehabilitation centre for spastic children in Landegem; Jacques Dolphyn (b. 1927), who built a number of fine country houses; Jean Englebert (b. 1928), the long-time chairman of the architecture section at the university of Liège; Jacques Gillet (b. 1931), who became famous for his 'sculptural home', which will be discussed further; Alfons Hoppenbrouwers (b. 1930), a driving force behind the Sint-Lukasinstituut in Brussels; Willy Serneels (b. 1933), who rigorously tried to apply geometric shapes; Jean Van Coppenolle (b. 1924), who in 1959 was awarded the Van de Ven prize for his own house in Linkebeek; Jean Vanden Bogaerde (b. 1929), who in 1966 caused a stir with his own house in Sint-Martens-Latem, and his friend Jos Van Driessche (b. 1930), who built a series of houses in the Waasland region reminiscent of F.L. Wright's work. One could also add Axel Ghyssaert (b. 1933), who was awarded the Van de Ven prize in 1963 for a bungalow in Zedelgem, and Lou Janssens (b. 1935) with a series of carefully constructed villas and terraced houses.

These names cannot be classified in a single category. Nevertheless, there is, if we compare them to the previous generation, a noticeable shift. The previous generation, which started out just before or just after the war, first and foremost believed in the necessity of modern architecture and its social duty. Belgium has never known an actual 'modern school', except if one wants to qualify the architectural circle of La Cambre as such. Yet there was a group that advocated innovation of the architectural culture. Their argument was that architecture had to be the expression of scientific and technical developments as well as of the new sense of life they created. There was clear social and political conviction. The new architecture could no longer be an expression of the former power structure, but had to give form to the new proportions of social democracy. Public housing especially became an important subject.

In the period between 1955 and 1965 these architectural ideals met a quiet death, though the mourning ceremony of 1968 was still a few years off. To most people in the profession it is clear that architecture, just as literature or theatre, cannot directly engage in politics and, if it wants to signify at all, can only look after itself and in the play of forces that determin society carry forth its own values as an intellectual and cultural project. They no longer strive for a homogeneous pattern, but aim at applying freedom of spirit in architecture as well.

Antwerp 1970

(Karel Vermeir)

While architects were mainly concerned
with themselves and the justification of
their art, organizing congresses,
formulating ideals, and setting up action
groups, the building trade simply carried
on as if nothing was the matter. Whole
streets disappeared to make room for
huge mutlifunctional complexes, as can
be seen around the 'Boerentoren' in
Antwerp.

Chapter 3

1965-1975

Revolution and repentance:
in pursuit of a frame of reference

Design and Utopia

During the 1968 uprisings architecture students and lecturers played an important role. It was as if architecture had become the battlefield on which conflicting interests could measure their strength against each other. Not only in Belgium, but all over the world ways were being sought to redefine and legitimize architecture.

'The force of the imagination' had free reign in utopian plans which ignored the limitations of reality. It dreamt of the world as a city in which *Homo ludens* could move about freely as a nomad. Constant had already described this in *New Babylon* (1956). Cities were being designed above and below the earth, above and below the sea. Apart from the fantasies, architectural thought turned towards the developments in philosophy and the social sciences. Architectural history too received renewed interest. Architects started writing their own history, which broke away from the dictatorship of art historical categories.

One name will serve to summarize this situation: the Italian architect and historian Manfredo Tafuri (1935-1994). In the early 1970s he fascinated architectural thought. 1968 saw the publication of his *Teorie en storia dell'architettura*. Reyner Banham in *Theory and Design in the First Machine Age* (1960) had already tried to give a new interpretation of modern architecture showing its embedment in the architectural tradition of classicism. Tafuri went further. He concluded that modern architecture is the ultimate end of a hystorical cycle that started out with the Renaissance. His study provoked many questions, which he tried to answer in *Progetto e utopia. Architettura e sviluppo capitalistico* of 1973. Tarfuri's articles in *Oppositions,* Peter Eisenman's periodical, were hailed as events. Especially his article 'L'architecture dans le boudoir' made an impression. In it he writes: 'Today, he who is willing to make architecture speak is forced to rely on materials empty of any and all meaning: he is forced to reduce to degree zero all architectonic ideology, all dreams of social function and any utopian residues. In his hands, the elements of the modern architectural tradition come suddenly to be reduced to enigmatic fragments, to mute signals of a language whose code has been lost, stuffed away casually in the desert of history.' After the apocalypse of architecture only empty signs are left, sublimely useless. In his analyses Tafuri regularly refers to the ideas of Walter Benjamin, who at the time, also in architectural theory, was discovered as a mentor and remained a constant point of reference.

Not only Tafuri followed Marxist lines of thought. Henri Lefebvre, the French philosopher, published *Le droit à la ville* in 1968. In it he does not approach the city as a product of the economy, but as a 'work', 'une œuvre', in which one invests for one's own sake as in a work of art. Numerous studies have been devoted to the subject of *La question urbaine,* Manuel Castells' standard work of 1972. In the same year he also published *Luttes urbaines.* One can consider Pierre Sansot's *Poétique de la ville* (1973) as a corrective to the one-sidedness of the ideological approach.

Reflections formulated about habitation itself were less adroit. Philosophy, ethnology, and the 'new' science of semiotics, which is the study of signs and symbols, each contributed their share. Dutch publications include F.Ph.A. Tellegen's *Wonen als levensvraag* (1965) and Libert Vander Kerken's *Filosofie van het wonen* (1965). In the newspaper *De Standaard* I myself at the time put the question 'Sterft de stad aan de stedenbouw?' (Is urban development killing the city?) and published an essay in 1967 at the Limburgs Universitair Centrum on *Het einde van de architectuur* (The End of Architecture). This was continued in 1975 in the essay 'Mensen wonen', published in the book *Omtrent Wonen.*

A separate place should be assigned to John Habraken's book *De dragers en de mensen. Het einde van de massawoningbouw* (1961). Habraken pleads for housing production to be restructured by means of prefabrication and standardization so that the occupant would be able to design his own home and thereby bring the monotony of general mass contruction to an end. This would require 'bearers' that would contain the whole housing infrastructure. Habraken's concept partly contributed to the design of utopian megastructures, which has tempted many architects over the years. It became institutionalized in the Stichting Architecten Research (SAR).

Building Living Thinking

Martin Heidegger is present below the surface of many texts. His memorable speech, 'Building Living Thinking', which he held in 1951 at the second Darmstädter Gespräch, became increasingly prominent, until towards the end of the 1980s it became an explicit object of study. Without wanting to get involved with the subject itself, Heidegger relates it to the totality of human existence. He concludes: 'Only if we are able to live [somewhere], are we able to build... Building and thinking are each by their nature indispensable to living. However, they are also both insufficient as long as they separately go their ways instead of listening to each other. They are capable of this if they both, building and thinking, belong to life, remain within their borders, and know that they have both originated from the workplace of long experience and continuous practice.'

Ethnology, the science of unspoilt existence, had already been introduced into the architectural debate earlier on. In Le Corbusier and Ozenfant's periodical *L'Esprit Nouveau,* which appeared between 1920 and 1925, the anonymous architecture of American silos was shown side by side with the timeless objects of primitive cultures. In the 1950s Aldo van Eyck, inspired by Marcel Griaule's writings, gave a lengthy account of the 'Miracle of Moderation' of the Dogon. The North-African kasbah is set as the counter-model to rationalist urban planning and architecture. An exceptionally influential study on the Kabyle house, 'La Maison ou le monde renversé', was included by Pierre Bourdieu in his *Esquisse d'une théorie de la pratique* (1972). As from 1964 the exhibition *Architecture without architects. A Short Introduction to Non-Pedigreed Architecture* by Bernard Rudofsky travelled the world. Architects likewise travelled to study the anonymous architecture of primitive cultures around the Mediterranean in Le Corbusier's footsteps, but also in Africa, Djenné, Morocco, M'Zab, and in America, the Pueblo Indians. In 1973 the Flemish television broadcast a film entitled 'Stedelijk wonen in de woestijn' (Urban living in the desert) about the cities in M'Zab.

Semiotics, following Roland Barthes's publication of *Eléments de sémiologie* in 1964, was at one stage hailed as the solution to every problem among architectural circles. In 1969 Charles Jencks published *Meaning in Architecture,* a collection of essays introduced by his own study on 'Semiology and Architecture'. In 1969 *Sémiotique de l'espace* appeared, with the subtitle 'architecture/ urbanisme/ sortir de l'impasse'. In it Jean Castex and Philippe Panerai published 'Structures de l'espace architectural'. Umberto Eco's *La Struttura assente* had appeared the year before, outlining the relationship between semiotics and structuralism. The influence of the chapter 'La funzione e il segno' on architecture should not be underestimated. Structuralism became the 'style' of the 1960s, or rather structuralism translated into the simple logic of the architect: if not directly equated with the bearing structure, it came down to the linking of equal fragments.

A new manifesto

Designers did not remain aloof from this tumult of ideas and trends. In 1966 Robert Venturi published Complexity and Contradiction in Architecture containing his 'Nonstraightforward Architecture: A Gentle Manifesto'. 'I like elements which are hybrid rather than "pure", compromising rather than "clean", distorted rather than "straightforward", ambiguous rather than "articulated", perverse as well as impersonal, boring as well as "interesting", conventional rather than "designed", accommodating rather than excluding, redundant rather than simple, vestigial as well as innovating, inconsistent and equivocal rather than direct and clear.' He concludes his manifesto by inverting Mies van der Rohe's 'Less is more' into 'More is not less', or 'Less is a bore'.

This essay appeared in a series on architecture published by the Museum of Modern Art in New York, where Henry-Russel Hitchcock and Philip Johnson had organized the famous 1932 exhibition on modern architecture, 'The International Style'. It also had significant influence in Belgium, together with the writings of Serge Chermayeff, Christopher Alexander, and Alex Tzonis. In Europe the most remarkable book undoubtedly was Aldo Rossi's *L'Architettura della città,* published in the same year (1966) as Venturi's book. In it Rossi tries to define the role of architecture in the construction of the city, the problem left unsolved by the modernists.

Walking cities

All these attempts to understand architecture and to redefine the modern ideal were outstripped by the wild imaginations of architects who rejected every limiting frame of reference. This time the inspiration came from England and Italy, two countries that had remained within the margins of the modern movement, and from Japan, which took no notice of European inhibitions. In the 1960s London saw the start of Archigram, whose spokesman was Peter Cook. In 1963 the group held the 'Living City Exhibition' in London. The titles of the projects on show speak for themselves: 'Computer City', 'Walking City', 'Blow-Out City', 'Plug-in-city'. The 'Walking City' consisted of enormous machines moving about like prehistoric dinosaurs, or of megastructures on and in which all necessary living units were brought together. The final chapter of Peter Cook's *Experimental Architecture* (1970) is entitled 'The future of architecture lies in the brain'.

In Italy it was the Archizoom and Superstudio groups that demonstrated the contradictions of modern culture in a poetic-ironical way. In 1969 'Il Monumento Continuo' appeared, a Cartesian spatial grid spanning the world and in which lovers could inhabit their own little corner without paying attention to the rest of mankind. In 1972 Rem Koolhaas commented upon it in 'Exodus' or 'the voluntary prisoner of architecture'. In 1978 his *Delirious New York. A Retroactive Manifesto for Manhattan* appeared, in which he opens our eyes to the reality of modern architecture and urban development. The 'Office for Metropolitan Architecture' (OMA) in Rotterdam fascinated the younger gen-

LUC DELEU

Vlissingen, pier, 1985, scale model
(SABAM)

In post-war Belgium novel cities such as designed by Archigram or the radical architecture of Metabolism are rare. It is only in Luc Deleu's work that we can detect something of it. In his proposal for the pier in Vlissingen he confronted general architectural expectations with present-day reality.

Basle, 'Deux petits arcs de triomphe', design
(SABAM)

Luc Deleu created a beautiful metaphor when combining the perfect architectural image, the triumphal arch, with the symbol of the new reality, the city highway leading nowhere.

eration, many of whom worked there for some time.

Japan at the time knew Metabolism, a short-lived but energetic movement in which the most prominent architects were involved: Kenzo Tange with his new city in the Bay of Tokyo, Arata Isozaki with his tree structures, Kurokawa with his propeller city – every one of them a virtuoso project, worked out in detail as if they were preliminary designs ready for execution. Interestingly enough, these three references once more bear the stamp of a national character.

Living architecture

In Belgium 1966 also seems to have been a year of awakening, without it giving rise to exuberant visions and matching designs. The Belgian situation was fantastic enough as it was. Several independent initiatives were suddenly being taken to blow new life into architecture, each of them inspired by overwhelming enthusiasm. However, this enthusiasm repeatedly proved insufficient and disappeared at the first confrontation with the existing structures. As elsewhere, in Belgium critical questioning goes hand in hand with the study of the tradition of modern architecture.

The first initiative came from Lucien Kroll and André Constant. In 1965 they organized an exhibition on contemporary Belgian architecture in the 'Colegio de Arquitectos de Cataluna' in Barcelona. The closing speech held by the 72-year-old L.H. De Koninck, to whom the exhibition paid a special tribute, was significant: 'Next year we shall gather again, this time not to enjoy one another's company, but to work, to think about a clearly defined theme, which will be prepared and introduced by competent speakers.' The next year never came. The exhibition was afterwards shown in Leuven on the occasion of a week-end seminar entitled 'L'homme et la cité'.

In 1967 Robert Courtois organized the exhibition of 'Les tendances nouvelles de l'architecture contemporaine en Belgique'. In October 1966, in 'De Blankaart' in Woumen, a group of Flemish architects started a series of study meetings aimed at formulating a new professional ethos, which the order of architects founded in 1963 apparently could not provide. Still in 1966 the Postuniversitair Centrum in Hasselt started up a course for architects, but this initiative likewise came to nothing.

The exhibition 'Antoine Pompe et l'effort moderne en Belgique. 1890-1940' had a more lasting influence. It was organized by Maurice Culot and François Terlinden in 1969, the year in which Culot also founded the ARAU action group (Atelier de Recherche et d'Action Urbaine) and AAM (Archives d'Architecture Moderne). Indeed, it looks as if he wanted to justify these actions, which resulted from the student uprisings at La Cambre, by studying the past.

In 1968 the Sint-Lukasarchief was founded. It focuses mainly on cataloguing and conserving the architectural patrimony of Brussels. The results of their study include the *Urgentie-inventaris van het bouwkundig erfgoed van de Brusselse agglomeratie* in 1979, as well as the exhibitions and catalogues *Brussel, breken, bouwen. Architectuur en stadsverfraaiing 1780-1914*

FOLON
Poster for a conference in Liège, 1969
Towards the end of the 1960s the world of architecture was in chaos. The conference in Liège for which Folon designed this poster was entitled: 'L'architecte n'a plus d'audience. Quel est l'avenir du domaine bâti?' Or, architecture as a scarecrow.

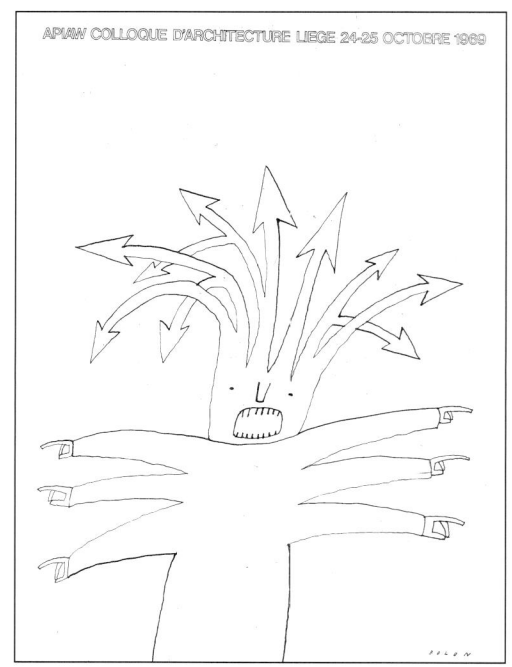

in 1979, and *Straten en Stenen. Brussel: Stadsgroei 1780-1980* in 1982. In 1971 the 'Construire en Belgique' exhibition took place, which was accompanied by a book with the same title. In the catalogue of *Interieur 1982* this manifestation was branded as an *in memoriam* to Belgian architecture after 1945 by the younger generation.

In 1968 the 'Etats-généraux de l'architecture' was founded. This body put pressure on the F.A.B. (Fédération des Architectes Belges) to organize a national congress of Belgian architects in Mechelen. Their conclusions were formulated as points of action, but nothing much ensued. In Liège, a year later, there was a colloquium with the telling title 'L'architecte n'a plus d'audience; quel est l'avenir du domaine bâti?'. The speakers included G. Bekaert, R. Braem, M.L. Burckhardt, Bruce Goff, G. de Carlo, M.B. Hamburger, H. van Lier, and A. Moles. To conclude the German architect Elmar Wertz put the question: 'Le colloque est-il une auto-défense spectaculaire?' Folon's poster showed a scarecrow pointing its arms in all directions. In 1971 SBUAM, which had actually ceased to exist in 1968, was officially closed down.

In February 1970 *La Maison* appeared for the last time. In March 1970 it was followed by *Environnement,* which only lasted a few years. The first issue contains no reproductions of buildings, but the speech made by Giancarlo de Carlo at the congress in Liège: 'L'architecture est-elle trop importante pour être confiée aux architectes?', and an article by John Habraken 'Pour qui, pour quoi? Réflexion à propos de l'habitat', ending with a photograph of a group of children who through the proposed SAR system will get the opportunity to create their own environment after we have taken ours with us to the grave. In 1970 a congress, which 'did not aim at being a congress' was held in a marquee on the Sablon in Brussels under the title 'Société en conflit', and in Tournai 'La foire aux architectes'. In 1973 A+ was founded to replace the ailing *Environnement.* The chairman of the order of architects and initiator of the magazine, Dan Craet, wrote: 'Through A+ we would like to fight the lack of ideas in architecture.' Not many ideas have originated from A+, unfortunately.

Troglodytes

This theoretical activity was accompanied by stagnant practice. For the sake of economy and prefabrication, the construction of schools was subjected to rigorous regulations. Only the postal services showed attempts to get out of the rut.

In the new world of the cultural centres that were being erected all over Flanders, 'Westrand' – the Flemish cultural centre in Dilbeek put up between 1968 and 1971 after plans by Alfons Hoppenbrouwers – tried to force a breakthrough. The 'Warande' in Turnhout (1965), designed by Carly Vanhout and Paul Schellekens together with Wauters and Schoeters, also

wanted to add a tangible presence to culture through its robust architecture. The same holds true for the cultural centre of Strombeek-Bever by Walter Steenhoudt.

November 1974 saw a unique initiative with the opening of the Stichting Veranneman in Kruishoutem by Christiaan Vander Plaetse, a forerunner of the Galerie Van de Velde in Antwerp. In the undulating landscape, on the top of a hill, this house of art dominates its surroundings in a friendly way. It is not set off against the other houses, but absorbs everything, nature and art, old and new, in timeless osmosis.

An attempt was made to save architecture by the Liège-based architect Jacques Gillet (b. 1931) together with the sculptor Félix Roulin and the engineer René Greisch in 1967. In Angleur the once functionalist Gillet built an organic sculptural house. Gillet had been converted under the influence of Bruce Goff. The latter had been invited to the Liège congress to proclaim the new message of liberated form. 'Why this sculpture

for living in?' Gillet wonders in *Bouwen in België 1945-1970*, 'Explanation would, in my view, come down to an attempt at justification, or at making it appear logical. There is nothing to be understood here, one can feel everything, subjectively... And if one later discovers to one's surprise that in order to solve the problem of building for the most people possible, one definitely should not have turned to industry as it is understood today, in the sense of the standardization of products, but one ought to have invented a different sort of industry. An industry whose standard is the core of matter itself: the molecule, the atom, the electron, the particle... I am dreaming of this wonderful industry of the tool made to suit the hand, materials to suit the body, space to suit the heart, of Architecture to suit the Occupant.'

Living or leaving

However, it is the universally praised 1972 master plan for the historical centre of Bruges that gives the clearest summary of the dominant views on architecture and town planning in this period. It was drawn up by the 'Binnenstad-steam Brugge' (Bruges Inner-City Team), chaired by Alderman Andries Vanden Abeele. The most prominent contribution came from Planning, but it also involved Prof. R.-M. Lemaire and city officials. The master plan did not intend to lay down definitive structures, but to provide a model for development 'in which growth and innovation will not take place at the cost of conservation and renovation'. Just as the formulation of their aims, the actual recommendations remain rather vague and can be interpreted in many ways when working out a concrete policy.

The way in which it was presented demonstrates on the one hand the lack of power of such a plan, and on the other the limitations of the concept on which it is based. This concept is worked out in the book *Wonen of Wijken*, which Jan Tanghe and Sieg Vlaeminck published for the Minister of Public Works A. Califice in 1978. Living here is not directly associated with a cave, as in Gillet's case, but with a nest. A more inspiring book, Italo Calvino's *La città invisibile*, was published the same year. It knew a greater success than any technical work.

JACQUES GILLET, FELIX ROULIN, AND RENÉ GREISCH
Angleur, sculptural house, 1967-1968, photograph 1970
(Gilbert Luigi)
Architects can explore diverse ways of breaking away from the restrictions of accepted codes. Gillet collaborated with the sculptor Felix Roulin and the engineer René Greisch to build a sculptural house, 'a space measured by the heart'.

Luc Deleu (b. 1944)

In 1969 Luc Deleu obtained an architecture diploma at the Hoger Sint-Lucasinstituut in Schaerbeek, Brussels. In 1970 he said farewell to architecture in four languages at the Vacuüm art gallery in Antwerp. He did not simply take his leave. From T.O.P. Office – his bureau for urban planning and architecture set up together with Laurette Gillemot in the Antwerp Cogels Osylei, which was being threatened with demolition – he waged a veritable guerilla war against the architectural Mafia. He bombarded them with plans and proposals announced in art galleries, with unflagging zeal took part in architectural competitions which he seldom won, and from time to time relaxed with a proper architectural project, such as 'Café de Schipper' (now transformed), which received the Maskens prize in 1975; the Mergits florist's shop; Jan Dirven and Bernard Blondeel's antique shops, all of them in Antwerp; and more recently 'Hotel Stock' in Albrandswaard near Rotterdam.

He regularly takes stock of his work through large retrospective exhibitions. He organizes his career in periods during which certain themes come to the fore. 1973 marked the start of what he calls 'Orbanism', urban planning and architecture on world scale, whereas from 1980 he was concerned with 'Scale and Perspective', and from 1989 with urban redevelopment projects.

The 'orbanistic' period was terminated in April 1980 with an exhibition in the Internationaal Cultureel Centrum in Antwerp, where he had previously laid 'The last stone of Belgium'. Under the title 'Vrije ruimte' (Free Space) he writes: 'So, between 1970 and 1980 my activities on the one hand focused on designing a world view in which the pressure on the soil would be decreased by means of rational and intensive use of the land (especially in urban conglomerates) and by combining the notions "mobile", "transport", and "living", on both land and water, which in the first place led to around 75 proposals and eight recommendations. On the other hand I investigated the new import within this world view of the profession of the town-planner architect, who does not necessarily have to build.'

On the role of the architect he says: 'The function of the town-planner architect (orbanist) has in "present times" even become something of a completely different order. Just as the (pictural) function of the painting (in Western art) completely changed after the invention of photography, the content and significance of town planning and architecture (orbanism) has changed. "Information" (the diminution of uncertainty) has now become an important field of work for the "present" orbanist; he is a medium, a trendsetter and/or urban jester, etc... He designs, publishes, acts, exhibits, realizes, or plays, etc... The "free space" has now become his ideal. Instead of infrastructures, which specify earth-space and renders it more one-dimensional, the orbanist now uses ultrastructures, which increase earth-space without diminishing the number of diverse possibilities.'

His proposals and recommendations range from planting

University of Antwerp, 1972, scale model
(Wim Riemens/SABAM)
For the competition held around the new university campus in Antwerp, Luc Deleu suggested converting three aircraft carriers so that the students and professors could cross the oceans.

'Manifest aan de Orde', 1979-1985
A year after graduating, in 1970, Luc Deleu formally bade architecture farewell. In 1978 he proposed the abolition of the Order of Architects and started his 'Manifesto to the Order', consisting of 150 applications for planning permission based on designs by the prospective owners themselves, but signed by the architect Luc Deleu. In a word: coming up for the right to individual taste.

fruit-trees along city boulevards, the import of urban agriculture and fishery, the abolition of public lighting and traffic regulations, and the establishment of social housing in public buildings through to the listing of houses due for demolition as monuments.

The declaration of Antwerp as a caravan city in 1978 was illustrated with a number of colourful site huts in front of the cathedral, the Museum of Fine Arts, the railway bridge, and the roundabout in the Cogels Osylei. In the same year Deleu formulated the 'Proposal to abolish the law of 20.2.1939', a law protecting the profession and title of architects.

Several projects were connected to these proposals. The project for Les Halles in Paris proclaimed the open building site as an urban landscape which constantly changed its appearance through circus tents. For the 1972 competition held for the new university campus in Antwerp, Deleu proposed a mobile university situated on three moving aircraft carriers, from which any location in the world could be reached within 24 hours. Apart from the exciting prospect for students of seeing the whole world during their years of study, it also involved the recycling of military equipment for peaceful purposes.

The first period also saw the 'museum for broken art', demolished in 1979, in the ruins of a factory in Turnhout and the 'neo-natural space' in Ravels, photographs of luxuriant vegetation in an abandoned warehouse. In 1978 he exhibited a homemade bird's nest and a series of Lego constructions, which are now being preserved in museums as works of art.

Deleu's most direct attack on architecture as an institution was his 'Manifest aan de Orde' (Manifesto to Order). In an incredibly short, not to say impossible span of time, from 1979 to 1983, he submitted no less than 150 applications for planning permission for individual houses. He openly admitted that he had given or sold his signature to people who wanted to build without an architect, which is illegal in Belgium. He considered these plans as ready-mades which, by placing his signature, he had declared as valid and legitimate architecture. He did, however, keep his options open. Being a professional, he corrected most of the plans submitted to him without interfering in the sense of 'aesthetic supervision'. In this way he could ridicule not only the aesthetic mishmash which architects pass off as architecture, but affirmed, in Adolf Loos's footsteps, the right of every individual to have his own taste.

Luc Deleu's work is never gratuitous. If he defends the right to kitsch and demonstrates its intrinsic value, at the same time he investigates the fundamental laws of form in architecture in his 'scale and perspective' project. It started out in 1980 with the discovery of a fallen sequoia in California. A photograph of it was exhibited under the title 'The fallen monarch'. Inspired by the tree, Deleu developed a whole series of studies of two identical structures, one lying and one upright.

He gave one of the most impressive demonstrations in the Montevideo space in Antwerp. In a disused port warehouse he lay flat an immense crane. He repeated the same principle with lampposts. At the 'Initiatief '86' exhibition, held on the occasion of 'Chambres d'Amis', he laid two power pylons next to each other, pointing in opposite directions.

As from 1983 he constructed triumphal arches of various sizes with containers in Basle, Neuchâtel, Antwerpen, Tielt, and Barcelona. His most impressive container construction is the one in Limerick, Eire (1994), an unconscious *in memoriam* at the death of his father. At the 'Torens van Babel' exhibition in the Montevideo space in 1984 he delivered 'containers in bulk', a heap of containers that looked as if they had fallen off an enormous lorry. In Hoorn, at the 'For Real Now' exhibition in 1990, he built a bridge across a canal by leaning two containers one against the other. For the international 'Housing the city' contest in 1989 Deleu designed two identical buildings for the Diagonal in Barcelona, one lying flat and the other standing upright.

His last period concerns urban redevelopment projects. As from 1986 Luc Deleu started researching the construction of the HST railway line and, in the first place, the way it would run through Brussels and Antwerp. In Brussels it would pass over the city and incorporate 'Europe Central Station' hanging

ARCH. LUC DELEU
Barcelona, 'Diagonal', scale model, 1989
(Wim Riemens/SABAM))
The most complete project in Deleu's 'Schaal en perspectief' (scale and perspective) series was his proposal for the Diagonal in Barcelona. Two identical buildings, one vertical and the other horizontal, accentuate the entrance to the city. 'Both these multifunctional buildings' says Deleu, 'were mainly conceived as luxurious social housing, but also incorporate functions such as a factory, a car park, a hotel, and a panoramic view. The buildings are complementary in that the horizontal one contains a sports deck and the vertical one a cultural deck.'

Luc Deleu
Antwerp, Montevideo arcade, 'Lying Crane', 1981

(Bernd Urban/SABAM)
Luc Deleu himself distinguishes between various periods in his work according to the themes on which it is based. As from 1980 he started studying scale and perspective. He convincingly demonstrated the force of this theme by laying flat a high crane in the Montevideo shopping centre.

Limerick, Republic of Ireland, container monument, 1994

(Hans Marters/ SABAM))
The cross of Limerick is one of Deleu's most impressive container constructions, a symbolically charged image of Ireland past and present.

LUC DELEU
Brussels, HST line / Europe Central Station, scale model, 1986-1989
(Wim Riemens/SABAM)
In 1986 Luc Deleu started studying the building of the HST railway line in Belgium, concentrating on the stations of Brussels and Antwerp. In Brussels the high-speed train flies over the city, with Europe Central Station suspended from high buildings functioning as pylons. In Antwerp, however, Deleu's HST runs right through the station hall.

'Antwerp, Your Next Cruise Stop!', 1993, sketch
(SABAM)
In response to the 'Stad aan de Stroom' competition in Antwerp Luc Deleu suggested leaving the city as it was, except for adding a dynamic element to its liveliest part: a cruiseport and a swing bridge across the Scheldt.

from high pylon buildings. At an average height of fifty metres the rails follow the line of the underground North-South railway link, as had been proposed in the nineteenth century. A moving walkway goes from North to South and affords a beautiful panorama of Brussels and its surroundings, another sort of urban beautification than that proposed by the Atelier de Genval. In Antwerp Deleu's HST runs straight through the entrance hall of the Central Station.

In 1990 he made another proposal for Antwerp as part of the 'Stad aan de stroom' contest. He left the existing city as it was, but, as for the HST in Brussels, he added a dynamic element. He named Antwerp as 'Your next cruise stop' and presented an abutment with a swing bridge across the River Scheldt in the liveliest part of the city centre. The bridge was never built, but more and more cruisers now call in at the spot.

Each of these projects could be analysed in its complex stratification, for each and every one of them at the same time offers fundamental insights into the city and architecture, and aptly, wittily formulates obvious solutions aimed at the absurdity of our accepted notions. In the catalogue of his last exhibition in the Museum of Contemporary Art in Antwerp (1991) Deleu writes: 'Although it now looks as if the building architect has to renounce every form of social reality, suppress a vision of the future that deviates from present thinking patterns, and compromise himself aesthetically speaking, I am convinced that the day will come for T.O.P. Office to realize its projects.' In 1993 Luc Deleu was awarded the Eugène Blanlin-Evrart prize by the Catholic University of Leuven. On the occasion he stated: 'To me this prize seems to be a homage to art in the first place, to its avant-gardism, its openness, its freedom from prejudice, its lack of inhibition.'

ANTWERP, YOUR NEXT CRUISE STOP!

Bob van Reeth (b. 1943)

Although like Deleu a former student at Sint-Lucas in Schaerbeek, Bob (or bOb, as he writes his name) van Reeth is not so much bothered by the architectural establishment. He was gripped by architecture itself, by invention, making, building. He did not rebel against existing notions, but went looking for places where the freedom and inevitability of architecture could still be found. He discovered the primary power of architecture in the brickyards of his native region, on the banks of the River Scheldt between Temse and Niel. He was surprised by their imaginativeness and the sometimes bizarre outbuildings proliferating behind the conforming blocks of houses.

He was still a student when in 1965 he converted a jeweller's shop and house on the Paardenmarkt in Antwerp. He left the skeleton and the front façade. It was its embedment in the street that inevitability caught his imagination. He demonstrated the possibilities contained in such an existing structure inside the house, but more intensely in the shop-front itself.

At the same time hailing and moving in against brutalism, which at the time was highly fashionable, he uses concrete, rough from the frame, in crystalline shapes that contrast with the high unframed shop-windows in which the sparkling jewels and watches lie. The free-standing frame of the unusually high door further emphasizes the entrance to the open space of the shop. The doorknob is an enormous watch. The mastery with which an unknown architect handled the whole range of

BOB VAN REETH
Mechelen, Klein Begijnhof, own house, 1969
The transformation of a dilapidated old house into his own home led Bob van Reeth to explore the essence of an architecure that would stimulate its occupants to regain some sense of freedom. Within the framework of the existing house he developed a spatial interaction that reaches its climax in the open staircase.

BOB VAN REETH
Antwerp, jeweller's shop, 1965
(Bastin/Evrard)
This jeweller's shop, Bob van Reeth's first work and carried out while he was still a student, contains the seeds of all the transformations he was to go through in his later work. At the same time saluting and breaking away from the brutalist movement so fashionable at the time, Bob van Reeth endows rough concrete with a crystalline form contrasting with the high glass surfaces without frames.

Antwerp, O.L.Vrouwe college, 1973

(Bastin/Evrard)

Confronted with a classical complex, Bob van Reeth revealed that the architectural construction process need not consist only of continuous change, but that it can also determine the building's final composition, which may include the use of references or quotations. The Onze-Lieve-Vrouwe college in Antwerp combines a light playfulness with strict control of the overall composition.

architecture, from constructive inventiveness, programmatic stunts, sidelong refences to current fashions, and contrasts of scale through to humour came as a total surprise and at once placed Bob van Reeth in the spotlight.

That his mastery did not apply only to smaller projects, but also held its ground in the complex commission of a large company building on an open green was later proved by the former publishers Walter Beckers in Kalmthout. Just as the jeweller's shop, the building was transformed and extended by Bob van Reeth over the years. It consisted of a clear structure that was playfully filled in, as if the permanent and sturdy nature of the architecture had here signed a pact with its changing and temporary appearance.

Nevertheless, it was not these first two buildings that determined Bob van Reeth's stormy career. They were no more than a sort of prologue that indicated the high level of his ambitions. The real manifesto lies in the Boote house in Mechelen (1969) and the transformation of a house in the 'Klein Begijn-hof' (beguinage) in Mechelen into his own home. The directness of the Botte house was defiant. This was no architecture in the normal sense of the word. A concrete skeleton outlined the structure within which free improvisation could take place. There was no projected formal ideal, as had been the case with Kroll. The ultimate result depended on the process of gradual appropriation of the structure, which in principle is endless.

Bob van Reeth approached the existing beguinage house in the same way. He wanted to return true freedom to the act of living. In this sort of non-architecture living becomes a real adventure, the discovery of an unknown world in and around oneself. Yet the spontaneity of this sort of construction, which referred to the 'power to the imagination' idea of 1968, should not be seen in too simplistic a light and be reduced only to its outward appearance. Already in his first works the freedom of the architecture was supported by a strong, geometrical structure. However, his followers, and there have been many, did not quite understand this.

When the van Reeth style was at its height, van Reeth himself was already a step further in the exploration of inspiring architecture. Not only the structural aspect was rendered more independent, but the pursuit of a more controlled form, which this structure contains, came to the fore. With his preference for lapidary definitions, van Reeth characterizes his work as the construction of ruins, that which is left after the use of a building and can always be interpreted anew.

In the Onze Lieve Vrouwe college in Antwerp a worn out wing of classrooms had to be replaced. This work, whose design dates from 1973, van Reeth conceives as a homage to the classical architecture in which it has to be integrated. Whereas in the past the fragmentary singling out of elements tested the unity of the structure to the full, clarity of the volume is predominant in his new approach. Yet within these limits van Reeth cannot help playing with the differentiation of the various parts. This results in façades with their own rhythmical articulation, which refers to a Palladian charged sense of rest. On the inside,

BOB VAN REETH
Mechelen, Botte house, 1969-1970
(Bastin/Evrard)

The Botte house is the most defiant example of the new approach to architecture. Its concrete structure indicates the limits within which improvision can freely take place. There is no preconceived formal model to which one can comfortably conform. In the interior we can also see the architect's radical coming to terms with the set and peaceful typology of the house.

behind the façades, the constructive inventiveness and the flexible playfulness of communicating spaces run their own course just as and maybe even more so than before. Convention and order here compete against liveliness and spontaneity.

The new wing of the Onze Lieve Vrouwe college is difficult to assign to a specific trend. However, just as the jeweller's shop on the Paardenmarkt hails brutalism without actually following it, this work was also influenced by what was happening in the world, and not only that of architecture. The introduction of an awareness of form goes hand in hand with the rediscovery of the historical dimension of our culture as well as with an awakening to the cultural dimension of architecture. Bob van Reeth continued his development along these lines, becoming increasingly concerned with ordering and controlling chance while making sure that order and control do not exclude chance, but uphold it as their vital principle.

After an unfortunate period during which one project after the other failed to be realized, his œuvre saw, as it were, a new start in the 1980s. In 1981 AWG ('architectenwerkgroep') was founded together with Marc Van Bortel, Mica Franck, and Geert Driesen. The effect of his new work is even stronger than that of the 1960s. The Van Roosmalen house on the Scheldekaaien in Antwerp, with its explicit reference to Adolf Loos's house for Josephine Baker, has had great success.

On the 'Scheldekaaien' (quays along the River Scheldt) in Antwerp van Reeth also built a café-restaurant near the Zuidterras and designed a large office building. However, the Van Roosmalen house and Zuidterras café sound like a new confession of faith. Inspired by the maritime architecture of pleasure boats, their construction is devoid of any gravity. Architecture here presents itself as a flexible, almost transparent appearance, whose dynamism – as in a dance – is inhibited by the geometry of the figures. His own house is closely in keeping with this.

At the same time Bob van Reeth took part in several competitions. For the new Sea Terminal in Zeebrugge he was inspired by the massive volumes of historical granaries, such as that of Ter Doest in Lissewege, and the characteristic towers on the polder plains. For the new development of Hoog Kortrijk he does not avoid drastic interventions and, just as Deleu with his cruiser port in Antwerp, wants to point out that large-scale constructions are apparently no longer possible in these times of faint-heartedness. For 'Stad aan de stroom' in Antwerp he proposed an actual ring road around the city, including the Linkeroever area on the left bank of the River Scheldt and designed two high, inhabited bridges, which harks back to a proposal by Léon Stynen. His entry for the competition around the kursaal in Ostend created quite a stir, but here again he took no notice of nostalgic sentiments and other prejudices: he proposed a square complex of buildings that runs straight into the sea.

While his light-footed work surprised people all round, he built on grounds that had been lying empty for decades in the centre of Antwerp. Here the architecture was inconspicu-

AWG, Bob van Reeth, Mica Franck, and Geert Driesen
Antwerp, own house, rear façade, 1982-1989
(Wim Van Nueten)
In one of his earliest texts Bob van Reeth pointed out the difference between the conventional, formal street-side façades and the wild, unrestrained construction of those at the back of the house.
He rendered an interpretation of this difference in the transformation of a mansion into his own house: the distinguished front façade, accentuated by few new elements, has been kept more or less unchanged, whereas the rear façade reveals the architect's personal imagination through the innovative way in which he has ordered independent elements.
The step-like composition of the rear façade against the straight block on the street side suggests something of the complex interior behind it.

ous, yet carefully thought out, claiming no attention for itself but ensuring that the urban pattern is repaired at that specific vital point in the city. At the same time a new office building rose within the walls of the historical Averbode abbey, which houses a publishing house. It is similar to his urban architecture in Antwerp. These last buildings, of which the publishing house was awarded the prize of the 'best company building' in 1994, not only show the wide range of possibilities within Bob van Reeth's architecture, but first and foremost shed light on his attitude; he is not in pursuit of originality in his own œuvre, but is inspired by the questions that every new commission puts to architecture.

AWG, Bob van Reeth, Mica Franck, and Geert Driesen
Antwerp, 'Zuiderterras', 1987-1991
(Wim van Nueten)

The Van Roosmalen house signalled the start of the renovation of the quays of the River Scheldt in Antwerp. Bob van Reeth gave a new impulse to the reconstruction of the pavilion on the 'Zuiderterras'. The round tower of the pavilion, the panoramic belvedere, the plinth with its portholes, and the pyramidal crowning of the central volume are at the same time playful evocations of a maritime iconography and allusions to architectural archetypes.

Averbode, office building, 1993
(Reiner Lautwein)

Within walking distance from the 'Zuiderterras', on an empty piece of land in the centre of Antwerp, Bob van Reeth put up an unobtrusive building whose architecture combines a polyvalent scheme with the recreation of a sense of urban openness. This approach can also be seen in the new office block which he built near the historical Averbode abbey.

AWG, Bob van Reeth, Mica Franck, and Geert Driesen
Antwerp, house, 1985-1987
(Bastin/Evrard)

With its explicit references to Adolf Loos's house for Josephine Baker and its salute to the refinement of boat construction, the Van Roosmalen house has become a new beacon on the quays of the River Scheldt in Antwerp. Here again, as in his own house in the beguinage of Mechelen and in the Botte house, we can see Bob van Reeth's pursuit of an architectural style devoid of rigidity and perfunctory arguments, a style that has become part of a lively cultural movement.

BRUNO ALBERT

Liège, 'Ecole des Hautes Etudes Commerciales', 1994

(Bastin/Evrard)

In keeping with other works of the late 1980s and early 1990s, Bruno Albert's 'Ecole des Hautes Etudes Commerciales' in Liège shows a sense of simplification and a return to elementary craftsmanship. Starting out from a covered atrium, the building develops from the inside. The closed exterior, which reflects the traditional style of the Meuse region, further underlines its introverted character.

Bruno Albert (b. 1941)

Bruno Albert, who graduated from the Institut Saint-Luc in Liège in 1966 and became Charles Vandenhove's long-time associate, has inconspicuously built up an impressive œuvre over the years. The surprising effects and turns in Bob van Reeth's work are not found here. He has striven for thorough craftsmanship from his first house in 1967 right up to his recent work in Amsterdam and Liège. His work has evolved in the margins of trends, which it neither rejected nor slavishly followed.

The promising small garden pavilion that he built in Esneux (1969) was conceived as a little wooden cottage, fresh and unconventional with its roof construction that wraps up everything and in a surprising way is directed towards a sort of light shaft that projects light from the woods into the interior. He built a house for the same owner nearby in 1984. Here the casualness of the first work has made way for an awareness of what is going on in the world of architecure. Albert wanted to take up a conscious position – it is a clear reference to Venturi –, but the power of the work in the first place lies in the clarity of the concept and the purity of its realization. The Herset house in Esneux may be seen as the prototype of an architectural trend that continued into the 1980s, a reaction to Dupuis's free plan.

The rest of Bruno Albert's work is not characterized by invention either, but rather by the incorporation of some or other idiom chosen as his point of departure. The restaurant of Vandenhove's institute for physical training at Sart Tilman or the new sports complex built there by Albert and René Greisch in 1981 are examples of this. The sports hall of the Athenée in Verviers, one of his best balanced works, is the clearest demonstration of his somewhat rigid, though thorough approach.

The recently completed school in Liège forms a climax. Bruno Albert here gives his own version of a type of building that is very successful at the moment and is being applied in various schemes. It is a return to the inwardly directed building that had been introduced in the nineteenth century, whether or not inspired by Bentham's 'panopticum', and which today triumphs as the American mall. It develops from the inside, from a covered atrium with which all the functions communicate. The recent 'Beaulieu Area' in Brussels by the Atelier Genval is based on the same principle.

Esneux, house, 1984-1985

(Bastin/Evrard)

The unrestrained character of Bruno Albert's earliest work gradually gave way to a sensitive interpretation of new lines of thought in the international world of architecture, broadening the architect's own vision and enriching the typology of the house. The house in Esneux, which alludes to Venturi, may be considered the prototype of a trend that was to attract many followers throughout the 1980s.

Pierre Arnould (b. 1947)

Pierre Arnould came, just as Bruno Albert, from the circle around Charles Vandenhove, who together with the engineer René Greisch dominated the architectural scene in Liège for years, not to say in the whole of Wallonia. He deserves mention for one work which he designed in collaboration with Greisch. It is the residential area 'Le Bernalmont' in Liège (1979), an ensemble of 39 houses on the corner of Rue Renardi and Rue du Haut-Pavé. It is a remarkably ambiguous work, a modern version of regional architecture, but made with so much flair that it almost becomes convincing. It looks as if the houses in the area already existed and have now been refurbished with new additions and unusual, striking colours.

This approach refers to that of Louvain-la-Neuve or to the renovation projects in Antwerp, but comes across better through its conscious choice of model and attention to detail. It also stands out against other new developments from the same period, such as 'Le Carré' in Cuesmes by Jean Barthelemy, who was likewise inspired by existing housing blocks, but tried to give them an unreal, modern appearance. In his commentary to 'Le Bernalmont' Barthelemy quotes an apposite sentence by Auguste Perret: 'Celui qui, sans trahir les matériaux ni les programmes modernes, aurait produit une œuvre qui semblerait avoir toujours existé, je dis que celui-là pourrait se tenir pour satisfait'.

Arnould's keen sense of interpretation of the old through the new, which he demonstrated in 'Le Bernalmont' and which suggests continuity, totally fails in his proposal for developing the Mont des Arts in Brussels. He gets completely lost in fashionable details. As an alternative to Charles Vandenhove's proposal it can only serve to underline the power of the latter.

Johan Baele (b. 1943) / Eric Balliu (b. 1936)

In 1967 Johan Baele and his old friend, Eric Balliu, founded B.A.R.O. (Bureau voor Architectuur en Ruimtelijke Ordening), almost at the same time as Tanghe's Planning. It immediately attracted attention because of its direct approach and 'brutalist' architecture. Its work is reminiscent of Marc Dessauvage's, but it also moves away from it, as Johan Baele puts it, because of its 'Zorba the Greek vitality'. 'Architecture again has to create a rhythm of spaces in which the searching resident is surprised and while dreaming becomes more aware of himself; architecture in which he discovers himself and meets others, in which he always remains free to choose: in the morning he may feel like the emperor of the world (right under his feet), in the evening like a 'sehnsuchter' (with the same globe on his shoulders). Architecture has to provide room for the romance of human imperfection.'

Modesty was not their motto. The tone was set with the Goethals house (1968) in the Hundelgemsesteenweg in Ledeberg with its concrete outside stairs, projecting terrace, crossing beams, and rough brickwork – all of them characteristics of 'brutalism' as described by Reyner Banham in his eponymous book of 1966. An impressive number of such houses were to fol-

low and in a milder form were imitated in turn. The daring of architecture seems to be typical of Ghent if – apart from Baele and Balliu – we take into account the work of Julien Lampens, Albert and Eric Lefebure's conversion of a neo-Gothic boys' school in Ghent, or that of Van Mossevelde.

The Meca-Pneumantics building (1968), in collaboration with the painters Willy Plompen and Jan van den Abbeel, was B.A.R.O.'s manifesto, not only because of its brutalist superposition of volumes, but especially through the application of colour and the contrast between the lively coloured surfaces or stripes and rough materials such as brick and concrete. However, little is left of the effect since it has been uniformly painted over.

Their work has vanished from the architectural scene as abruptly as it appeared. Both Baele and Balliu have pursued a career in education. Under his own name Balliu built the St Macharius school in Ghent (1966-1984), a striking accent in the area. Originally designed as a steel structure which could be filled in with closed capsules where necessary, it eventually became a concrete construction whose different volumes seem piled one on top of the other.

ERIC BALLIU
Ghent, Saint Macarius school, 1966-1984
(Bastin/Evrard)

The present appearance of the school, as if it were built with blocks, only vaguely reflects its original design. It was conceived as a metal construction into which different parts of the composition could freely be inserted and was intended as an open centre for the renovation of the whole neighbourhood.

BARO, JOHAN BAELE AND ERIC BALLIU
Ledeberg, house, 1968
(Bastin/Evrard)

BARO (Bureau voor Architectuur en Ruimtelijke Ordening) was founded by Johan Baele and Eric Baillu in 1967 and was to redefine brutalism in a series of houses. The house in Ledeberg, with its concrete staircase, projecting terrace, crossing beams, and rough brick is a fine example of this. Its explicit design gave rise to several less outspoken versions.

◁ PIERRE ARNOULD AND RENÉ GREISCH
Liège, 'Le Bernalmont', residential area, 1979-1985
(Bastin/Evrard)

This ensemble of thirty-nine houses constitutes a surprising new version of the traditional architecture of the Meuse region with its characteristic door and window frames. These spacious homes are grouped around a semi-public courtyard.

Yvan van Mossevelde (b. 1940)

Yvan van Mossevelde's work couples the tendency towards emphatic forms, which is typical of Ghent, with distinction and classicism. He does not see architecture as a manifesto, but as the expression of perfect mastery. This in the first place comes to the fore in the company buildings he has designed. In his book Pierre Puttemans lists a number of these: the steel plant of Chertal by André Constant and Jean Godart, the combustion furnace of Gosselies by Urbat, the IBM building in Diegem by Walter Bresseleers, a printing office by Luc Delhaize and Michel Jaspers, and the cotton mill in Kortrijk by Yvan van Mossevelde. A few more could be added to the row, but few possess the distinctive character with which van Mossevelde endows each of his works.

This mastery comes out best in the offices for Batibo Investments in Drongen (1977), in which van Mossevelde's detailed steel construction shows that the quality of his work is not dependent on the concrete masses he liked to use in the beginning. The closed concrete walls of the factory in Kortrijk reappear in the house he built for a collector in Deurne (1970), in a house in Sint-Denijs-Westrem (also 1970), and in a doctor's surgery in Ghent (1973).

An exceptional place in his œuvre – and in the whole of the architectural landscape at the time – is taken up by the unconventional house in Merelbeke of 1973, a perfect square defined by a brick plinth and a glass-and-light crowning. The brick plinth continues into the garden. Van Mossevelde is clearly concerned only with architectural problems and solutions, even when commissioned with a housing estate such as the one in Deurle (1977). Just as all his works, this can be considered a model for other, mostly modest, housing estates. Apart from those by Arnould and Barthelemy just mentioned, there are other examples by the hands of Jos Van Driessche, Pierre Huyghebaert, Eugène Vanassche, and Paul Schellekens. Each work taken on by van Mossevelde is endowed with aristocratic perfection. He does not stick to a particular style or material, but to an approach that puts a prime on the perfection of the individual work, with a notable tendency to let the work in this way distinguish itself from the rest and not sink into banality.

Werner De Bondt (b. 1943)

If we want to outline the architectural geography of Belgium *anno* 1970, it was the time when Antwerp reappeared on the map. We have already mentioned Luc Deleu and Bob van Reeth, who actually both came from outside, having studied in Brussels. The Antwerp profile does not show their unconventional streaks, but is to some extent inspired by Georges Baines. The work of Werner De Bondt, Claire Bataille, and Paul Ibens can be seen as prime examples. They are introspective and deliberately opt for extreme purity.

Werner De Bondt went his own way from the start by focusing on the intelligence of the work, in the modernist tradition, with conviction and perseverance. He cannot claim an extensive œuvre, but his realizations demonstrate a deliberate attitude. He started his career in Marc Dessauvage's firm, but he soon became involved in the world of theatre at the Herman Teirlinckinstituut in Antwerp. Here he designed the acting area and for years concerned himself with the décors for the plays the students performed. This is not to say that his architcture should be seen as décors, though it has something to do with the pent-up tension and import of his strict formal vocabulary.

A substantial part of his work consists of conversions. One of the first was the transformation of the Royal Palace on the Meir in Antwerp into the Internationaal Cultureel Centrum. The reconversion of the Ancienne Belgique in Brussels is also by his hand. The design of the Esprit Superstore (1988) in Antwerp, together with the Milanese architect Antonio Citterio, must be the most typical example of his approach, first and formemost because of the collaboration itself. 'One has to like architecture in order to understand it,' says De Bondt,. 'If one wants to give the greatest priority to the quality of the building and is also convinced that this quality is closely connected to the way in which the process of building takes place, then a customer such as Esprit and a design by Citterio are a godsend. The enthusiasm is not based on the embodiment of an autobiography, but on the fact that six architects can work on a building – of which the customer himself expects that it will be top quality – with an ample budget, with proper resources, and for a whole year.' Indeed, this is exceptional in a Belgian context.

In Werner De Bondt's eyes an even more important factor than this collaboration is 'the conviction that historically speaking we are still in the period of modern architecture and that the real problems are those of all times'. This position clearly comes to the fore in a number of exceptional houses he

ANTONIO CITTERIO AND
WERNER DE BONDT
Antwerp, Esprit Superstore, 1987-1988
(Gabriele Basilico)
A significant part of Werner De Bondt's œuvre is made up of transformations. One of the first was the interior arrangement of the Royal Palace on the Meir in Antwerp, opposite which he designed the Esprit Superstore in collaboration with the Milanese architect Citterio. Of the existing building they kept only the outside walls.

realized. This exceptional quality definitely does not lie in the far-fetched nature of his formal vocabulary. De Bondt unabashedly uses that of modernism: the cubic volume, the white surface, capacious glass. Here, however, modernism has left behind its dogmatic character. It no longer draws attention to itself, but to what can be passed on.

WERNER DE BONDT
Schoten, house, detail, 1985
(Hans Biezen)
In this house Werner De Bondt does not shrink from using the modernist idiom: the cubic volume, white planes, and ample use of glass. He is 'convinced that in historical terms we are still in the period of modern architecture and that the real problems are those that belong to all ages.'

◁   YVAN VAN MOSSEVELDE
Drongen, office building, 1977-1978
(Bastin/Evrard)
The refined metal construction of the office building in Drongen demonstrates that Yvan van Mossevelde is less concerned with the choice of material than with having control over form. Jacques Wirtz's layout of the garden further emphasizes the purity of the architecture and its interaction with nature.

Claire Bataille (b. 1940) and Paul Ibens (b. 1939)

Shop buildings also appear among the works of Claire Bataille and Paul Ibens. Their work mainly consists in the arrangement of existing interiors in a style that is close to De Bondt's, though it is less tense. Their work is more abstract, more formal. Even if it has to be adapted to the existing specifications, it tries to integrate them into a pure geometrical style. It is concerned only with the beauty of proportion, the intensity of light, the colour of the materials, and the progression of lines and refuses to attach any meaning. An important element in these interiors is the furniture, which they often design themselves.

Most of these interiors and shops date from the 1980s and 90s. An earlier work of the 1970s is the Villa Corthout in Schilde which was designed in collaboration with Lieven Langohr, according to a strict pattern which excludes every form of expressive coincidence. The light metal construction indicates the visual rhythm within which the building specifications can be freely interpreted. The overall effect is one of total transparency, of almost complete absence of form. All that counts here is proportion and alternating rhythm. Although this poetic construction cannot be said to rebel against the brutalist fashion of the time, it certainly does not take part in it. There is no brick or concrete. The ensemble is beautifully set in Jacques Wirtz's layout of the garden.

A more extreme application of these principles can be seen in a villa in Dworp (1990). A rhythmical grid dominates a light metal construction, in which the living areas are defined by means of closed, but mainly transparent or semi-transparent glass walls. However, here the orthogonal structure is set off by the beautiful arch of the roof, which has been lifted, as it were, to let the light flow into the interior even more abundantly.

Paul Schellekens (b. 1939)

The Turnhout School, led by Paul Schellekens, has already been mentioned in the context of Paul Neefs's work and is poles apart from the timeless character of the Antwerp School. Indeed, it is closely related to the Ghent School in that it is a flaring up of the desire to construct exciting and unusual forms, often resembling the brutalist idiom of raw materials and sharp contrasts. Jacqmain refers to 'the amateurism of a generation too eager to seduce'.

In Braem's choice of architecture for *Openbaar Kunstbezit 1976* he draws attention to Turnhout, though not without some reserve. 'These buildings show how talent can follow the wrong track,' he wrote. More specifically Braem saw the work of the Turnhout architects as 'regionally inspired contemporary architecture'.

Schellekens graduated from the then 'Nationaal Hoger Instituut voor Bouwkunst en Stedebouw' in Antwerp in 1964 and set up a partnership with Carly Vanhout the following year. Vanhout's own house and studio (1965) in the Parklaan in Turnhout immediately indicated their direction through its sumptu-

The rigid pattern of this transparent villa, which is organized around a central patio, excludes any form of arbitrariness. The light metal construction indicates a visual rhythm within which the scheme could freely be carried out. In a period when bricks and concrete dominated, this architecture brought a breath of fresh air. Jacques Wirtz's garden layout beautifully complements the house.

CLAIRE BATAILLE AND PAUL IBENS
Antwerp, Verso, shop interior, 1994
(Bart van Leuven)
Claire Bataille and Paul Ibens's work
mainly consists of arranging existing
interiors, especially of shops. Even
though the architects constantly have to
adapt their designs to existing structures,
they try to incorporate these into a clear
geometry and so create an independent
framework within which man and object
can meet each other in a sublime
atmosphere.

ous approach. The emphasis on the horizontal line makes it a conspicuous feature of the surrounding landscape.

In the same year they were commissioned with the cultural centre 'De Warande' in Turnhout. The range of their projects dating from the 1960s is impressive: housing estates, a convent, and private houses. In 1968 the straight line of most of these is broken by Shellekens's own house. It unites everything under a single saddle roof reaching down to the ground – a representative example of this architectural approach that will not accept what is normal, but continuously spins out an expressionistic metaphor. One of their most complex houses is the Klaver house in Oud-Turnhout (1975). The Crabbe house in Zoutleeuw dates from a year later.

Paul Van Aerschot (b. 1938)

Paul Van Aerschot was one of the first to graduate from the new architecture department at the Catholic University of Leuven, which is why the school has been able to have some influence among architects. After graduating, Van Aerschot remained in Leuven as a lecturer. He started out as an architect in 1961, in collaboration with Felix and Pepermans, with a residential area for students in the Arenbergpark. The strict pragmatism of the project clearly did not come from him. The first work he designed on his own, the far-reaching transformation of the Paus college in Leuven (1967), evinces a need for greater complexity and more creative imagination. In the stately architecture of the Paus college he felt at home. Whilst showing great respect for the existing building, he managed to give it a personal touch.

In the detached house designed for Professor De Meester his characteristic approach via geometric patterns overlapping one another can be fully appreciated. Apart from the numerous houses he has built in and around Leuven, he has also left his mark on the urban landscape. In close association with his work on the Paus college he built a library for the faculty of theology opposite the city park. In 1990 the large De Somer auditorium was added. Built according to a strict grid-like pattern, Van Aerschot's library develops the interplay of open and closed spaces within this structure. This can be perceived in the complex interior as well as in its effect on the façade facing the park, which opens and closes its side of the street in a single movement.

The auditorium completes the university complex between Beriotstraat and Tiensestraat. In a comment on his own work, which at the same time sheds light on that of many others of his generation, he writes: 'Geometry, its shapes and laws as a theoretical frame for design and the technical archetypes of the architectural tradition that are still useful now can be seen as the main architectural components of the Pieter De Somer auditorium... This intellectual approach to architecture is a rhetorical exaggeration, which, in a certain sense, can also be said of the auditorium itself. As a symbol of academe it offered the designer an exceptional opportunity to proclaim his ideas about the essence of architecture *ex cathedra,* as it were.

PAUL SCHELLEKENS
Zoutleeuw, house, 1976
(Bastin/Evrard)
Paul Schellekens can be seen as the forerunner of what has been called the 'Turnhout School'. Together with Carly Vanhout he has realized an extensive œuvre, the climax of which is the cultural centre 'De Warande' in Turnhout. The house in Zoutleeuw is typical of the period during which he used the roof as a fourth façade.

PAUL VAN AERSCHOT
Leuven, Pieter De Somer auditorium, 1984-1989
(Bastin/Evrard)
Paul van Aerchot defined his auditorium, situated between Beriot- and Tiensestraat, as a lecture on architecture: 'Geometry, its shapes and laws as a theoretical structure for design and the still useful technical archetypes of our architectural heritage can be distinguished as the most prominent architectural components of the Pieter de Somer auditorium.'

At the risk of coming across as pedantic and therefore missing his goal, the architect has taken his educational tools in hand. Lesson number one, vocabulary. This is a wall, the exterior, its inside, a ledge, a coping stone. This is a façade, a street wall, a rear façade, a side wall, a garden wall, a retaining wall. Each tick of the ruler indicates a pillar. This is a roof, a cornice, a socle, a plinth. This is the main building, those are annexes. Now geometry. The square, triangle, and circle are the basic forms of Western architecture and symbolize a rational world of thought. Here they are not merely theoretical models, but concrete, formal themes that can be discerned in the ground plan, volumes, and decorations.' The lesson continues in this vein until the architect remarks: 'However, the public turn away bored. They did not come here for a lesson, not even for a story, but for a feast. And behold, the curved walls become broad, inviting gestures, the carpet is rolled out at the entrance, the side wall of the library becomes an unrolled parchment on which, once it is white and smooth, the menu will be written out.'

Radical architecture

Paul Van Aerschot's lesson is clear, but gets lost in the tumult. During the eventful decade between 1965 and 1975 architecture was almost imperceptibly, but steadily sinking away. The realization of large projects such as the university campuses, at Louvain-la-Neuve in particular, was carried out in a minor key. It was no longer accompanied by enthusiasm, but by increasingly harsh criticism. Even before they were completed these buildings had become anachronisms and did not mark any starting points for the younger generation to build upon. 'Radical architecture' with all its dreams and Utopian ideas proved to be nothing but a Fata Morgana.

If in the preceding decade it was hard to choose between the multitude of names, in this period it is difficult to point out individual figures who created a distinct profile for themselves in their work. In face of criticism architects withdrew into themselves and, as Van Aerschot suggests, tackled the elementary principles of their profession and the fragments of tradition that still remained. The idea of making an impression by means of architecture was abandoned. If architecture could still have meaning, it was as a work that through its internal coherence would confront the occupant with a reality which each architect had captured by working out his own strategies.

MAURICE CULOT AND LEON KRIER
Venice, 1st Architecture Biennale, 1980
Leon Krier and Maurice Culot, the
founder of AAM (Archives d'Architecture
Moderne) and of ARAU (Atelier de
Recherche et d'Action Urbaine), together
brought out an anti-modernist manifesto
at the first architecture biennale in
Venice, their suggestive sketches
representing the ideal city.

Chapter 4

1975-1985

Post-modernism and integralism: 'View from the windows of my house'.

Post-modernism

The storms besieging the architectural landscape towards the end of the 1970s heralded the far-reaching changes yet to come. The 1970s were the years of 'post-modernism'. Joseph Hudnut had already used the term in 1945 to describe the 'Post-modern House'. However, it was only in 1974 that Charles Jencks introduced it as a characteristic of an architectural style during a congress held at the 'Technische Hogeschool' in Eindhoven. *The Language of Post-Modernism* was published in 1977. In it Jencks indicates the precise moment that saw the death of modern architecture and the birth of post-modernism: on 15 July 1972 at 3.32 p.m. the Pruitt-Igoe building by Minorou Yamasaki (1952) in Saint Louis, U.S.A., was demolished.

In 1975 the Museum of Modern Art in New York – where the International Style had been on show forty years earlier – held a large exhibition on the architecture of the 'Beaux-Arts', the bogeyman of modern architects. The European architectural heritage year in 1975 signalled the end of the Reconstruction and the expansion it had brought about. The themes celebrated in 1978 and 1985 were respectively 'the village' and 'urban renewal'.

At the first architecture biennale in Venice (1980) Paolo Portoghesi brought together various strains of post-modernism under the title 'La Presenza del Passato'. The central theme of the exhibition was the street, the 'strada novissima', in which twenty architects of different schools presented their 'wares' side by side. It included figures ranging from Ungers to Moore, Gehry to Hollein, Koolhaas to Krier (Culot), and Graves to Isozaki. Nothing and nobody was to be excluded. One of them, Massimo Scolari, pointed out that the debate on architecture had lost its central theme. On the square at the end of the street even formal criticism was assigned a space, with contributions by Charles Jencks, Vincent Scully, and Christian Norberg-Schulz. In 1981 the exhibition was repeated in Paris and in 1982 it was followed there by the exhibition 'La Modernité, un projet inachevé'. This was the title of an influencial essay by Jürgen Habermas written in 1980. Together with Jean-François Lyotard's *La condition postmoderne* (1979), this short text formed the central focus of the whole debate.

In 1984 a further attempt was made at introducing post-modernism as the theme of architecture, through the 'Revision der Moderne. Postmoderne Architektur. 1960-1980' exhibition at the Deutsches Architekturmuseum in Frankfurt. The museum itself was an example of post-modern architecture: in a nineteenth-century villa Oswald Mathias Ungers had built 'a house within a house', a pure prototype of a house at the centre of the transformation of pompous domestic architecture. At the same time the organizer of the exhibition, Heinrich Klotz, published *Moderne und Postmoderne. Architektur der Gegenwart. 1960-1980,* in which he summarizes the break between post-modern architecture and modernism with the slogan 'Nicht Funktion, sondern Fiktion' (not function, but fiction).

Lost years

With regard to Belgium, *Architecture moderne en Belgique* (1974) by Pierre Puttemans and Lucien Hervé marked the end of an era. It ends with the hopeful prospect that 'the excellent geographical location of Belgium may contribute to the avant-garde role this country can play in the definition of a new architectural style'. The avant-garde, however, had already disappeared.

In the opening lines of *Die Furie des Verschwindens* Hans Magnus Enzensberger writes: 'Almost without protest they excluded themselves in the 1970s, without giving any guarantees for posterity.' The answer to the question 'Alles of Niets' (all or nothing) – which Braem had asked in his address to the 'Koninklijke Vlaamse Academie' in 1971 – was: nothing. Together with increasing doubt concerning the economic system and the disappearance of dynamism in the building sector it was not only pluralism and eclecticism that came to the fore, as Jencks thought, but also an outspoken form of integralism that completely ignored any living style of architecture.

In 1951-1991 *Een tijdsbeeld* Marcel Smets calls the 1974-1991 period 'a time of hesitation and challenge'. He writes: 'We ended up in nostalgic praise of the congenial and comforting past and imagined that the mechanism of senseless consumption could be halted by encouraging conservation, ecological cycles, and recycling. Whether consciously or not, until the late 1980s the professional world (of town planners and architects) therefore took no part in the reassessment of the New. Their attention went almost exclusively to the creation of conditions within which our heritage could be reused. The focus on revaluation underpinned all the temes dominating the professional literature: restoration, reconstruction, renovation, and rehabilitation. The concern for spatial coherence, which presented itself as the answer to the disparate interventions of previous periods, was anchored in a reduced definition of the problem. It was still modelled on what already existed, on the dangers and insufficiencies of the moment. It was taken for granted that urban development could be controlled voluntarily and that regulating steps taken by the authorities would suffice to reduce the pressure of social renewal to an acceptable level. In order to retain the charm of the medieval street layout, the flow of traffic was brought down to a minimum. In order to conserve the small scale of historical buildings, those functions that could not be fitted into them were avoided.'

As an example of this tendency Marcel Smets refers to the structural plan for Bruges and to Louvain-la-Neuve. Maurice Culot, the most prominent exponent of this trend, openly puts it that the whole of modern development should be regarded as a blunder and a sign of stupidity and that we ought to return to architecture and town planning as they were before the industrial revolution.

The third way

The attack on modernism had been started in 1969 by Maurice Culot and François Terlinden in 1969 with the reinstitution of the cross-grained modernist Antoine Pompe in the exhibition 'Antoine Pompe et l'effort moderne en Belgique 1890-1940'. Indeed, the actual history of modernism contradicted the doctrinarian version given in history textbooks. In *Modern Movements in Architecture* (1973) Charles Jencks mapped out its antagonistic trends. The Pompe exhibition coincided with the foundation of the 'Archives d'Architecture Moderne' (AAM). As from 1975 this institution published a periodical in which Culot's battle cries resounded as an omen of Prince Charles's invectives against modern architecture yet to come.

In 1978 AAM published *Architecture rationelle*, the title referring to Aldo Rossi's *Architettura razionale* of 1973. In it Robert L. Delevoye, the director of La Cambre, notes the failure of the semiological approach and hopes for a 'third way', that of typology: 'L'approche typologique apporte non seulement une dimension imprévue mais le lieu même d'une action réciproque et constante entre la critique et la pratique, entre le passé et le vécu, entre l'exigence théorique et l'impératif du construire. Ce qui revient à dire –qui est sa richesse- qu'elle enferme simultanément un problème de lecture et d'écriture'. The collection also contains the essay by Anthony Vilder entitled 'The Third Typology'.

Culot did not leave it at mere words. By founding the 'Atelier de Recherche et d'Action Urbaine' (ARAU) he joined the battle for the conservation and renovation of the inner city of Brussels. He won the day when he protested against the erection of office blocks in the Marolles area, but it was a pyrrhic victory. In fact, practically nothing was altered as to the existing development and any change that occurred was for the

Brussels, Carrefour de l'Europe, 1995
(Bastin/Evrard)
The present-day Carrefour de l'Europe shows the application of the principles advocated by Maurice Culot and ARAU: urban architecture which, though it might be modelled on the pre-industrial city, lacks its spirit and discipline.

worse. The conserved city was a city no more, but was transformed into a theme park for consumption. The conservation and renovation of a few passages and alleys can at best slow down the process and cannot possibly lead to a new urban culture or architecture. The whole approach becomes painfully comical if one now sees how in less than no time urban repair à la Culot and Krier has produced even worse monotony and simplism than the modernism they despise.

The buildings on the Carrefour de l'Europe in Brussels are a clear example of this. Kroll's work is based on a similar misunderstanding. What ARAU has achieved can be seen in the strings of so-called post-modern office blocks – designed by, amongst others, Jaspers and his 'Bureau d'Art Urbain – ranging from the Cera branch in Leuven to the new Kredietbank building in Brussels. Compared to these blown-up shapes, the products of the Atelier de Genval are little gems.

Simultaneously with ARAU action groups were set up in almost every city with the enthusiastic cooperation of architects trying to regain some of their credibility. Urban renovation became the new pretext for architecture. The projects in Antwerp around the Vleeshuis and in Huikstraat have already been mentioned, as has the work done by Planning on the Oude Burg in Bruges. Another noteworthy instance is the renovation of the Rue des Brasseurs in Namur to which R.M. Lemaire contributed, or else commercial operations in shop-

ping centres such as the Zilverpand in Bruges.

The successful firm of Michel Benoit (b. 1941) and Thierry Verbiest (b. 1942), which operates under the name AUSIA (Architecture/ Urbanisme/ Sciences Humaines/ Ingénierie/ Associés), seems to have taken out a patent on this sort of 'accessible' architecture that combines every cliché imaginable. In 1968 they had won the Bonduelle prize for a new city in the Lasne valley, whose configuration to some extent influenced that of Louvain-la-Neuve.

Between 1969 and 1979 they built 'La cité de l'amitié' in Brussels, a series of more than 300 housing units incorporating accommodation for the disabled and the elderly, and in 1973 the 'De Drevekens/ Les Venelles' complex. In the same year they designed a group of 350 lodgings for the campus in Woluwe-Saint-Lambert. In the book dedicated to their architecture, Francis Rambert calls their work 'à la recherche de l'urbanité perdue'. AUSIA has been especially successful in France.

Suburban alternatives

The Krokus group in Mechelen – founded by the architect Bob van Reeth, the town planner Marcel Smets, and the sculptor Jean-Paul Laenen in 1973 – was one of the action groups mentioned. Perhaps the term 'action group' is inaccurate, as this was in fact a study group looking for alternatives. Not only did its members live in the area they wanted to renovate, but their approach was also based on actual architectural improvement rather than deceptive packaging. The project at one stage knew such a success that in 1976 it was shown at the 37th Venice Biennale – which was no longer dedicated to art, but to the environment and participation – as the model of Belgian urban renovation.

In the Belgian pavilion Krokus was surrounded by photocollages by Filip Tas on the city as 'Heroes Place', colour slides by Joseph Willaert entitled 'Zicht vanuit de vensters van mijn huis' (View from the windows of my house), and hyper-realistic paintings of zebra crossings and drainpipes by Marcel Maeyer. However, this whole mythology of urban renewal is put into perspective elsewhere at the Biennale, in the installation by Ettore Sottsass Jun., who presented 'The invention of the pole' as the ultimate escape from the impasse of architecture. With poles that could be coloured at will one could create the sky

Henri Guchez and Manolo Nunez
Wasmes, psychiatrical institute, 1981-1984
(Bastin/Evrard)
The hypertrophical image of Henri
Guchez's work sharply contrasts with the
ecological trend. Together with Manolo
Nunez he designed the psychiatrical
institute in Wasmes, a picture book full of
architectural reminiscences.

above one's bed or armchair, one could hang them with the washing or festive flags, or suggest a door.

The Biennale also brought the first exhibition of architecture in the salt plant alle Zattere. The chaos could not have been worse. Besides so-called participating architects such as Giancarlo de Carlo, Lucien Kroll, and Herman Hertzberger, it also included Hans Hollein and a group of Americans who under the title 'Suburban Alternatives' exhibited works by Emilio Ambasz, Reimund Abraham, Peter Eisenman (showed with an ice-cream), John Hejduk, Richard Meier, Charles Moore, Cesar Pelli, Robert Stern, Stanley Tigerman, and Robert Venturi. Another remarkable exhibition in San Lorenzo in Venice was dedicated to rationalism in Fascist architecture. Finally there was the special exhibition on the Deutsche Werkbund with as its climax the Weissenhofsiedlung in Stuttgart of 1927.

The embedment of Krokus in this international environment is more significant than might seem, for it reveals the sea change that was taking place in architectural awareness at the time. Architecture had to lay down the robes of the Grand Inquisitor to reflect on its past without feeling the need to glorify it any longer. Architects were no longer trying to be heroes, but men among men – as directly and honestly as possible, without any illusions. This was what Krokus was aiming at.

However, they had still a long way to go, as can be seen in the only work that Krokus actually realized: the laying out of a minute playground near the beguinage in Mechelen. The preparatory study and proposals which Krokus drew up for the commune of Overijse were never taken any further. In the meantime – and in perfect keeping with the laws of inertia – the trend to modernize the old city continued for a while as if nothing were the matter. 'Liège 2000', 'Gent Morgen', 'Leuven 2000' – so many competitions and preparatory studies that only produced megalomaniac proposals leading nowhere, not even to an interesting spectacle.

JAN BRUGGEMANS AND MARC SOMERS
Neerijse, own house, 1979-1980
(Bastin/Evrard)
Instead of the exuberance of
spontaneous building – which aims at
reflecting the complexity of life –
Jan Bruggemans here proposes the strict
discipline of geometry, through which the
inhabitant can free himself from
architecture.

LUC SCHUITEN
Overijse, 'Orejona', own house, 1976-1977
(Luc Schuiten)
The title of Hans Magnus Enszenberger's
Die Furie des Verschwindens can be literally
applied to the architectural trend that
aims at absorbing traditional
architectural practice into spontaneous,
self-built construction determined by
natural cycles. However, even this radical
rejection of an architectural culture is
fated to involve both expression and
tradition.

The architect as an eccentric

The fact that post-modernism did not leave Belgian architects unmoved can sporadically be seen in the evolution of their œuvres, most explicitly perhaps in that of Charles Vandenhove. An image of Hors-Château has served for the cover of a collection of essays on post-modernism in philosophy and literature. However, what usually happens with such intellectual or artistic trends in Belgium is that they but seldom come to the surface. This certainly has been the case of post-modernism, for the Belgian orientation has in a sense always been post-modern. Indeed, neither Pierre Puttemans' book, nor the study by Francis Strauven on Belgian architecture between 1970 and 1980 make any mention of it. Apart from the work of architects working within this decade, it also manifests itself in that of a few characters who still interpret this new freedom as a form of lawlessness.

The period after 1975 saw the emergence of the ecological trend, in which spontaneous do-it-yourself construction as well as the use of natural cycles and solar energy came to the fore. The self-built 'ecological' Orejona house (1976) by Luc Schuiten (b. 1944) in Overijse is a prime example, but it did not stand the test of time.

However, purely formal hypertrophy had to prove that anything was possible in architecture. This can be seen in the work of Denis van Impe (b. 1953) such as in Mageleinstraat in Ghent (1980); in Ruud Vael's post office in Jezusstraat in Antwerp (1979); or in the work of Henry Guchez, who renovated the ruins at Grand Hornu, put up an imposing block of flats that have never been occupied right next to it and, in collaboration with Manolo Nunez, built a psychiatric institution in Wasmes (1981) that resembles an architectural fairground. The remarkable water-tower of Kattenberg in Ghent (completed in 1976) by Dirk Bontinck (b. 1945) may be classed alongside these buildings which in a non-architectural way attempt to lift the boundaries, i.e. the means of architecture, and to create a sort of architecture that is architecture no more.

This decade could be ignored, were it not that it saw the creation of a number of works heralding a new approach. It was a period of incubation, the fruits of which were only seen after 1985. The architect had become an eccentric, as Jo Crepain put it, who withdrew into his own houses, each with its own features: for instance, strictly geometrical as in the house by Jan Bruggemans (b. 1945) in Overijse (1979), or else indulging the playfulness of an imagination trying to unite the multiplicity of life in a single object, such as the house by Roger Demartelaere (b. 1946) in Leefdaal (1980).

Jo Crepain (b. 1950)

The post-modern self-consciousness of architecture at the time found its most striking expression in Jo Crepain's œuvre. In 1988 he received the first 'Premio Internazionale di Architettura Andrea Palladio'. Not that awards are all-important; Charles Vandenhove, for example, never received a single honour. Nevertheless, the awarding of the Palladio prize to a Belgian architect came as a complete surprise.

Jo Crepain graduated from the then 'Nationaal Hoger Instituut voor Bouwkunst en Stedebouw' in Antwerp in 1973 and was able to start working quite soon. As early as 1974 he received the Maskens prize for the Roels house in Kapellen. In 1975 he became a lecturer at the 'Academie' in Ghent and in 1985 at the renamed 'Hoger Architectuur Instituut van het Rijk' in Antwerp, which was to become the 'Henry van de Velde Instituut'. His early work contains references to Georges Baines, but through these references one can already see the signs of a more explicit formal expression inspired by Bob van Reeth's work. The De Schutter block of flats in Kapellen (1979), which received the 'Baksteen' prize, marked the completion of this evolution. It demonstrates an affirmative formal approach that rejects any coincidence, but creates a 'pure' form full of figurative references.

In the 'Villa van de waanzin' (Villa of Insanity), a Lego construction of 1985, Crepain expresses his personal fantasy. 'An eccentric withdraws from society and builds four villas: one for a foggy coast, one at the cradle of civilization in the desert, one in peaceful high mountains, and one in the hostile rain forest. Four identical villas which he occupies in turns for a year so as to experience spring, summer, autumn, and winter once in each of them. Four identical villas, each with a crypt, two identical halls, a roof terrace, and four towers in four colours situated on the four points of the compass. Each tower has a piece of music that is continuously repeated: for the black tower, Heitor Villa-Lobos's *Chorus 10*; for the glass tower, Igor Stravinsky's *Sacre du Printemps*; for the yellow tower, Meredith Monk's *The Tale*; for the blue tower, Eric Satie's *Gymnopédies*. The villa, then, is an amplifier of emotions, the villa in inevitable confrontation with the elements of nature, the villa as the protector of cultivated taboos. The villa of insanity.'

This text says more than the architecture itself. It reveals the desire to involve architecture again with life as a whole without its loosing its identity. In the De Wachter villa in 's Gravenwezel (1985) architecture is not the neutral framework where the occupant settles, but defines the scenario to which he knowingly submits himself as an escape from banality and apathy. 'Three temples (reminiscent of Rome and Athens) connected to one another stand along a no man's land where light and space reign supreme and whose only function is experience.'

Concerned as he is with this impossible upgrading of architecture, Jo Crepain initiated the so-called WISH competitions ('Wedstrijd Ideën Sociale Huisvesting - Social Housing Ideas Competition), the acronym indeed expressing his hope for more sensible popular housing. They were held between 1984 and 1985. Towards the end of 1988 E. Vandevelde, the director of the national housing association, could not help remarking that 'unfortunately few of the winning projects have been completely or even partly carried out'. L. Wouters and F. Mostien's work yielded impressive results in the Twee Netenstraat in Antwerp, but they had in fact already deserved their reputation in the field of social housing by then. The realization of a small housing development in Tervuren by Jan Maenhout also positively distinguished itself from he traditional social housing.

We shall return to Jo Crepain's participation in the competition for the Carrefour de l'Europe in Brussels further on. His later work is characterized by two company buildings: one for the Van Cauwenbergh firm in Rumst and one for UCO in Ghent, which in 1992 was declared the 'best company building' of the year. In both instances the architect worked with an elongated, closed volume that is modified and interrupted. In Ghent the most striking feature is the six glass cones above the roof, which allow daylight to enter into the interior with its rhythmical columns. At night their effect is created by the illuminated interior so that they reveal the true nature of this architecture, which is not averse to spectacular effects.

Ghent, office building, 1992
(Bastin/Evrard)

During a period of growth at the end of the 1950s, the 'Union Cottonière' put up a glass office block (designed by the German architects Kelter and Feltes) on the Bellevue in Ledeberg, which became a landmark in the Ghent cityscape. In the wake of the firm's slimming-down in 1992, an old company building that had remained on the terrain was transformed into offices. The most prominent feature of this elongated building today is the glass cones on the roof, which allow a soft light to enter the building during the day and create a striking effect at night.

Floor

Jo Crepain
's Gravenwezel, house, 1982-1984
(Bastin/Evrard)
In the De Wachter house in 's Gravenwezel Jo Crepain combined three
volumes which at the same time reveal
the subdivisions of the scheme. They
serve as 'three temples (reminiscent of
Athens) that are connected to one
another via a no man's land where light
and space dominate and whose only
function is perception.'

Paul Robbrecht (b. 1950) / Hilde Daem (b. 1950)

Paul Robbrecht and Hilde Daem's architecture is of a completely different nature. Robbrecht graduated at the Sint-Lucasinstituut in Ghent in 1974 and for some time worked in Marc Dessauvage's studio. His work does not aim at effects, but at an intrinsic substance, a domain of its own that refers neither to external factors, nor to the public. Robbrecht calls this the 'being in itself' of architecture, 'unlike art, which refers to an exterior world'. One of their first works made their position clear.

With the De Mol house in Kortrijk (1979) they deliberately put all functionalist conventions behind them, reclaiming the right to architecture in house design, which is not to say that architecture became disconnected from comfort. 'The moment architecture has come to be, it starts leading a life of its own and slips from the architect's hands. The concept becomes a secret and the architecture submits to well-being. The strong emphasis on well-being –*commoditas*- in architecture as a technique and the inevitable disguising of the concept endue the architecture with its own sense of poetry. It is precisely this reconciliation between distance/concept and embracing/well-being of everyday life that can be most clearly seen in the house as an architectural project.'

This approach could not have been more clearly expressed than by returning to the classical principles of symmetry and static, clearly defined volumes. The requirements did not determine the architecture, which found its ultimate freedom and development within a composition that was based only on itself. The affirmation of this insight has been an important feature of recent architectural history. It did not concern a particular image or style, but rather the laying down of laws of architecture as well as a return to a form of architectural grammar in which the autonomy of architecture could be established. It did not concern an example that could be imitated, to the extent that even Robbrecht and Daems themselves never used it as a model.

The exploration of the borders of the territory of architecture itself almost automatically led the architects to its relation with contemporary plastic arts. The 'interventions-inventions' together with Christian Kieckens in the house for the collector Mys in Oudenarde (started in 1984) not only play upon the relation between architecture and the work of art, but also with that between architecture and the existing environment. The changes brought in the Mys house all took place while it remained occupied. These were punctual interventions in the sense that they were stops along the way, which while exploring and confirming the existing elements almost imperceptibly transformed them into something completely new. The architecture, both existing and new, created a house in which art as well as the occupant can be put up.

Apart from the bank building in Kerksken (1987), almost all works by Robbrecht and Daem have something to do with art. The bank building is the exception that proves the rule: through the absence of art it demonstrates the autonomous

PAUL ROBBRECHT AND HILDE DAEM
Antwerp, 'Katoennatie', renovation, 1994
(Kristien Daem)
The relation between architecture and art is one of independence, even though art may be fully integrated – which it is in the transformation of 'Katoennatie' on De Waghemakerestraat in Antwerp. Here Paul Robbrecht and Hilde Daem called in the Spanish artist Christina Iglesias to design the skylights.

Brussels, Galerie Hufkens, 1989-1992

(Kristien Daem)

The exploration of the limits of architecture led Paul Robbrecht and Hilde Daem to its relation with the plastic arts. Galerie Hufkens in Rue Saint-Georges in Brussels receives art in a space that is both clear and differentiated. Though hidden behind the white façade of an existing mansion, it reveals all its beauty in the new rear façade.

Kerksken, bank, 1987-1989

(Kristien Daem)

This difficult site with its sharp and obtuse angles led the architects to create clearly outlined exterior volumes, emphasized by a colonnade. The inside brightly unfolds in the semicircle of the entrance hall, on which the whole interior is oriented.

role of its architecture. The static structure is loaded – just as it was to some extent in the De Mol house – with a dynamic tension of geometrical patterns and their mutual interaction, so that the materiality of the object fuses with the immateriality of the play of light. Archetypal elements – such as façades, walls, transitions and passages, stairs and towers, horizontals and verticals, closedness and openness, interior and exterior, speed and inertia, light and shadow – are all invested with emphatic qualities.

This is not an attempt at attractive architecture that has to blend in with the banality of the street. The colonnade that screens and protects the volume on both sides facing the street aggressively demarcates the unity of the site and the transition from the exterior to the interior, giving the architecture an almost sacral character, 'an unforgettable place for art' that has remained empty.

In 1986 Robbrecht and Daem were engaged to fit out the 'Initiatief 86' exhibition in St Peter's abbey in Ghent. The highlight of the exhibition was the architecture in which René Heyvaert's work was housed. In the following year they held an exhibition at Galerie De Appel in Amsterdam, entitled 'Floor for a sculpture - Wall for a painting', with work by the sculptors Isa Genzken and Christina Iglesias (with whom they were to collaborate later on) and the painters René Daniels and Philippe Van Snick. 'Neither the floor nor the wall has anything to do with some or other technique for presenting art. Nor should they be regarded as a sculpture or an installation. They are purely architectural elements being confronted and/or brought in relation with art,' Robbrecht says.

This temporary installation was the preparation for the transformation and interior arrangement of two art galleries in Brussels, Galerie Meert-Rihoux in Rue du Canal (1988), to which a flat was added in 1991, and Galerie Hufkens (also with a flat) in Rue Saint-Josse (1990). In Galerie Hufkens the street-side façade was conserved, as well as the party wall and a part of the staircase, against which the bright new construction was placed. It would be hard to imagine a stronger constrast between the two parts, and yet they seem to fuse and form a single spacious house. The two lower storeys house the gallery and the upper floor contains the apartment.

The flat in Galerie Meert-Rihoux is situated on top of an existing building and looks like a strange crystal that has somehow ended up in a chaotic rocky landscape. Its strangeness and isolation is further emphasized by Isa Genzken's sculpture, a pure frame dangerously leaning over the abyss and fulfilling the same role as the screens in the De Mol house or

PAUL ROBBRECHT AND HILDE DAEM
Sint-Martens-Latem, house, 1993
(Bastin/Evrard)

Whether they are working on a transformation in the city centre or a new construction in the open fields makes little difference to Paul Robbrecht and Hilde Daems. In both cases they want to use architecture to define a place with a strong and individual character without its being isolated from its surroundings. They place clearly defined fragments along a never-ending course.

PAUL ROBBRECHT AND HILDE DAEM
Brussels, Galerie Meert-Rihoux, 1989-1991

(Kristien Daem)

Just as the Muys house and Galerie Hufkens, the Galerie Meert-Roux in Brussels constitutes an intervention in an existing structure. The living quarters are situated in a flat on te roof, resembling a strange crystal in a chaotic rocky landscape. Its isolation is underlined by Isa Genzken's sculpture, which dangerously leans over the abyss.

the colonnade of the bank in Kerksken. For Katoen Natie in Antwerp they converted two warehouses into offices. The character of the existing architecture was enhanced by their intervention and transfigured by means of a series of skylights by the hand of Christina Iglesias.

In 1992, on the occasion of Documenta IX, they built a number of temporary pavilions in the Auewiese. They were also responsible for the general interior arrangement of the whole Documenta. In both cases one could see a succession of fragments combining a strong identity with a free and undirected course, Gilles Deleuze's rhizome. The pavilions were bought up by Almere, the new polder city near Amsterdam, and fitted out as permanent exhibition rooms. With the 'Fiamminghi a Roma' exhibition in the Brussels Palais des Beaux-Arts (1995) they faced the challenge of dealing with both the Renaissance-like closed architectural concept and a homogeneous, yet fragmented space.

One of their most recent works, a detached house for a collector in Sint-Martens-Latem, also contains strong emphasis on the fragmentary approach combined with archetypal elements. The house originates from a combination of these and constitutes a tentative synthesis thereof. It is architecture without end, architecture in progress, as it were. The certitude of the beginning no longer consists in clear definitions, but rather in controlled use of architectural components, both material and immaterial, which seem to discover one another with a degree of wonderment.

Marie-José Van Hee (b. 1950)

Marie-José Van Hee belongs to the same circle as Robbrecht and Daem and often collaborates with them. Although their approach to architecture is similar, Van Hee's work has its own indisputable character. Often working in unsatisfactory conditions, she manages to place accents that are at the same time assertive and controlled. A fine example of her approach is the corner house that she built in the Tinnepotstraat (1982), a narrow street in the inner city of Ghent. Through its symmetrical composition and its closed volume with few, carefully placed openings, it has acquired an elevated and even majestic air. It does not interrupt the streetscape, but enriches it by means of a subtle, though effective shift in the typology. Apparently architecture needs nothing more to express its own dignity than intelligence and sensitivity.

The success of this modest house is repeated in her later work with ever decreasing means. Van Hee's work in collaboration with Johan Van Dessel in Brussels, a bank in Uccle (1978) and a house with a shop in Laeken (1988) demonstrates the same subtle manipulation of architectural elements through the ingenious layout of the ground plan, the composition of the volumes, as well as in the play of light. Here again the most striking feature is the effect of the openings in the protective exterior wall. They are not merely present, but cut into the wall and invest it with a constant tension, which is mirrored in the tension between the banality surrounding the work and the intensity of the new building that has been inserted in it.

The complex incorporating accommodation, offices, and a shed built for the firm Van Hee-Coppens in Deinze (1990) bears out the continuity of this approach as well as the role of architecture in an everyday environment. Indeed, the architecture is a silent, yet uninhibited exaltation of reality, which it transforms without withdrawing from it. The various volumes are organized asymmetrically around a courtyard and are explicitly connected to one another by means of a series of opened-up walls, similar to colonnades, which lead a life of their own both in- and outside.

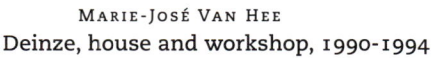

MARIE-JOSÉ VAN HEE
Deinze, house and workshop, 1990-1994
(Bastin/Evrard)
The house and industrial buildings in Deinze constitute a quiet, though uninhibited tribute to the banal reality of everyday life and work. The various volumes are organized around a courtyard and are mutually connected by a colonnade.

MARIE-JOSÉ VAN HEE AND
JOHAN VAN DESSEL
Laeken, house, 1988-1991
(Bastin/Evrard)
The tension of the skin around a building is convincingly demonstrated in Marie-José Van Hee's Pay house in Laeken. The openings in the wall reveal very little of the interior arrangement, although they do suggest the intensity of what is happening on the inside.

Eugeen Liebaut (b. 1952)

The work of Eugeen Liebaut, who set up his own firm in his native city of Aalst in 1979, brings to mind Edward Hopper, the painter of the striking commonplace that, because it is painted, loses its commonplace character to become intriguing and mysterious, close to the spectator and nevertheless strange. Liebaut perceives the commonest reality with wonder and wants to make this commonness reveal its strangeness through the interventions he performs on it.

The atmosphere of the city of Aalst, which has a history of social engagement through characters like Daens and Louis-Paul Boon, is not unfamiliar with this. The city's industrial relics are now being robbed of their true character by the urge to renovate, which is what Liebaut is trying to counteract. He does not want to erase the past, but to absorb it and let it be itself by confronting it with a contemporary presence. His own house, a working-class home dating from around 1900 and which he converted between 1979 and 1984, can still count as a declaration of his architectural principles. He left the shell unchanged, but inserted a number of elements into it that transform its lack of potential into a stimulating experience. Liebaut himself unwaveringly refers to its 'mysterious tension'. Indeed, this tension can only be brought about via the existing typology, the associations embedded in the materials, and in the new interpretation thereof.

The confrontation with living in a working-class area from the industrial age is carried further with the sort of space cabin that Liebaut has put down in a meadow somewhere to serve as his weekend cottage. A closed container made of wood, without any windows except for a skylight resembling a cockpit and two doors right opposite each other in the longitudinal sides, is elevated from the gound by metal legs. This incongruous space cabin endows the act of living somewhere with a motive force. A similar principle was applied later in his conversion of Plateau, an interfunctional centre for the performing arts in Brussels (1988). The extension of a house in Hedersem shows another version of this.

The dual nature of living somewhere is literally embodied by the Gees house (1981) in Erpe-Mere near Aalst, deliberately situated near a motorway. Two striking volumes, clearly referring to the archetypal detached house, are connected with each other via a chimney reminiscent of industrial architecture. Liebaut hereby creates his own archaeology, as it were, which he can then use without restriction. The use of materials, form, and colours is remarkable. The open façade with its regularly punctuated rhythm strongly contrasts with the improvised half-finished closed wall on the other side of the house. They are linked together by the clarity of the volume alone.

In his later work Liebaut no longer needs such explicit methods, as is borne out by the Vanderpooten house in Dilbeek (1989) or the Leysen house in Wezembeek-Oppem (1990). Both these examples at the same time incorporate and abolish the typology of the house as a closed box. The right angle of two façades is complemented by a curved front, in the Vander-pooten house clearly to avoid a corner, in the Leysen house to complete this and the adjacent house with a single third façade consisting of a smooth segment of a circle. The interference with the typological image is not diminished, but remains implicit. In these works the subtle formal play is not directed only at itself, but constitutes a sort of revelation of the complex contradictions that determine the private house today: hesitating between security and spectacle, rest and motion, introvert and extrovert tendencies, frontal and evasive positions. Arthur Wortmann writes on the Vanderpooten house in *Archis*: 'Apart from the fact that the house corresponds to the specific demands of the location and the building requirements, it is impossible not to recognize in it references to Le Corbusier and John Hejduk's work. However, these references are not an end in themselves; it rather seems as if Liebaut has appropriated the thoughts of a number of Masters, as if his own handwriting has started showing traits of theirs.'

Indeed, Liebaut's work not only applies a more or less abstract typology, but also positions itself with reference to the history of architecture, most clearly in the case of the Vanderpooten house. The new house was built straight opposite an earlier one designed by Alfons Hoppenbrouwers. Liebaut studied with Hoppenbrouwers at the Sint-Lucasinstituut in Schaerbeek (Brussels), where he has himself been teaching since 1981. The contrast could not have been more striking. Liebaut's work, just as Hejduk's, stands at the extreme of what architecture can achieve through its own means. It is confronted with the dilemma described by Jean Genet at the beginning of *The Thief's Journal*: 'If I, listening to my heart, choose a world in which I delight, then at least I have the power to discover in it the many meanings I want to see: *there is a close relationship between flowers and convicts*. The frailty and fineness of the first are of the same nature as the brutal insensitivity of the latter. (What agitates me is the fluctuation from one to the other.) If I have to represent a convict (I mean an ideal convict, a man in whom all the *qualities* of the punished are brought together) – or a criminal – I would deck him out with so many flowers that he would disappear under them and become another, giant, new flower.' This may serve as a suitable metaphor for the metamorphosis that architecture can impose on relentless construction.

EUGEEN LIEBAUT
Weekend house, 1987-1988

Eugeen Liebaut demonstrates the sobriety of his poetic approach in this weekend house, designed on the site of a ruin.

The temporary quality of the building is elevated to charm, play, and mystery. The long sides contain double doors with only peep- and airing holes. One only has a view when the doors are open or if one goes up into the cockpit on the roof.

Herdersem, house extension, 1988-1989
(Bastin/Evrard)

The inventive way in which Eugeen Liebaut transforms houses is strikingly demonstrated in this house in Hedersem. Not only does the elegant structure of the extension formally enrich the house, but it also serves to regulate the climate inside.

Erpe-Mere, house and studio, 1981-1984
(Ger Van der Vlugt)

In 1979 Eugeen Liebaut started transforming a working-class house of the beginning of this century and made it into a striking confrontation between different worlds. In the house and studio in Erpe-Mere he first created the typological framework of the house and industry, through which he conformed with planning regulations, only to fill in this framework in a free and even capricious way.

EUGEEN LIEBAUT
Dilbeek, house, 1989-1991
(Bastin/Evrard)

In his recent work, such as the Vanderpooten house in a typically suburban development in Dilbeek, Eugeen Liebaut returns to the immaterial character of the international style, but adapts it to his own principles. Here he has combined the right angle of the rear and lateral façades with a curved façade, which goes against the rules applied in the rest of the development.

EUGEEN LIEBAUT
Brussels, 'Plateau', transformation, 1988-1990
(Martien Van Beeck)

The interfunctional centre for the performing arts 'Plateau' in the Rue du Berger in Ixelles was installed by Liebaut in an old school hall. The stage and hall have become interchangeable.
The apartment suspended from the truss hardly interferes with the space, but seems to be lightly floating in it.

Christian Kieckens (b. 1951)

One so often comes across Christian Kieckens in connection with other names that it looks as if this cannot be mere coincidence, but that it must be a deliberate attitude. No matter how much the history of architecture may concentrate on names, they are in fact irrelevant. It should be about what they stand for, that is, the reality of architecture. In the Belgian situation, where the world of architecture has very little structure, this is even more pertinent. It is about spiritual families. Kieckens somewhere quotes a title by Claudio Monteverdi, 'A voce sola in dialogo'.

Christian Kieckens regards Pieter De Bruyne (1931-1987) as his spiritual father. De Bruyne was an inspired designer of furniture, obsessed by the secrets of Egyptian geometry and in his work looking for the key to free us from all forms of subjectivity. These objective aesthetic laws applied to both architecture and furniture, to anything created by man. With his 'Hommage aan Pieter De Bruyne' (1981) Christian Kieckens not only honoured his mentor, but also took his leave to explore new ways.

He collaborated with Jos Vanderperren from 1980 to 1983. They formed the 'Detaai' group which, according to Kieckens himself, dissociated design from 'scale' and brought it back to 'size, constructed according to a specific system of proportions recurring throughout history'. From 1984 to 1986 Kieckens worked together with Paul Robbrecht and Hilde Daem. This collaboration again cannot be considered coincidental, for they too approach architecture as an intellectual exercise.

This concern with architecture also was the reason why Christian Kieckens, together with Marc Dubois, dedicated himself to the 'Stichting Architectuurmuseum', which for ten years tried to create an architecural awareness in Flanders. The foundation's declaration of principles was worded for the competition and exhibition for a museum of architecture (1983), based on Oswald Mathias Ungers' thematic approach to architecture: 'Architecture that does not deduce its themes from itself is like a painting that tries to be nothing more than a photographic reproduction. Only architecture itself can be the theme and contents of architecture.' Kieckens adds: 'The series of "architectural museums", both fictional and real, is an attempt at creating a first confrontation between various contemporary visions on architecture and museums. We are not concerned with a functional solution, but with an intrinsic philosophy that forms the basis of the concept.'

Year after year exhibitions were organized at the Museum of Decorative Arts in Ghent, dedicated to 'the house as architectural typology', 'young architects in Belgium', 'young interior designers', and 'architecture is' (a project by Johan van Gheluwe), but special attention was also paid to the works of Alvaro Siza, Mario Botta, Le Corbusier, Wiel Arets, and Wim van den Bergh. In 1986 and 1987 the 'Jonge architecten in België' exhibition toured Belgium and the Netherlands. The exhibitions were accompanied by publications, at first in the form of monographies, later in the form of a periodical. The 'Stichting Architectuurmuseum' also successfully organized architectural trips. The climax of their activities came with the exhibition in the Belgian pavilion at the 1991 architectural Biennale in Venice, 'Architetti (della Fiandra)'. However, it also practically marked the end of the foundation.

All these activities, to which have to be added teaching at the Hoger Architectuurinstituut Sint-Lucas in Ghent (1980-1990) – where he had graduated in 1974 – and at the Henry van de Velde-instituut in Antwerp (from 1987 on), have meant that his architectural œuvre is relatively small. It also has to be taken into account that at the special exhibition on his work between 1990 and 1993 in Galerij S65 in Aalst a large number of his designs were marked 'not executed'.

The work he has carried out is limited to the arrangement of exhibitions, conversions of existing buildings, and furniture. Among the exhibitions, 'Architetti (in Fiandra)' in Venice and 'Interieur 94 in Kortrijk come to mind. Among the conversions the most remarkable include the transformation of a nineteenth-century mansion on the Kouter in Ghent (1992) into a bank with art gallery. The magnificence of the old mansion was recreated in its original proportions and brought to life by the addition of 'floating' surfaces and stairs transforming the existing static space into a dynamic whole.

CHRISTIAN KIECKENS
Ghent, bank, 1992
(Reiner Lautwein)
By transforming a 19th-century mansion on the Kouter in Ghent into a bank with an exhibition room Christian Kieckens revealed its hidden proportions, blowing new life into them through a few discrete interventions.

Philippe Samyn (b. 1948)

It is no easy task to situate Philippe Samyn within this school of architects believing in a certain degree of autonomy for the architectural form. Born in Ghent, he studied civil engineering at the Université Libre de Bruxelles, whence he graduated in 1972. He added to this a degree as an architect in 1985, but had already set up an office in 1980, equipped with the latest technologies. According to Belgian standards it is a large firm, employing up to 40 people at times with a worldwide network of associates.

Nevertheless, Samyn distinguishes himself from commercial firms, to whom it does not matter whether they are selling architecture or washing-powder. As a typical engineer he has a strong belief in the 'universal builder', a type secretly dreamt of by all architects, who creates form out of the inventiveness of construction and discovers beauty in the laws of numbers. However, Samyn is realistic enough to realize that things are not all that simple. Even though, as he puts it, he discovers 'the same proportions and order in the pillars of an African hut, the temple of Sukhotai in northern Thailand, the temple at Karnak, the Parthenon, and even in the houses of the Far West', he is also aware that the history of architecture has continuously been creating new images according to a timeless architectural concept.

It is the contrast between the image and reality he is concerned with. He dreams of the ultimate, perfect structure of the dune: 'a heap of sand, mobile and under vertical pressure. For, even if the wind displaces it, which inevitably implies a change in shape, it nevertheless remains a structure'.

Samyn's openness towards formal elements makes his œuvre fascinating, but at the same time capricious, for even the purest technology functions in terms of culturally determined images. This even appears in one of Samyn's most impressive works, the OCAS research centre for steel applications in Zelzate (1989), where the power of the clear image puts technology in the foreground. The centre stands as a sculpture in an undefined landscape, on an empty spot between a sea canal and the motorway.

In the same year Samyn designed an office building for Eric Boulenger in Waterloo, a round 'Chinese' temple in wood, composed of receding floors with a segment left out for the entrance. These two works differ less from each other than might appear at first sight. Samyn would explain the difference with reference to the location and materials. The most striking aspect is the continuity of the approach, in which a simple concept is chosen as a foundation to be consistently and abundantly developed down to the last detail. The structure is the form; it is decoration and in some cases even furniture. Indeed, it therefore acquires a sort of timelessness in that it is based on itself alone. This timelessness contains in it attention for the 'eternal' values of architecture – Perrault's 'absolute beauty' –, which Samyn cherishes with the greatest care, such as the quality of the materials, physical conditioning, the incidence of light, orientation, appearance, and even maintenance. Samyn

PHILIPPE SAMYN
Brussels, Brussimmo offices, 1990-1992
(Bastin/Evrard)
In the Brussimmo building in Brussels Samyn has succeeded in endowing the strict, technical rationality of the building with a brilliance that takes it beyond practical concerns.

once admitted: 'Best of all I would like to build a very traditional house. But one, for instance, with a façade made of fabric so that it could be washed every week.'

In the Brussimmo building on the corner of Rue Belliard and Rue de Trèves in Brussels (1990), Samyn rethinks the typical office block, in particular as regards ideal utility, even if its use may vary. The structure consists of two rows of five columns, which support the concrete floor slabs and allow the free division of every floor. The glass skin of the building is double, as often occurs in Samyn's work, with a gap of almost a metre and catwalks to facilitate maintenance. The bearing structure of the façade is made of aluminium on the outside and of wood on the inside. Though completely transparent, the wall does not lose its consistency and marks the transition between interior and exterior. In the greyness of the Brussels office landscape this building brings a breath of fresh air. Just as André Jacqmain's Foncolin building (1955), it focuses on the complex reality of our time without submitting to superficial decoration or commercial exploitation.

The simplicity of construction in the inner city of Brussels is contrasted with the research and distribution centre of the Walloon timber industry in Marche-en-Famenne (1992). Despite its simple balloon shape, the centre does not exclude technical *tours de force*. It is reminiscent of the laboratory designed by Samyn for a chemical plant in Venafro, Italy (1989), for which he was awarded the 1994 European prize of Industry. Samyn has recently erected a membrane construction beside the Brussels-Luxembourg motorway at Wanlin, the first true monument on the Belgian motorway network.

Office baroque

There is no precise end to this decade, which is directed towards the future, towards a new beginning. When in 1977 Gordon Matta-Clark installed his 'Office Baroque' in Antwerp, it marked the end of architecture as a symbol of what Richard Nonas called the 'hard-shelled cultural reality we meant to push against'. In a building destined for demolition, opposite the Steen in the centre of Antwerp, Matta-Clark cut elegant figures in the walls and floors so that via this negative transgression the whole building became transparent. Gordon Matta-Clark himself says about his work: 'The very real nature of my work with buildings takes issue with the functionalist attitude to the extent that this kind of self-righteous vocational responsibility has failed to question or reexamine the quality of life being served.' 'There is no way of describing a system without resorting to the vocabulary of architecture... The image of the world itself is caught in the architectural analogy.'

For the new generation Gordon Matta-Clark's attitude forms the foundation for a lucid way of dealing with architecture. They no longer interpret it as a means to correct the 'badly constructed universe', in Bontridder's words, and to replace it by a pure cosmos. The want to deconstruct architecture itself by investigating its historical bases, using architecture not as a solution, but as a means to understanding reality. Indeed, this is a new beginning.

Philippe Samyn
Zelzate, OCAS, 1989-1991
(Bastin/Evrard)
In the research centre for steel applications, situated on a useless piece of land between a channel and the motorways in Zelzate, Philippe Samyn has created a powerful image by building a long steel bridge between the two shells. The overall impression is taken up in a single glance. The bridge contains offices and the laboratories are below the shells.

HOOGPOORT: STÉPHANE BEEL,
XAVEER DE GEYTER, ARJAN KARSENBERG,
AND WILLEM-JAN NEUTELINGS

Brussels, Carrefour de l'Europe, 1983, sketch
The occasional Hoogpoort team saw the
Carrefour de l'Europe competition as an
opportunity to put outdated notions of
urban architecture as something
disconnected from present-day reality
behind them.

The empty triangle is not filled in with
architecture, but is prepared for the lively
activity reflected by the towers and
buildings along the edges. This is an
explicit reinstatement of the modern
tradition.

Chapter 5

1985-1995

A new beginning: 'Bright Young Gods'

'Bright Young Gods'

Chronologically speaking, the mid-1980s is an ideal point at which to start this last chapter, for it was precisely 1985 that saw the first constructions that can be regarded as a manifestation of the generation of 'young gods' who entered the world of architecture as leisurely as if it were a discotheque. They are contemporaries of the Flemish writers who in 1986, not without somewhat inflated egos, called themselves 'Bright Young Gods'.

In an article published in *Ons Erfdeel* (January-February 1989), entitled 'Jonge architecten ontmaskeren de architectuur' (Young Architects Unmask Architecture), I introduced the young generation: 'This young architecture appeals more to enthusiasm than to understanding, more to joining in and enjoying than to detached appreciation. It has clearly left all its inhibitions behind. It is not concerned with building for eternity. It also takes no notice at all of petty criticism. Just as it originates from the intense enjoyment of inventing and making something, it creates a space for the enjoyment of discovery and experience. It is in this intelligent play with the facts of present-day reality that its only norms are contained. It justifies itself through its existence. Bad luck for those Scrooges who will not let architects and builders have their fun.'

'Their force lies in this lack of inhibition. These young architects were born in an architectural no man's land. They have an open playing field. Of course they have eyes in their heads. They know what the world has to offer and they even shamelessly go along with it. It is only here in Belgium that they appear as a total surprise.'

'They will take on the responsibility for continuity themselves. They create their own examples and thereby build up their own tradition. They are not after originality, which is precisely why their hands are free to draw original links between all possible phenomena that appear both in and outside the complex world of architecture and construction. Nothing is excluded in advance, nor do they join anything in advance.'

'Through this attitude the perception of the generation working in the 1970s is put into question, which enables their work to be reappraised as well. It would be out of place to speak of a conflict between generations, for it is precisely this concept that has been superseded. What remains is those architects who have something to say and those who have given up.'

Nevertheless, the division within the architectural profession is becoming increasingly clear; on the one hand there is the industry of spectacular architecture, on the other hand there is the marginal art of an architecture in pursuit of the intensity of the work. The rare large-scale commissions that are still given go to those architects who without reserve offer their services to the megalomania of customers who can only judge the quality of what they have built in terms of the money they have invested in it.

Money also plays a role in the 'alternative' architectural practice, but mainly in that there is a lack of it. One would be tempted to see limited budgets as a characteristic of good architecture and confirm Victor Bourgeois's remark that 'Le salut de l'architecture c'est la dèche,' were it not that his own work so flagrantly contradicts this.

Deconstructionism

New denominations are continually being thought up to justify architecture, as if it needs a flag to sail under. The most common of these is modernism itself, followed by postmodernism and, thanks to Charles Jencks, late- and neo-modernism. Some people even speak of retro-modernism, which is not so strange if one takes into account that it is precisely through contemporary architecture that we are rediscovering the true nature of the modern. These terms often derive from other fields, such as philosophy or science, before they are applied to architecture – mostly with some delay, as in the case of structuralism. Sometimes they originate from attempts at ordering and making particular phenomena of architectural practice a subject of discussion, such as brutalism. Whatever the case may be, these terms rarely appear in the actual work done by architects.

Towards the end of the 1980s a new term was added: deconstructionism. Deconstructionist architecture was the subject of an exhibition held by Philip Johnson and Mark Wigley at the Museum of Modern Art in New York (1988). Johnson explicitly pointed out that he was not aiming at launching a new style, which had been the case with the 'International Style' in 1932, but only wanted to focus our attention on a number of architects who despite certain common characteristics, could not simply be lumped together. They were the architects that fascinated the younger generation at the time, also in Belgium: Frank O. Gehry, Daniel Libeskind, Rem Koolhaas, Peter Eisenman, Zaha M. Hadid, Coop Himmelblau, and Bernard Tschumi.

Deconstruction is the term used by the French philosopher Jacques Derrida in the 1960s to describe his method. It was a way of thought no longer aimed at the setting up of systems, but at the questioning of systematic thought itself. Derrida 'adapted', or deconstructed texts by others.

Psyché, the 1987 collection in which his texts on architecture appear, was given the subtitle 'inventions de l'autre'. It contains 'Point de Folie – Maintenant Architecture', about Tschumi's creations in La Villette in Paris, '52 Aphorismes pour un avant-propos', and 'Pourquoi Peter Eisenman écrit de si bons textes'. In it Derrida warns against deconstruction being taken as an architectural metaphor that can be applied literally.

It is impossible to imagine the architectural scene today without Derrida and deconstructionism. Derrida shares this role as mentor with his less prominent compatriot Gilles Deleuze, whose terms such as 'rhizome' and 'pli' have had a profound and lasting influence on architectural thought. In a contribution to *Lotus 72* (1992) Ignasi de Solà Morales describes Deleuze's position as a reply to the uncertainty of a time without any direction. Just as Derrida, he does not propose a theoretical discourse, but a watchful and temporary line of thought based on interpretation.

It was especially with *Mille Plateaux* (1980), written in collaboration with Felix Guattari, that he made his breakthrough in architectural circles. 'What they offer', says Solà Morales, 'is a system of changeable concepts that do not claim durability, but have the power of being tools that can be fashioned for every circumstance. These concepts appear to follow sideway routes, trying to find unexpected links and to use science, history, and culture in an uninterrupted attempt to bring about an interpretational and therefore critical discourse – a discourse which, temporary as it may be, would clarify the present situation.'

The term 'deconstructionism' has inspired many architects to design buildings that had to create the impression of no longer being 'constructed'. In Belgium this misunderstanding has led to a sort of publicity architecture. Dirk Coopman's showrooms in Lokeren and his shop ('Minit One') in Ghent are prime examples of this. However, their architecture have little to do with a deconstructionist way of thought.

Carrefour de l'Europe

The organization of exclusive, often international competitions is a striking phenomenon in recent Belgian architectural history. In the first place it provides an indication of the authority assigned to architecture as a medium. Little has changed in the actual situation, for practically nothing has issued from these competitions. Nevertheless, they are very different from those held in the 1970s, such as 'Gent Morgen' or 'Leuven 2000'. They are directed towards a concrete approach, though this does not necessarily imply that they are eventually carried out.

Let us return to the open spot at the Carrefour de l'Europe, which we last saw when discussing the North-South railway link set up during the Reconstruction after the war. Since halfway the nineteenth century this spot has posed a problem for town planners, as it is situated on the North-South axis and the border between the popular lower city and the more prestigious upper part around Place Royale and the Parc Royal. There have been constant attempts to heal this urban wound ever since the completion of the Central Station.

In 1960 a special construction plan for the 'Ilot Sacré' around the Brussels Grand' Place was approved by the local authorities. In the competition held in 1961 Robert Courtois's proposal for the Carrefour de l'Europe was awarded the first prize. A second competition was held the year after, this time won by Baudon. Five years later, in 1967, the Van den Boeynants government gave Charles De Pauw a 99-year lease to build a car park on the Carrefour de l'Europe. In 1969 the recently founded ARAU protested against the designs for a car park by Polak and Van Meulekom. Luc Deleu, still a student at the time and a pupil of Willy Van Der Meeren's, also got involved in the debate.

In order to calm everybody down the city council held another competition in 1970. No first prize was awarded, but the second prize was won by Planning. However, the Tekhne research consultancy firm was commissioned to make a synthesis of (or a compromise between) the proposals entered for the competition. In 1975 Planning submitted a new proposal, and in 1976 ARAU finally presented an 'aesthetic alternative'. This last term is significant; indeed, their proposal concerned neither urban development nor social planning, but an aesthetic image. In it the triangle of the Carrefour de l'Europe is used to create an idyllic pre-industrial city, very similar to the present buildings except that the houses have now been replaced by hotel rooms.

A last attempt at seeing the Carrefour de l'Europe as a test to town planners was made by the 'Classe des Beaux-Arts' of the Académie Royale de Belgique when it made this controversial area the subject of the Bonduelle competition in 1983. This last episode is interesting in that the entries demonstrated various visions of life in the city today and particularly since it involved the new generation for the first time.

The prize was awarded to Georges Baines's project. Baines remained faithful to the principle of the closed block filling the empty part of the city and repairing the streetscape.

JO CREPAIN
Brussels, Carrefour de l'Europe, 1983, model
The last attempt to use the Carrefour de l'Europe in Brussels as a test for urban planning was undertaken by the Académie Royale de Belgique, who made this controversial spot the subject of its Bonduelle competition. The prize was awarded to Georges Baines. Whereas he repaired the walls of the buildings and laid out a park in the middle, Jo Crepain transformed the area into an autonomous element with a long wall on the side facing the Central Station. There are three curved buildings, which are stylistically linked to the architecture of the city centre.

The Boulevard de l'Impératrice is flanked by a long façade with colonnades and forms a closed front opposite the station, the post office, and the Sabena building. The interior section is transformed into a public park with a boulevard leading to the heart of the city. Jo Crepain also isolates it from the Boulevard de l'Impératrice, but behind this screen he reflects the radiating lines of the typology of the old town centre. Van Volrick's proposal breaks away from this pattern of restoration by occupying the whole triangle with an immense amphitheatre directed towards the city centre.

The Hoogpoort team, made up of Stéphane Beel, Xaveer de Geyter, Arjan Karsenberg, and Willem-Jan Neutelings, used the opportunity to bring to an end those old-fashioned ideas that had little or nothing to do with the dynamism of present-day reality. The space is used to create a bustling centre where old and new have a role to play. Even more clearly than in their actual proposal, the group's approach comes to light in a series of sketches made to illustrate the chaotic mix of urban activities. The buildings are conceived as dynamic elements rather than formal entities and contribute to the attempt at ridding architecture of its alienation and rigidity in order to integrate it into real life today. Hoogpoort's proposal was dismissed as a joke, despite the fact that it is closely connected to everyday reality.

The demolition in 1985 of the yeast plant in Bruges absurdly demonstrated how pertinent and realistic the Hoogpoort team's ideas were. The monumental factory had to disappear because it did not fit in with the model of integration, which rejected everything that was different. In Bruges one can see the sort of worn-out architecture that has replaced it and what remains of the dynamism and contrasts that make a city what it is and give life its colour.

VICTOR JOCKIN
Bruges, yeast factory, 1924, demolished in 1985
The strong protest voiced against the demolition of major urban monuments – such as the yeast factory in Bruges or the Royal Warehouses in Antwerp – should not be seen as a reactionary reflex that is against all forms of change. It is a plea for diversity. The yeast factory in Bruges had to disappear because it did not fit into the integration model that does not tolerate anything that is different.

REM KOOLHAAS
Zeebrugge, Sea Trade Center, scale model, 1989

(Hans Werleman)

Rem Koolhaas does not paraphrase what is recognizable, but proposes new types. Nevertheless, he too refers to history when he calls his design an inverted Tower of Babel. The dome, shaped like a gigantic mooring post, contains all the functions of the building and brings them together in a single, whirling space.

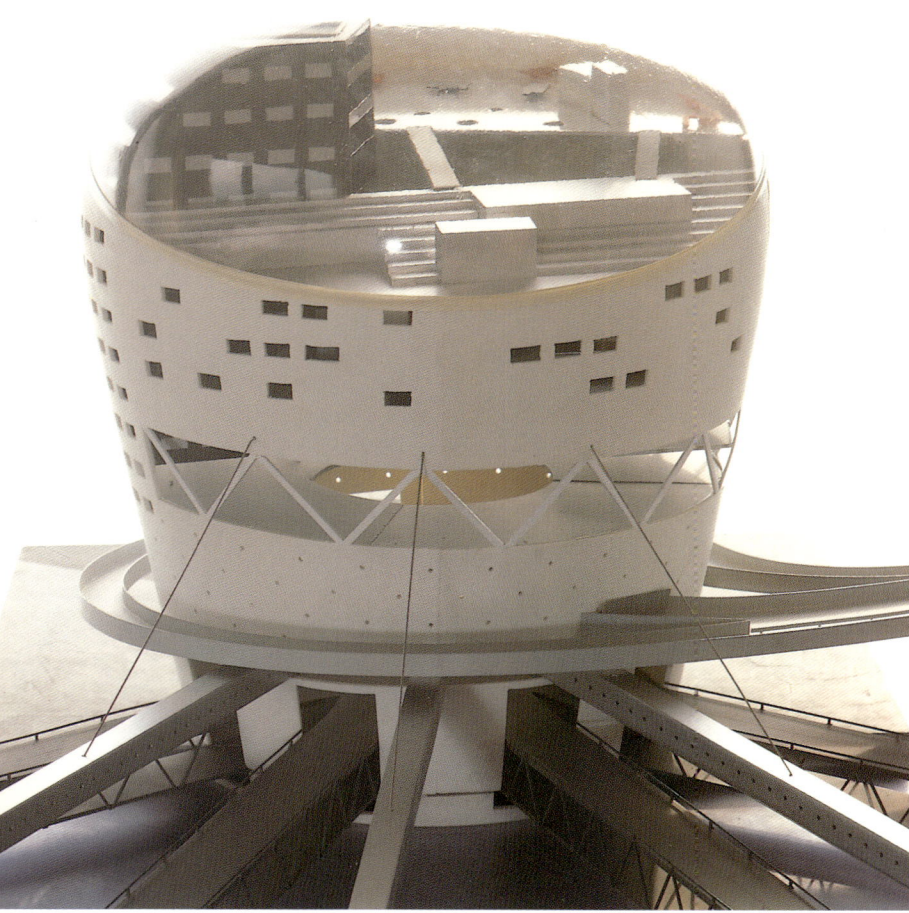

Sea Trade Center

The competition for the Sea Trade Center in Zeebrugge (1989) was an innovation in that architects from both Belgium and abroad were invited to submit designs for the new terminal: Charles Vandenhove and Bob van Reeth (Belgium), Tadao Ando (Japan), Santiago Calatrava (Spain/Switzerland), Norman Foster (Great Britain), Frank O. Gehry (United States), Rem Koolhaas (Office for Metropolitan Architecture, the Netherlands), Fumihiko Maki (Japan), and Aldo Rossi (Italy). Of these nine only four entered designs. Their designs were well matched, but produced very different interpretations of the question at hand. As Bob van Reeth remarked, it was one of the few occasions when architecture had been honestly approached in its intellectual dimension.

Maki's project was the most poetic. Its title, 'A Voyage into a Mirage', perfectly describes it. The bare surroundings are transformed into a fairy tale: a deck appears in a green park like a Fata Morgana, a round plateau inside which the traffic is caught up and laid still. On the plateau itself the party is going on. In his explanation Maki refers to Hokusai, Watteau, the Navajo Indians, and even to Greta Garbo.

Aldo Rossi, in association with Claude Zuber, also conceived the terminal as an autonomous area, a city on the interface between sea and land. He does not call his project a 'mirage', but an 'acropolis', the archetype of human settlements and of European history. On a square base in which the technical services involving arrivals and departures are housed, a number of buildings are ordered around a central tower resembling a cross between an industrial water tower and a belfry. Below there is an enormous domed hall reminiscent of nineteenth-century stations, with a closed amphitheatre above only affording a view of the sky. Here architectural archetypes are blended with technological achievements, which makes history present and places the present in a historical perspective. The Bonnefanten Museum in Maastricht, which opened in 1995, gives an idea of what this architecture is like.

Koolhaas's approach is totally different. He does not paraphrase what is recognizable, but presents a new type of building. He himself calls it an inverted Tower of Babel. The dome, shaped like a gigantic mooring post, does not absorb the dynamism of transport in static architecture, but rather exalts it in a space brimming with energy in which all the elements of the scheme are brought in relation with one another. An idea of what could have been can be gleaned from Euralille's approach in his 'espace piranesien' and his congress hall. For a moment the Zeebrugge project created the impression that architecture was being taken seriously in Belgium. Indeed, it would have been fantastic had any of the five proposals been carried out.

ALDO ROSSI AND CLAUDE ZUBER
Zeebrugge, Sea Trade Center, scale model, 1989

(Wim Van Nueten)
Aldo Rossi suggested an acropolis for the terminal in Zeebrugge, the archetypal settlement seen in the unfolding of European history in coastal areas. He combines architectural archetypes with technological innovations; history becomes present and the present acquires historical depth.

◁   FUMIHIKO MAKI
Zeebrugge, Sea Trade Center, scale model, 1989

The competion held for a new terminal for the port of Zeebrugge constituted an innovation in the Belgian context. It was the first in a series of such contests in which the authorities showed their intention to carry out a conscious architectural policy. With his design, entitled 'A Voyage into a Mirage', Fumihiko Maki wittily plays upon this by creating a sort of fun-fair.

Hoog-Kortrijk

Inspired by the Zeebrugge experiment, the local authorities in Kortrijk and the 'Interkommunale voor Streekontwikkeling Leiedal' organized a competition in 1990 for the urban development of the Hoog-Kortrijk district. The architects invited to take part were Stéphane Beel and Bob van Reeth (Belgium), Bernard Huet (France), Bernardo Secchi (Italy), and Rem Koolhaas (the Netherlands). Huet was unable to complete his project due to ill health. As in Zeebrugge, the four projects that were submitted are of a standard that makes serious discussion on town planning possible, something new in the history of Kortrijk. The havoc wreaked upon its inner city by urban development is comparable to that done during the Second World War. Hoog-Kortrijk itself knew only the principle of proliferation. Time and again plans were drawn up only to be abandoned after initial attempts to carry them out.

The plans by Stéphane Beel and Rem Koolhaas take this chaotic situation as their point of departure to develop strategies aimed at optimizing and intensifying it. In his explanation Koolhaas says: 'If the main attraction of the Leiedal has until now consisted in the freedom that reigns there – the space and apparent absence of limitations – then the trick is not to destroy this quality through planning. Scanning the area as if through a magnifying glass, we have in our plans used minimal means to identify a number of points with heightened potential.'

In his project Bob van Reeth proposes a radical intervention in the urban pattern by shifting the railway line to the motorway. On the traffic interchange he sees a proper city radiating out from the centre, similar to eighteenth-century city plans such as that of Karlsruhe.

The winner was Bernardo Secchi's project. Inspired by the topography, he emphasized certain aspects to give the whole a recognizable structure. Secchi also most explicitly wanted to involve the 'new city' with the old. Although he was commissioned to work out some sections in more detail, such as the new cemetery and the Grote Markt, practically none of these plans have been carried out to date.

'Stad aan de Stroom' - a city at the waterside

The approach in Antwerp was different. A group of architects, town planners, and representatives of the social sector found that something had to be done to rid the inner city of Antwerp of its melancholy and founded the 'Stad aan de Stroom' work group towards the end of 1989. As in most European ports, the harbour activities in Antwerp are largely withdrawn from the city proper, leaving behind a ruinous landscape.

An international architectural competition combined with a multiple assignment seemed a good way to put the local authorities under pressure. These at first played the game, but afterwards it appeared that they were playing cat and mouse. Nevertheless, the method of an independent work group offers ideal opportunities for town planning. In contrast to Zeebrugge

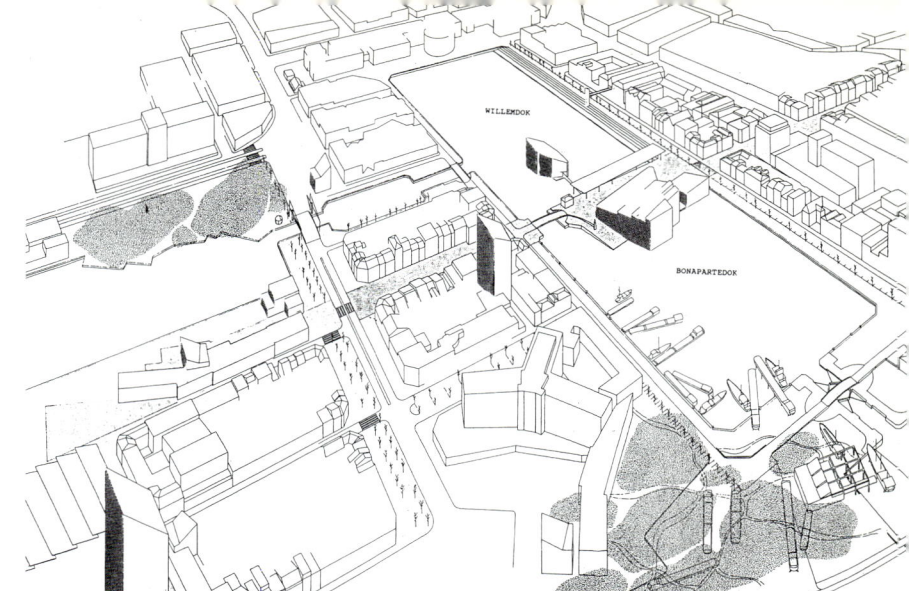

or Kortrijk, the Antwerp project was not incidental, but a permanent yet flexible institution.

The competition was a great success. Three locations had been proposed: 'het Eilandje' in the north, the 'Zuid' district in the south, and the zone between the quays on the River Scheldt. These three were very different, but each of them had a key position in terms of town planning policy. As the general competition was coupled with a multiple assignment its results did not receive the attention they deserved.

Luc Deleu's proposal for transforming Antwerp into a cruise stop with a jetty at the Steen in the centre of the city and a swing bridge to the left bank was not accepted. Ben van Berkel's proposal, which the jury referred for further study, was likewise rejected. Those invited for the multiple assignment submitted fascinating, but divergent proposals. Yves Lion converted Antwerp into an idyllic park with the bend of the Scheldt closed to shipping. Beth Gali thought up a sensitive remodelling for the quays with woods in the 'Zuid' area. Bob van Reeth linked the right and left banks of the river with each other, and Rem Koolhaas worked out a new city on the traffic interchange of the 'Zuid'. An international jury presented the plans by Manuel de Solà Morales for 'het Eilandje' and the quays, as well as Toyo Ito's for the 'Zuid' district to the city council for execution.

For a while the prospects looked promising. In September 1992 the two complete projects were presented to the public after being accepted in principle by the authorities. They were carried along with the enthusiasm surrounding Antwerp '93. The development and architectural scheme of the European cultural capital, 'Open city', concentrated on the neglected nineteenth-century belt. In February 1994 the celebrations were at an end and 'Stad aan de Stroom' was dissolved by the city authorities. The plans by Solà Morales and Ito, which had taken three years' work, disappeared into the drawer. In contrast to other European ports, such as Rotterdam, Barcelona, Hamburg, or Genoa, Antwerp yet again let a beautiful opportunity go by. André Loeckx noted: 'Dismay and anger are making it virtually impossible for me to write about the dismantling of "Stad aan de Stroom". The decision taken by the Antwerp bench of aldermen is so primitive that it does not even deserve a formal charge. A combination of abuse of power, incompetence, and short-sightedness has erased four years of innovative and expert involvement in the city. That is all there is to it.'

Solà Morales' proposal explicitly combined a vision of the city today with a spatial, architectural form. Nevertheless, its main quality lies in the fact that it was not conceived as a set plan, but as a strategy taking into account the time factor, with clear and efficient aims. Each decision depends on the previous one and influences the next while at the same time the future is left open. The specifications can, without doing damage to the original conditions, constantly be modified.

The remarkable thing about the two 'Stad aan de Stroom' proposals is that they both perfectly fit in with new concepts of the city today and yet are fundamentally different. In contrast

Manuel de Solà-Morales
Antwerp, 't Eilandje, design, 1992
Invited by 'Stad aan de Stroom', the Spanish architect Manuel de Solà-Morales made a design voor 't Eilandje in Antwerp, a derelict area from which the port activities have largely disappeared. He establishes a balanced interaction between the area and the city, renewing it without changing its character.

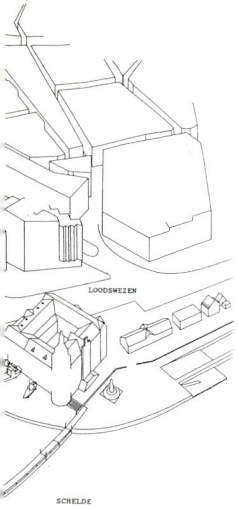

TOYO ITO
Antwerp, 'Het Zuid', design sketch, 1992
In contrast to de Solà-Morales's plans for 't Eilandje, the Japanese architect Toyo Ito did not integrate his designs for a cultural park on the filled-in southern docks and a residential area on the railway yard of 'Het Zuid' into the existing urban context. He considered these as independent elements that ought to be able to stimulate new developments.

Toyo Ito proposed a model of a residential area, putting behind him a number of architectural taboos concerning house design. The new area unfolds according to a linear pattern at right angles to the River Scheldt. The functions are kept strictly apart. The orthogonal character of the new residential area sharply contrasts with the dynamism of the traffic junction on which it borders.

to Solà Morales, Tyo Ito did not try to integrate his project into the existing city, but rather added new fragments to it. He descibes his intervention as placing an obstacle within existing streams to create new, unexpected whirls. Indeed, his interventions are clearly defined. He transformed the filled-in southern docks into a cultural park, creating an undulating landscape, an evocation of the water that had disappeared, which contrasts with the geometry of the dockyard walls.

The new residential area, which he designed at the rail-way-yard of the 'Zuid' area, also possesses an independent character. In contrast with the configuration of the old 'Zuid' district with its star-shaped pattern of streets, the new area is developed in a linear sequence at right angles to the river. This orthogonal layout forms a beautiful pendant to the nearby spaghetti junction, an oasis of peace and clarity.

One cannot be unaware of the beauty and intelligence of his projects, not only in Antwerp, but also in the rest of Belgium. If one takes into account the tireless efforts of Domus Flandria and other responsible institutions to improve public housing, it is shocking indeed that a project such as this is allowed to go to waste.

Living among architecture

The model town Papeye in Aalbeke near Kortrijk and various other model towns have followed a different approach. However, one can doubt the wisdom of inviting various architects to design show villas in model areas, reminiscent of the Weissenhofsiedlung in Stuttgart. This comparison actually is too flattering and inaccurate, for the circumstances are entirely different. These doubts also arose among the architects invited to work on Papeye – Frank Delmulle, Xaveer de Geyter, Stéphane Beel, Luc Reuse, William Lievens, Rudy De Backer, Eugeen Liebaut, Dirk Defraeije, Koen Van de Vreken, and Philip Deceuninck – in the catalogue accompanying an exhibition on the project, held in 'deSingel' in Antwerp (1992): 'Nevertheless, there is something sterile about this group project, something boring. Partly because of the uneven quality of the designs…, but probably also because this project demonstrates the architects' own pursuit of architecture, a pursuit that faces no opposition, which *is not carried by opposition, encounters no obstacles… and tumbles down.*' Papeye is the direct opposite of what Ito pro-

posed for Antwerp, even though he too allowed for collaboration between various architects. An initiative such as Papeye can only be successful in very specific circumstances. Indeed, the very concept of a 'model area' evinces a hopelessly outdated view of the role of architecture.

The competition for the renovation of a block of buildings in Kortrijk (1990), organized by 'Eigen Erf en Huis' and the local authority, is closer to Ito's approach: they did not collect architects, but asked them for their ideas and proposals in order to work out a project with only one of them. The prize-winning team – Henk De Smet, Marleen Goethals, Bart Van Schuylenbergh, and Paul Vermeulen – were inspired by the typical hybrid form of the nineteenth-century development in order to create recognizable coherence amidst all the variety.

In 1991 and 1992 the Ghent city authorities worked out a structural development plan and held competitions for public housing in poor areas, the so-called 'Wonen in Gent' (WIG) competitions. These were respectively won by Bruno Dercon, Pieter T'Jonck, and Leo Van Broeck, and by the design bureau Nero, which is made up of William Lievens, Rudi De Backer, and Marianne Hofstede.

The most striking initiative was the competition held by the Ghent authorities for mixed housing on the grounds of the Hollain barracks (1992). The terrain is adjacent to the listed site of the Klein Begijnhof and is bordered by the Lower Scheldt as well as by a major arterial road – a situation that is as prestigious as it is challenging when it comes to formulating a new way of living in the city.

Just as was the case in Zeebrugge, the jury and the city authorities were confronted by five fascinating, but divergent proposals. These ranged from a brilliant reinterpretation of the 'Unité d'habitation', with everything down to allotments, by Luc Deleu through to an intriguing evocation of a village within the city by Paul Robbrecht and Hilde Daem in collaboration with Marie José Van Hee. The projects by Stépahane Beel and the team formed by Henk De Smet, Marleen Goethals, and Paul Vermeulen provide refined developments of the scheme through a succession of blocks.

The prize-winning design by Willem-Jan Neutelings proposes a new version of the closed beguinage community around an open square similar to what can be seen in Hors-Château in Liège, only in a more direct form, once more endowing architecture with obviousness. One can only hope that the project will survive all the complicated procedures unharmed and that it will be able to prove itself once it is being lived in.

WILLEM-JAN NEUTELINGS
Ghent, Hollain barracks, design sketch, 1992
Five architects were contacted for this multiple commission to build social housing on the grounds of the Hollain barracks near the 'Klein Begijnhof' in Ghent. The commission was finally awarded to Willem-Jan Neutelings, who proposed a modern version of life in the closed community of the beguinage.

Developments

In model towns architecture remains in the background. It comes to the fore again in normal urban developments. This is its rightful place, where it interrupts the routine of the commonplace. The architecture in such developments is often by the hands of the younger generation and designed in the margin of other professional fields, such as education or the media.

Jan Meersman (b. 1956) together with Guido Driesen, and Jan Thomaes formed the team that won the competition for the Belgian pavilion at the Expo 92 world fair in Seville. One of Meersman's earliest works was the conversion of a storey in a corner building in central Antwerp (1983). He removed everything that was unnecessary from a constructional point of view and played upon the contrast between the light evenly entering from the street side and the closed front of the walled-in building opposite it.

The directness of this approach is also demonstrated by the house built in a wooded area in 's Gravenwezel (1988). Under an open hood construction the space is divided by parallel wall sections situated along the longitudinal side of the house, which determines the interior arrangement. A closed wall separates the house from the street and here too, though less emphatically than in the flat, serves to reflect the light from the woods. It could not have been simpler. However, this simplicity works precisely because of its accuracy. In the noise surrounding similar commissions, this house is remarkable for its purity of tone.

If Meersman's is a regular version of the well-known type, René Jacobs endows it with a radical form and transforms it into a white container with the sole addition of a glass staircase, a cut-off angle, and the curved lid forming the roof. With this austerity he follows the example set by his Dutch compatriots Frank and Paul Wintermans in a house built in Mol in 1982: Northern minimalism and rigour amidst abundance and capriciousness? Despite its extremeness, John Körmeling's house in Hedersem takes in an intermediary position. It makes use of industrial constructions not so as to elevate them to architecture, but to enrich architecture itself through their intrinsic beauty. The architectural exchange between North and South has now changed its course. Whereas there is only one Dutch architect currently working in Belgium, several Belgian architects are carrying out major assignments in the Netherlands.

The house in Kuringen consists of eight steel porticoes covered with a tight skin in which openings have been left at obvious places. Behind the almost completely blind eastern façade there is a circulation strip leading to the living-room, which opens up the interior both upwards and lengthwise. From here one has access to the various rooms, a scheme that is often applied nowadays.

The house on the Lege Voorde in Waarschoot (1991) by Guy Châtel (b. 1956), who has been running the firm O.A.S. Architecten-Ingenieurs in Ghent together with Marc De Kooning since 1991, does more than just filling a gap on a plot of land. It

RENÉ JACOBS
Kuringen, house, 1991-1993
(Bastin/Evrard)

It would be hard to discern the typical design of the suburban home in the white container which René Jacobs transformed into his own house. Its obvious shape stems from the rigorous logic of the specifications. The interior is accessible via a high passage reaching from one lateral façade to the other and from the floor to the roof.

constitutes an obvious statement about the opportunities offered by an extreme situation in which architecture could seem pushed aside. However, it does so by starting from the elementary principles that all construction carries in it. The typology of the house is still discernible, but it is enriched by incorporating other typologies.

Many young architects yield to this temptation, but the remarkable aspect of Châtel's work is that he integrates all these references and reminiscences into the obvious character of the new object. There are three blind walls on the street side demarcating a secret zone, which can be entered through a hole that also affords the opportunity to cast a quick glance into it. The ground floor, containing the bedroom and study, serves as a socle for the living area on the first. From this area under the open framework and with the high light of the sawtooth roof from behind, protected on all sides by the closed wall, one can look out onto the garden and the landscape.

In Wachtebeke, a few villages further, still in East Flan-

JAN MEERSMAN
's Gravenwezel, house, 1988-1990
(Reiner Lautwein)
This house in the woods of 's Gravenwezel, designed for a graphic artist, is
remarkable for its simplicity and
directness. Amidst the luxuriant plants
its clear construction transforms the
plain materials into an open space in
which the light can have free play.

ders, we can witness the 'oblique' architectural notions of Erik Lefebure (b. 1955), which are in sharp contrast with the orthogonal thinking behind the house in Waarschoot. Obliqueness, of course, is to be understood literally in this case; for Lefebure it forms the basis of logic itself. It all started out with a dyke house into which the architect moved with his family. When it became too small and started coming apart at the seams, the architect let it go ahead, allowing closed volumes and open greenhouses to arise at random along the longitudinal axis of the house according to the ground available. It looks something like a car crash.

However, this most striking part of the house is nothing more than the exterior of something that must be a real adventure on the inside. It is not a demonstration of principles. Lefebure says of himself that he is not a frustrated architect, but even delights in the cottagey houses he is asked to design. His work is not a heavy esoterical idea materialized, but a playful experiment with the possibilities construction offers. It is an attempt that does not submit living in a house to some clichéed image, but intuitively looks at what the result will be.

In Wallonia the best on offer as to young architecture consists of a few modest houses, in which the existing typology has been reconsidered with great care. In a house by Benoit Laloux in Champlon-Famenne (1983) the basic idea is a square ground plan with a central spiral staircase connecting three floors. This closed volume is enlivened with a portico and a segmental arch. It is accessed via a stately, rounded flight of stairs as if it were something grand. Despite this stately entrance, the roof is made up of solar cells.

The houses by John Berhaut (b. 1942) in Embourg are more direct. Arthur Wortman commented on them: 'In the houses he has built up to now he has always been striving for exceptionally economical use of the financial means available. This has consistently led to compact volumes, simple constructive systems, and good insulation, to the point of embedding them into hilly grounds. This is why Berhaut's houses are practically without passageways and usually have the simplest of sloping roofs... Who looks at the house will discover that it has been well thought out, that its obvious presence has been created with a high degree of workmanship. Yet it does not seem contrived. The house is there. It is there as a house.'

GUY CHÂTEL AND MARC DE KOONING
Waarschoot, house, 1991-1993
(Hilde D'Hayere)
Guy Châtel's house constitutes a
statement on the ability of architecture to
exist in a situation where it seems to
have been supplanted. It does this by
means of the elementary nature of all
architecture. The typology of the
traditional house is still discernible, but it
has been radically changed because of its
combination with other typologies.

ERIK LEFEBURE

Wachtebeke, house

(Bastin/Evrard)

In his own house Erik Lefebure gives his enjoyment of architecture free rein. His starting point was a small house on a dike. As the family's needs grew, so did the house – randomly and in all directions, according to a non-conformist logical system.

JOHN BERHAUT

Embourg, own house, interior, 1979

(Bastin/Evrard)

In a number of houses, starting with his own against a slope in Embourg, John Berhaut has demonstrated his conscious approach to useful architecture. His architecture, which Arthur Wortmann described as architecture of few words, is subservient to the specifications and its surroundings.

New monuments

Asingle exception apart, we have in the last few chapters discussed only one-family homes, a sharp contrast to the large scale architectural commissions of the Reconstruction period seen in the first two chapters. Indeed, larger commissions that are even slightly connected to contemporary architecture have to be cherished.

William Lievens (b. 1948), who runs the design office Nero, built the cultural centre 'De Herbakker' in Eeklo from 1991 to 1993 after an original proposal in 1987. It forms part of a series of public institutions, such as a library, a museum, academies of art and music, and a square for public events. The way in which the free space, occupied by imposing buildings, and half the village street are brought together is most inventive.

The organization of the ground plan corresponds to this intention. The entrance is on the inner courtyard and protected by a substantial canopy. The large entrance hall and foyer integrate the public space into the building. The glass street-side façade, which is lit up with varying intensity at night and also serves to illuminate the foyer, makes the building seem transparent.

His greatest merit lies in having used an unassuming sort of architecture to establish the transition between provincial conservatism and a dynamic urban culture that is open to what is going on in the world today. It demonstrate the town of Eeklo's planning policy which, as Filip De Pau puts it in *Yearbook Architecture Flanders 1990-1993*, 'in keeping with the spirit of our times, often changes track, but shows overall continuity'. This continuity does not depend on a formalist planning method, but on an inductive, pragmatical approach. In this context the design bureau Nero have built a noteworthy block of social housing units, and Stéphan Beel's design for an office building for the 'Christelijke Mutualiteiten' are ready to be carried out.

So far, the province of Limburg has not appeared in our account of half a century of Belgian architecture despite the fact that after the war it founded its own school of architecture, which is housed at the university centre of Diepenbeek in a building by Adolf Nivelle (b. 1930). It is hard to define the influence of schools on the architectural landscape, but a general view will suffice to notice it beyond any doubt.

One of the most active members of the young generation, Alfredo De Gregorio, was commissioned to collaborate with the firm Jaspers on the design of the new Gallo-Roman museum in the centre of Tongeren, near the Onze-Lieve-Vrouwe basilica. The new museum resembles a large showcase, as if it wants to entice visitors rather than invite them. It follows a procedure contrary to that of William Lievens in Eeklo. Whereas the latter charges and intensifies the urban character of the area, the museum marks a point where the city virtually disappears into nothing. The border between past and present is clearly outlined; we have to penetrate the glass and dare to enter the darkness inside the building.

Koen Van Synghel (b. 1964) is one of those young architects who only occasionaly make designs. His main task is that

NERO, WILLIAM LIEVENS,
RUDI DE BACKER,
AND MARIANNE HOFSTEDE
Eeklo, 'De Herbakker', cultural centre, 1991-1993
(Bastin/Evrard)
After an original proposal made in 1987, the cultural centre of Eeklo was built in 1991 according to a new design. Its main feature is that it combines a series of public institutions: this free space is inventively structured by the new building.

ART & BUILD: PIERRE LALLEMAND,
MARC THILL, PHILIPPE VAN HALTEREN
AND ISIDORE ZIELONKA
Brussels, ULB, library, 1994
(Bastin/Evrard)
Because of its triangular shape the new library of the Université Libre de Bruxelles on the Avenue Franklin Roosevelt performs a crystallizing role amidst the diverse buildings of the university. The triangle was originally intended to be built in brick so as to make its formalism less striking and, according to the architects, give it a more democratic appearance.

of presenting architecture from Belgium and abroad in the media. Apart from his work in collaboration with Pascal Van der Kelen – the VIP boxes for the Flemish Opera in Antwerp and Ghent – he also designed a block of service flats for the aged in Kruishoutem (completed 1994) which, though not a public building, could acquire this function through its strong presence.

Van Synghel has placed nineteen flats in a light curve around an existing row of trees in a charming, somewhat neglected garden adjoining a surviving old building. They are reminiscent of holiday houses and constitute a new injection of life not only for the occupants, but for the whole area. This careful architecture with its interplay of surfaces and colours draws less attention to itself than to what it is all about. Here the elderly are most certainly not considered a section of society that has been written off. It is a stimulating place that in an unassuming, yet beautiful way brings to life its slumbering surroundings, partly thanks to Dirk Vandekerkhove's layout of the garden.

In 1994 Mauro Poponcini (b. 1956), together with Patrick Lootens, won the competition for Belgacom's new regional headquarters in Hasselt. A central feature of his work is the opposition between the timeless and the ephemeral in architecture. He learnt from Paul Van Aerschot, for whom he worked for some time, that 'only by means of a constructive geometrical system can space be ordered in a meaningful way and spatial coherence be established'. However, he applies this constructive geometry in a playful sense. There is nothing abstract about it. After all, Poponcini is fascinated not only by geometry, but as much by the various changing, graceful, and even fashionable forms it takes on.

In his carpet design entitled 'Ostacoli Imprevisti' he expresses 'this dialogue between classical order and frivolous formalism, between the timeless and the temporary'. Against the dark background of the rectangle there are a number of colourful figures, half recognizable and squeezed in below a smaller, pale rectangle. The carpet may be considered a model for the Belgacom design. The building's 30,000 m^2 floor surface is spread over a low volume developed along a transparent central axis and adapted to the various environments in which it is situated. By means of courtyards even the car park below the building receives natural light. The architects have reached an impressive point of balance between the neutrality and flexibility of the organized grid on the one hand and the expressiveness of some elements – for instance, the three conical volumes marking the training centre – on the other.

There is a sharp contrast between this 'Flemish' work and the library of the Université Libre de Bruxelles (U.L.B.) on the Avenue Roosevelt, completed by Pierre Lallemand in 1994. Perhaps this is the last time that we can speak of Belgian architecture as such. The last chapter ended with Philippe Samyn's work, whose formal approach distinguishes itself from Flemish architecture. A similar distinction can be seen in the work produced by Art & Build, a firm that also includes Philippe van

KOEN VAN SYNGHEL
Kruishoutem, service flats, 1994
(Bastin/Evrard)
On the outskirts of the town Koen Van Synghel has arranged nineteen service flats in a slight curve around an existing row of trees. Through the freshness of their architecture they bring the area to life, which is beautifully supported by Dirk Vandekerkhove's layout of the garden.

Halteren, Marc Thill, and Isidore Zielonka. Another point of comparison lies in the fact that both Samyn and Lallemand have been commissioned by the U.L.B.: 1993 saw the completion of the auditorium on the Erasmus campus in Anderlecht by Samyn. In both cases the elegant perfection of the architecture is able to bridge all divergences of taste – indeed, it is more about taste than about a convincing sense of form. In Anderlecht Samyn opted for a circle. Lallemand chooses a triangle, which gives his library three façades. It is through this binding shape that the shining building can function as a crystallization point within the old U.L.B. campus.

ALFREDO DE GREGORIO AND
MICHEL JASPERS
Tongeren, Gallo-Roman museum, 1994
(Bastin/Evrard)
The new museum resembles a huge
show-case in which the monumental
buildings around it – the Roman tower,
the Gothic basilica of Our Lady, and the
neoclassical lawcourts – are reflected and
behind which, in the dark, the traces of
the past are preserved.

MAURO POPONCINI AND PATRICK LOOTENS
Hasselt, Belgacom, scale model, 1994
The competition for the new Belgacom
offices in Hasselt was won by Mauro
Poponcini and Patrick Lootens. With this
initiative Belgacom again took up the
company's glorious tradition. The low
volume, articulated by the narrow
transparent nave, can be easily adapted
to any environment.

Reconversion

The specific problem seen in recent years, that of abandoned industrial, railway, or harbour sites, is not limited to cities like Antwerp, Bruges, Kortrijk, Ghent, Charleroi or Liège. We are confronted with it everywhere. Although the problem is more than pressing in Liège, hardly anything is being done to alleviate it through reconversion. The case is known even outside Belgium, as appears from a study carried out at the Technische Universiteit of Delft by Mark Graafland. In Antwerp the railway-yard of the 'Zuid' district belonged to the 'Stad aan de Stroom' project.

In Leuven a number of preliminary studies have been commissioned. 'Projectteam Stadsontwerp', led by Marcel Smets of the University of Leuven made an attempt at developing a new strategy for approaching the Vaartkom and, following on from this, for the reuse of railway grounds situated within the agglomeration.

This was most comprehensively worked out in the set of instruments for town planning worked out by Projectteam in 1992, in which architecture and urban development go hand in hand. It concerned the centre of Hoeilaert, a town in the Ijse valley bordering Brussels, which had, together with its grape growing, largely lost its spatial identity and developed into an amorphous residential area. The topography of the town was taken as a basis for its structural coherence, which contained both the increase of buildings in the centre and the openness of a new park. The buildings themselves were designed by Joan Busquets, Gonçalo Sousa-Byrne, and Stéphane Beel.

For a moment it looked as if the reconversion of the abandoned coalmines in the Kempen region would also lead to large-scale projects. However, Rem Koolhaas's sketches for the transformation of the mine at Waterschei and the entries for the architectural competition for the mining town of Winterslag – which was won by the team Goedele Desmet, Ivo Vanhamme, and Jean-Michel Culas – are still lying there as signs of impotence or unwillingness.

Marcel Smets concludes in *Jaarboek Architectuur Vlaanderen 1990-1993*: 'The final balance of this intensive period is still very uncertain. Right now, at the beginning of 1994, there is certainly no cause for euphoria: despite the grants awarded, no stimulating project for the Limburg mining area seems to be coming off the ground. In Kortrijk Secchi has been commissioned to design a cemetery and to lay out the Grote Markt, but his structural plan is not being used as a systematic criterium during negotiations about actual dossiers submitted for planning permission. In Leuven the authorities have commissioned the designers of the development plan for the station area with the drawing up of special construction plans, but they are being lobbied behind the scenes to accept another proposal. In Antwerp the city authorities are refusing to make the necessary funds available to enable 'Stad en Stroom' to continue their action.'

Only in the field of the reconversion of individual buildings or building complexes have there been any results. The

MARCEL SMETS
Hoeilaart, development plan for town centre, 1992

The 'Projectteam Stadsontwerp', founded by Marcel Smets, have become known for their proposals for the reconversion of the 'Vaartkom' and the railway yard in Leuven. The team proposed a new strategy in which the town planner is given an interactive role among the various parties concerned. The development plan for the town centre of Hoeilaart is the most detailed version of their approach to urban development.

▷ STÉPHANE BEEL
Zoersel, house, collage, 1985

In the Van Pelt house in Zoerzel Stéphane Beel combines all the registers of contemporary architecture, ranging from meeting the requirements of modern comfort to referring to Utopian dreams. This villa in a typical housing development creates its own world, which may contain anything from Alpine meadows to palmy beaches.

conversion in 1992 of a nineteenth-century school in Leuven into flats by Ludo Bekker was awarded a prize for architecture by the City of Leuven as well as the Flemish Community's prize for housing. Despite his limited budget, the architect managed to involve Guy Rombouts and Monica Droste, who have something to do with the alphabet and schools. In Antwerp the group Biecorff c.v. – Hugo Kinnaer, Johan Bruynserade, and Koen Ooms – can also claim a few sensible transformations. In Brussels quite a number of existing buildings have received new destinations.

In Wallonia the reconversion of individual buildings is likewise in full swing. One of the most striking examples is Charles Vandenhove's conversion of an old orphanage, 'Le Balloir' situated on the River Meuse in Liège, into a reception centre for children and a rest home. The transformation of a workshop in Liège by Bruno Albert for the publisher Pierre Mardaga adds a fresh note to the area. We have already discussed Guchez's approach in Le Grand Hornu. A large number of industrial buildings have been converted into museums. However, these changes and interventions are but rarely a match for the force of the existing architecture.

Stéphane Beel (b. 1955)

The first time that the young generation came to the fore was during the competition for the Carrefour de l'Europe in Brussels in 1983. They presented themselves under the title 'Hoogpoort', derived from the address in Ghent where a few of the participants had settled, with among them Stéphane Beel. Some elements of the Brussels project recur in his œuvre.

Beel starts out by accepting the *status quo* in architecture. He knows the tension between the banality of the mimetic model and the urge to reinvest the commonplace with its original power. He chooses neither one nor the other, but situates his work amid this ambivalence. There can be no question of pure architecture. He does not want to present architecture as a gift from above, but to let it be born from the social field of force, which it has to influence as well as transcend.

Judging from the prizes awarded to his work – in 1988 and 1990 the International Eternit prize, in 1989 the Eugène Baye prize, in 1990 the Durox and the 'Beter verbouwen' prize, in 1991 the Charles Wilford prize, in 1992 the Ytong prize, the prize of the Flemish Community and honours in the Mies van der Rohe prize, and in 1994 the prize of the Akademie der Künste in Berlin – he has certainly succeeded in establishing his reputation as an architect. However, he has for the moment not received any official commissions in Belgium yet. Fame as an architect can often count as a negative criterium, as it may frighten prospective customers. Moreover, in Beel's eyes architecture is as much a matter for the customer as it is for the architect. He has nevertheless had the opportunity to design semi-public buildings in addition to commissions for private houses.

In one of his earliest works, the Van Pelt house in Zoersel (1985), Beel convincingly set out his views on the role and possibilities of contemporary architecture. The white villa in a typically Belgian housing development indicates the variety of levels at which architecture can operate at the same time. It belongs there and is a villa in the literal sense of the word, similar to those found in any city or town. It takes into account all the demands and expectations of a villa, but to the extent that it immediately moves away from its stereotypical image. Without one realizing it, the architect has defined a new typology and a new approach to architecture.

After all, it is clear that this villa affirms itself as an autonomous work of architecture, which not only has an impact on the occupant and its surroundings, but also claims its place within the intellectual and architectural debate of the moment. That Stéphane Beel is aware of all these different layers of architecture is demonstrated by a beautiful collage he has made. In it the Zoersel villa appears somewhere in an imposing mountainous landscape, the ultimate example of a building plot, with in the foreground a family of goats, one of which – the symbol of the client and/or the architect – looks at the spectator, surprised at his interest.

Apart from the house in Zoersel, the pair of semi-detached houses built for Nijs in Anzegem (1987) and the doctor's surgery and house in Mortsel (1988) are worthy of mention. However, in order to understand Beel's œuvre, we have to look at the conversion of a building for the 'Spaarkrediet' in Bruges (1988).

This conversion contrasts with the villa in Zoersel in various respects. Whereas the villa rises out above the landscape, the office building disappears as if carved into the magma of the city. The scheme in Bruges inevitably is more complex, as it concerns the provincial headquarters of a bank, incorporating the necessary office and conference space, an agency with a counter and direct access for the public, and an annex housing an exhibition room – all of this organized around an atrium. Here again the architecture evinces an obvious logic, beyond which it manifests its autonomy.

The comparison between these two buildings invites further analysis of the architect's personal style, his unmistakably personal tone, preferences, hints at the formal vocabulary in fashion, and his ironical reserve. However, this personal style has been emphasized ad nauseam, which goes against the grain of this sort of architecture. Although it cannot escape from a personal style, its primary aim is nevertheless to say something via this inevitable characteristic.

In contrast with this work from the first phase, in which we can distinguish the explicit need to define the aims of the architecture, his later work loses this orientation towards the public and becomes completely absorbed in itself. In 1989 Stéphane Beel designed a mobile studio for Jef Cornelis's programme, 'Container'. It could be plugged in anywhere, 'like a parasite,' says Beel, 'as adaptable as a cameleon to the programme's requirements and locations, mobile and ready for broadcasting within minutes both at the BRTN itself [Flemish radio and television] and elsewhere in the country'.

Beel conceived it as a collapsible box. It contains the essence of his architecture, that is, of architecture as a whole. Its first, most striking feature, is that place becomes placeless. Like a suitcase, the container can be put down, used or lived in anywhere. Just as the Zoersel villa ended up in an alpine meadow, the container can land anywhere. It can be loaded onto a lorry, a ship, or an aeroplane to travel with its owner. However, it is different from a camper not only in that it is not automobile, but also because it manifests itself as an architectural object, a new version of the nomad's tent.

When closed it looks like a precious object. However, it can be flipped open on all sides, creating an open space, a collapsible stage like that of the medieval travelling theatre, a real interior that every time becomes the centre of perception. This interior is perfectly equipped and always fully available. Yet this machine does not boast with its technical innovations, which remain invisible. Just as a real-life nomad's tent, the container is covered in cow hides which give it colours and patterns foreign to the world of technology.

Stéphane Beel has called the Villa M. in Zedelgem 'an aeroplane in a paddyfield', which again, as with the container, suggests the placelessness and mobility of contemporary archi-

STÉPHANE BEEL, PIETER BROUCKE,
AND PAUL VAN EYGEN
Bruges, Spaarkrediet bank, 1988
(Bastin/Evrard)
The transformation of the bank in the centre of Bruges is one of the first large-scale works carried out by the new generation of architects. They approach their work without any prejudices and want to involve it in the hustle and bustle of modern life. Architecture no longer dictates, but readily reacts to any given situation. It needs this resistance to produce reality.

Stéphane Beel, Luc Morel,
and Paul Van Eygen
Bruges, BACOB bank, 1988-1991
(Bastin/Evrard)

Situated next to the motorway – which brutally cuts off an entire residential development – and on the edge of a surviving wood, the bank building transforms the whole area through its sharply outlined presence. The severity of the volume on the side of the motorway brings out the effect of the staircase wells on the other side as well as the dynamism of the ground floor.

A regular feature of Stéphane Beel's work is this pursuit of maximum tension through minimal means. The pent-up energy is not discharged, but holds together all the fragments, even the most frivolous.

Stéphane Beel
Kortrijk, Tack tower, renovation and enlargement, design sketch, 1993
(Brigitte Meuwissen)

The Tack tower on the Buda island in Kortrijk is the remaining part of a brewery. It is situated near the town museum. Stéphane Beel's minimal intervention has transformed this industrial building into a production centre for the arts while retaining its strong character. The essential public amenities are situated behind a mostly transparent screen.

Zedelgem, Villa 'M', 1987-1992

(Lieve J. Blancquaert)

Stéphane Beel has likened the Villa 'M' to 'an aeroplane in a paddyfield'. Even though its elongated shape was clearly inspired by its location, the house is not caught up in its surroundings. Built parallel to an existing garden wall of a castle, the various parts of the house are ordered in a row according to a logical pattern: the parents' quarters are at one end, those of the children and guests on the other. These two sections meet up in the central part of the house.

tecture. Even if its shape was clearly inspired by the location it can, just as was the case in Zoersel, leave again to traverse and reveal another landscape.

An immense channel beam set on its side is enough to create an interior. In the neglected vegetable garden of a château the girder has been placed with its closed side parallel to a surviving piece of wall. An entrance way is almost automatically formed, a passage from the open surroundings to the relative closedness of the interior on the other side of the wall. It also simply demarcates the boundary.

His recent work evinces the same qualities, both radical and sensitive: the annex to the De Clerck house in Kortrijk (1989), as well as the villa Neutelings in Brasschaat (1992) and the villa in Rotselaar (1993). Apart from the private sphere of the home, the larger projects confirm the efficiency of his approach. Some of them have not yet been carried out, for instance the Raveel museum in Machelen/Zulte and the conversion of a brewery tower into a cultural meeting point in Kortrijk – which one hopes will both be realized in the near future – or the new SWIFT offices in La Hulpe (a reference to Le Corbusier's convent La Tourette), which seems to have been cancelled altogether.

The realization of two other designs, the Bacob building in Bruges and that of the Economics Faculty in Kortrijk, proves the vitality and poetic force of his apparently minimal, banal architecture. The new regional headquarters of Bacob, for whom Beel had already built a branch office in Ostend (1989), also resembles a plane that has landed or a ship that has been moored at an empty spot somewhere along the motorway. With its sharply outlined presence the building transforms the whole area, the motorway, the remains of a forest, and the housing development bluntly cut off by the road.

The commission for the Economics Faculty in Kortrijk was also awarded to Stéphane Beel after an exclusive competition. However, the assignment involved more than just the design of a new faculty. It concerned a general proposal for the development and reorganization of the existing built-up area according to Secchi's plans for the Hoog-Kortrijk district. Beel started out by determining a building zone that would define the most important element of the campus development, i.e. a concentration of buildings and flexible phrasing. According to the architect's explanation, this would 'recuperate precious features of the original planning, which have been ignored or contradicted in later developments'.

The oblong strip marked by a gallery parallel to the street in the first place indicates the position of the university in the landscape. 'The university manifests itself,' Beel says. 'Essential points of contact between the university and its environment are being supplied; the campus no longer appears as an autonomous institution, withdrawn from the world.'

Here, as in all of Beel's work, minimal interventions are used to maximum effect. The building of the Economics Faculty, which also forms the main entrance to the campus as a whole, is the first step in carrying out the general plan. The building seems to neutralize gravitation. On ground level the landscape runs through below the building. One of its wings, which is at an angle with the street, is closed and indicates the boundary of the building. The other wing, partly glazed, remains completely open on the ground floor. At every point the whole building is present, its interior and exterior, its top and bottom, identical and different. The means used here are even more limited than in the Bruges bank building, but here again they are exploited to their full potential with a playful sense of lightness.

STÉPHANE BEEL AND BART MACKEN
Rotselaar, villa, 1994
(Bastin/Evrard)
Stéphane Beel's villa in Rotselaar is
conceived as a flat block shaped around
an open spot in the woods so that the
natural environment is interfered with as
little as possible. The block, floating above
the slope, is supported by pillars
mirroring the slenderness of the tree-
trunks around them. Anchored on the
street side, the occupants live like birds
in the sky or like Italo Calvino's baron in
the trees.

STÉPHANE BEEL, DIRK HENDRIKS,
AND PAUL VAN EYGEN
BRTN, mobile studio, 1989

For Jef Cornelis's 'Container' programme Stéphane Beel literally designed a container, 'as adaptable to the programme's requirements and locations as a parasite or a cameleon, mobile and ready to broadcast in a minute, both at the BRTN [Flemish radio and television company] and abroad.' It can be taken along everywhere, just as a suitcase or a nomad's tent.

The same thing occurs in the renovation of the so-called Tack tower in Kortrijk, for which Beel made a design in 1993. The industrial relic is left untouched, but it is made accessible to the public through the minimal addition of the necessary functions behind a largely transparent screen. Together with the layout of the immediate vicinity it revalues the whole area and constitutes an example of how to deal with the city and our industrial heritage in an uninhibited and inspiring way.

Willem-Jan Neutelings (b. 1959)

Willem-Jan Neutelings was a member of the Hoogpoort team that entered for the competition surrounding the Carrefour de l'Europe in 1983. In the same year he designed 'Huis te B.' (House in B.), a villa in Brasschaat, in which he both unmasks and rehabilitates the concept of a Belgian villa. Completed in 1985, it was to signify the breakthrough of the young generation, together with Stéphane Beel's villa in Zoersel. While he was still studying at the Technische Universiteit in Delft, Neutelings worked at Rem Koolhaas's OMA in Rotterdam and was, amongst others, the project architect of the Danstheater and collaborated on the project for a new town hall in The Hague.

He graduated in 1986 with a dissertation that was at the same time a theoretical analysis, entitled *De Ringcultuur* (Ring-road Culture), and a project about architecture along the ring roads around cities. The study was published by Mil De Kooning in his magazine *Vlees en Beton*. Mil De Kooning, together with Marc Dubois and Christian Kieckens (Stichting Architectuurmuseum), Carolina De Backer and Katrien Vandermarliere (deSingel), and Marc Felix (Archipel), has done everything in his power to promote the work of the younger generation.

In keeping with the tradition set by Le Corbusier and following on from Koolhaas's retro-active manifesto, *De Ringcultuur* opens with a proclamation in bold print. 'The European metropolis is undergoing spontaneous rejuvenation through the RING-ROAD MECHANISM. This mechanism is able to transform a peripheral zone into a spatial and programmatic element in the city. Once this zone has reached its critical mass, it becomes the pivot of its own RING-ROAD CULTURE. At the moment we are in the middle of a wave of peripheral development encouraged by the new mass culture. Jogging tracks and multipurpose halls, theme parks and rock palaces, DIY stores and chains of motels, allotments and furniture paradizes, commercial fairs and tyre dealers, sports complexes and commuter garages: mass activities are threading around European cities like necklaces, between centre and suburb, along the drawn out city highways. Here the modern RING ROAD generates its own aesthetics of mobile velocity and special effects, of large-scale construction and concentration of emptiness. Here modern culture condenses from physical pleasures and mass events, from condensed distribution and disseminated communication. Here the RING ROAD functions as the décor and the breeding ground of an era; as the Rosetta stone of urban development, it draws the portrait of an age. Therefore, it is both incomprehensible and irresponsible of architects and city planners to ignore this process completely: while they devote themselves to stylistic debates and cosmetic exercises, the largest share of construction is taking place in the periphery under the exclusive control of economic and bureaucratic forces. It is NOW that we have to develop models and strategies for the peripheral urban development of today and tomorrow. It is NOW that we have to give form to our time.'

In a word, the architect will not give up. Architecture belongs to the changes every day brings. We experience its beauty through dynamic perception. 'The principle of dynamic perception has the same determining influence on the present-day metropolis as the discovery of perspective had on the city of the Renaissance... The duty of architecture no longer is the creation of space, but the orchestration of programmatic activities.' The ring-road has become the paradigm, 'the sign of modernity: with a minimum of spatial amenities, a maximum of mass events can be activated'.

The 'House in B.', Neutelings' first work, is a fragment of the ring-road culture. Indeed, the metropolis does not end at the ring-road, nor does the ring-road end at the metropolis; it is everywhere. 'House in B.' – the name is significant in that it fulfils the same role as names such as 'Chez Moi' or 'Mon Rêve' – consists of heterogeneous fragments that are so closely brought together that they form a new sort of coherence. Neutelings describes the three elements as a submarine (the section containing the utilities, kitchen, bathroom, and swimming-pool), a small Italian *palazzo* (living-, dining-, and bedrooms), and a post-war petrol station (entrance and terrace). However, these associations with typological layers of meaning do not prevent the house from focusing on the occupant's direct comforts in the first place.

The same lack of inhibition that characterizes 'House in B.' can also be seen in his approach to other assignments, which is even freer and less emphatic. Designed in collaboration with Marc De Kooning, 'Ringzicht' (1988) is a group of three houses on the corner of a street on the verge of the Antwerp ring road at Berchem. In it heterogeneous elements again combine in the interplay of reference and reality, where architecture revenges itself on its disguise. The curve of the street corner is indicated by the blue garden wall. Two volumes, one wrapped in aluminium and the other in wood, are lifted from the ground and look out onto the landscape with its hidden, but audible ring road. They are connected to each other via metal bridges that are covered with corrugated plastic of the type found in DIY stores. This is the paradox of the cliché taken to extremes: the cliché itself has been elevated to originality.

Neutelings shows how the same approach can generate diverging results in his third housing complex on the quayside of the River Scheldt in Antwerp. It was also designed in collaboration with Marc De Kooning and bears the name 'De Kaai' (The Quay) (1988). Indeed, its most striking feature is the broad gesture with which movement is created in this façade on the quay, as if through a soft beating of waves. Here again, the ground plan is made up of the juxtaposition of parallel strips that find their expression in the composition of volumes and use of materials. The strip with the utilities is contained in a high, narrow volume on which the the box with the curved façade, strikingly covered with iroko, seems to hang. The ground floor, its rhythm punctuated by supporting pillars, is taken up by garages which, however, can easily be adapted to other uses. The staircase is shifted in between the new house and the existing buildings as a separate volume.

Neutelings has worked out his notions on the ring-road culture more explicitly in his studies on the 'Patchwork Metropolis', a fragment of 'Randstad Holland', and on the abandoned docks and quays in Hamburg. The synthesis of all this is found in the immense project for the European Patent Office in Leidschendam near The Hague, with which Neutelings was commissioned in 1990 after an international competition. The plans were as good as ready when the commission was cancelled for political reasons.

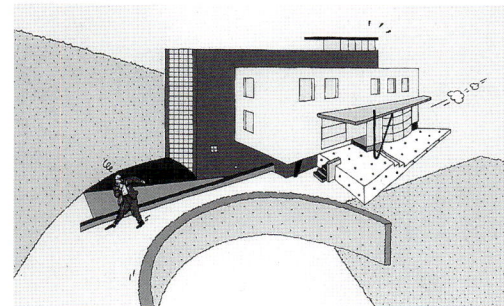

WILLEM-JAN NEUTELINGS,
AND LUC DELEU
Brasschaat, 'House in B.', 1983-1985

Through his lucid approach to this classical theme Willem-Jan Neutelings has been able to meet all the requirements of building a country house in a forest, and yet to put this architectural cliché into perspective. As a result it defies actual identification and allows both the architecture and the occupant a greater sense of freedom.

Willem-Jan Neutelings himself describes the three zones of which his villa is composed as a submarine (a high disc containing the kitchen, bathroom, and swimming-pool), a small Italian *palazzo* (containing the living-, dining-, and bedrooms), and a post-war petrol station, which forms the entrance and the terrace. The villa in Brasschaat, a status symbol *par excellence*, has become the hero of a comic strip.

◁ **Antwerp, design ring road, 1986**

Willem-Jan Neutelings wrote his final dissertation on the 'ring-road culture' (*Ringcultuur*), the latest cultural and architectural style developing along the ring roads of cities such as Antwerp. In it he wrote: 'European metropolises have seen a spontaneous rejuvination, the RING-ROAD MECHANISM. The ring-road mechanism is able to transform the peripheral zone into a spatial and programmatic element of the city. Once the peripheral zone has reached its critical mass, it becomes the generator of its own RING-ROAD CULTURE.'

217

WILLEM-JAN NEUTELINGS
AND MARC DE KOONING
Berchem, 'Ringzicht', houses, 1988-1990,
(Bastin/Evrard)

As if trying to illustrate what he meant by 'ring-road culture', Willem-Jan Neutelings built a set of three houses on the corner of a street above the verge of the Antwerp ring road. Two separate volumes, totally different as to character and situated on different streets, collide with each other, which creates a fascinating border area. The large horizontal aluminium volume is divided into two duplex apartments in the two lower storeys. The top floor contains a penthouse with a roof terrace. In the small vertical cedarwood volume around the corner there are two small flats that can either be made to communicate with the larger ones, or be used independently.

Xaveer De Geyter (b. 1957)

Xaveer De Geyter is the third member of the Hoogpoort team that has distinguished himself through important works, although his main activity lay in his participation in Rem Koolhaas's OMA. Amongst others, he was the project architect of Villa dall'Ava in Saint-Cloud, a suburb of Paris. The trio Beel, Neutelings, and De Geyter collaborated again in 1991 on a group of three villas on the Lege Kaart in Brasschaat, of which those by Stéphane Beel and Xaveer De Geyter have been completed to date.

Beel's villa perfectly fits in with the classical work discussed earlier and practically forms a synthesis of it. De Geyter's work is not concerned with bringing the tension in the design to rest. The architect does not hide his intentions. He conceals the villa in the sand, so that from the street side one can only see the drive and a glass carport. Apart from via the carport, the house below can be accessed by means of a ramp ending in the living area. At the front, imbedded in the dune and illuminated via a system of patios are the children's rooms. At the back, separated by a larger patio, we find the communal rooms and the master bedroom.

The whole scheme is contained in a square that is closed on three sides and opened up towards the garden, designed by the late Yves Brunier. In both the interior and exterior we meet with different, unexpected, mostly stimulating images – sometimes deliberately formal, and sometimes appearing to be based on almost industrial, organizational logic. Intellectual taboos are completely absent, as is the dichotomy between the elevated and the banal. Of all the attempts made to endue suburban residential areas and architecture with a new, contemporary value of perception, this must be one of the most radical.

XAVEER DE GEYTER
Brasschaat, house, 1990-1993, collage

Three architects of the Hoogpoort team, Stéphane Beel, Xaveer De Geyter, and Willem-Jan Neutelings collaborated on a set of three villas on the Lage Kaart in Brasschaat. Two of these have been built. In contrast with Stéphane Beel's villa, which is sharply set off against the trees, that by Xaveer De Geyter seems to be concealed in the terrain. From the street one can only see its roof with the drive up to the garage and the slope leading to the centre of the house. The whole scheme is arranged around three patios.

XAVEER DE GEYTER
Brasschaat, house, 1990-1993
(Catherine Bogert)

Of all attempts to transform life in suburbia into a conscious experience, that by Xavier De Geyter has been the most radical. Just as in Le Corbusier's Villa Savoye, the motor car features as an essential part of the concept. The drive continues through the architectural landscape and comes to an end in the central patio with its extension into the garden.

The house in Mariakerke, the first design of which dates from 1988, is in no way inferior to this. On the limits of a typical development, it constitutes a monument to the Belgian house in that it has been blown up from the inside – in all the senses of the word. However, the most remarkable fact is that comfortable living has not only survived from this operation, but, as was the case in Brasschaat, is regenerated by it. The final shape of this house is the result of ingenious manipulation of the planning regulations, which for instance prescribe a sloping roof. The high front façade, temporarily supported as it were by a crate and partly transparent, is oriented towards the development. The rear façade looks out onto a rural area with the rests of a seminary garden. The closed side façade looks as if it consists of enormous slabs of broken stone, a very popular material. Here the irritation created by such gaudy villas has been transformed into a game full of compassion, which makes the world not only more bearable, but even fascinating.

Mariakerke/Ghent, house, 1988-1992
(Bastin/Evrard)
The villa in Mariakerke may be considered as a monument to the Belgian home. It turns all the restrictive urban planning regulations to its advantage. It exalts the sloping roof and makes an enlargement of the ashlar walls. The whole weight of the superstructures seems to rest on a wooden crate.

Henk De Smet (b. 1954) / Paul Vermeulen (b. 1962)

The team formed by De Smet and Vermeulen has already been mentioned in connection with the housing competition in Kortrijk. Henk De Smet had, before his association with Vermeulen in 1990, already caught the attention in 1984 with the extension of the Noordstar and Boerhave insurance company in Ghent, a beautiful building by Marc Neerman dating from 1932. De Smet intelligently reflected the lines of the existing volume to create an ensemble in which old and new are perfectly integrated.

Unity of form is hard to discern in their work together. It even looks as if they are against it as a matter of principle and formulate a new basic concept adapted to every new assignment. For instance, in the case of an office building for Apple Computers Belgium, which has not been carried out, this has led to an adapted version of Le Corbusier's Villa Savoye; in that of the enlargement of a villa in Deinze the result has been an ingenious construction of glass staircases. It has also brought about their most remarkable work, namely 'Woning K. te Z.' (House K. in Z.).

In one of those numerous impossible housing developments – which do not seem to disturb their inhabitants at all – in a forlorn village in the Scheldt valley to the south east of Ghent and strewn with undefinable, pathetic middle-class villas, there suddenly arises one of those semicircular sheds made of corrugated iron that are used by farmers to store their agricultural machinery. It is reminiscent of the emergency housing set up near the front after the First World War, some of which is still in use today. This tunnel, or to put it in more architectural terms, barrel vaulting, contains a complete house. The house and vaulting are completely different. The vaulting is like a part of nature, a bulge in the ground, in which habitation finds its primary protection. The force of the elementary shape of this shed, which has been left untouched and is the colour of the soil, is sharply set off against the gingerbread houses surrounding it.

Below its fine arch the independent structure of the scheme is laid out along a longitudinal wall dividing the space into two uneven sections. The structure is clear and rigid, but has the effect of a maze. The dome, as it is popularly called, has not been interfered with except for a single skylight. The light enters through the open sides of the vaulting, a double-sided Plato's cave. Nevertheless, this is not an architectural manifesto, but the spontaneous liberation of architecture and habitation from the images to which they have been confined. It is a transformation in which accepted concepts such as innovation, originality, individuality, even beauty and ugliness lose their meanings.

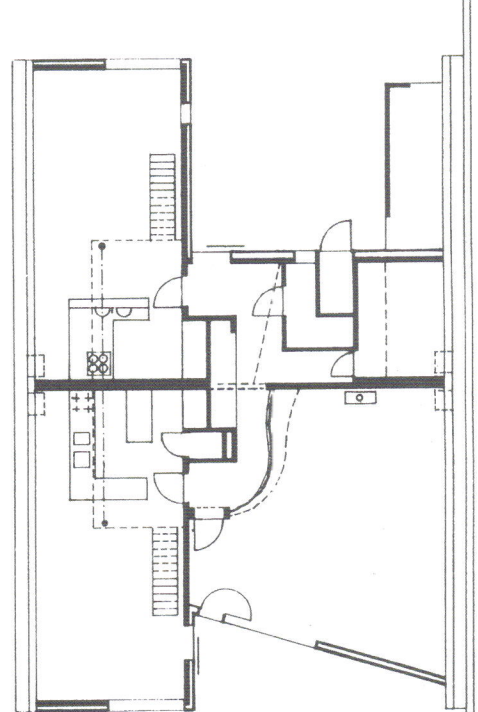

WILLEM-JAN NEUTELINGS,
AND MARC DE KOONING

Berchem, 'Ringzicht', houses, 1988-1990,
(Bastin/Evrard)

As if trying to illustrate what he meant by 'ring-road culture', Willem-Jan Neutelings built a set of three houses on the corner of a street above the verge of the Antwerp ring road. Two separate volumes, totally different as to character and situated on different streets, collide with each other, which creates a fascinating border area. The large horizontal aluminium volume is divided into two duplex apartments in the two lower storeys. The top floor contains a penthouse with a roof terrace. In the small vertical cedarwood volume around the corner there are two small flats that can either be made to communicate with the larger ones, or be used independently.

Kris Mys (b. 1956)

Kris Mys, who mostly collaborates with Geert Clarysse, has named his firm 'WAWW!' (What a Wonderful World!), a title that would have suited this book. As if he had chosen his customers himself, each and every one of his works is stunning. In 1985 he converted a depot in the 'Zuid' area in Antwerp into an exhibition venue and loft apartment. The 500 m² ground floor is reserved for two art galleries, the first and second floors respectively contain the living quarters with a kitchen and the bedroom with a bathroom. All Mys did was freeing the construction to reveal a wonderful empty space, which he made livable through minimal interventions. In order to avoid any associations with the bourgeois interior he used industrial appliances to fit it out.

Kris Mys's approach was even more clearly shown in his transformation of the former Loppa shop building in Antwerp, commissioned by the same client. But this belongs to the past. All that remains are traces of the original design, such as the monumental steel spiral staircase which through an open hole leads from the street to the showrooms. These showrooms were also kept completely free, shining emptiness in the fulness of the city. All the equipment needed was freely placed in the space as a set of temporary equipment, below a ceiling painting à la Michelangelo.

This shop is not an isolated example. In the same period several commissions from young fashion designers led to remarkable results. What cannot yet be done in a private house or public building, is enthusiastically applied in these experimental shop-fronts, highlighting the link between architecture and fashion. Similar to Kris Mys's work is that by Peter Cornelis in Brussels. In 'Stijl' (1984) and 'Stijl+', two shops designed by him, the existing shop and all its scars are basically left untouched. Nevertheless, the introduction of new elements is all the more prominent. They are no longer conceived as loose fragments in the space, but form a coherent structure challenging the existing space. We could also refer to arrangements by Guido Driesen, Eugeen Liebaut, Jo Crepain, Mauro Poponcini, Martine De Maeseneer, Dirk de Meyer, Johan Decoker, and especially Claire Bataille and Paul Ibens amongst many others. The difference between the semi-public space of the shop and the private quarters of the house has become virtually non-existent.

Kris Mys himself showed in the hairdresser 'Soap' on the quays in Antwerp that a radical approach such as his need not exclude frivolity and colour. Here again we can see the transformation of an existing building, typical of all Mys's work to date, which includes the transformation of a number of houses in Antwerp and the reconversion of an industrial building into offices in Brussels.

The most remarkable of these is the conversion of a listed house on the roundabout of the Cogels-Osylei in Berchem (Antwerp). Again his changes are both thorough and minimal: to the rear façade he has added a rectangular box which opens up the house towards the garden and the inner area, but the most striking intervention occurs literally in the middle of the house, where it is torn open from top to bottom by 'the largest showcase in Belgium', filled with toys and other curiosities. The stairs wind upwards around the showcase, revealing not only the objects displayed in it, but also the rooms surrounding it. This architecture is neither beautiful nor refined; it is obvious and indespensable. It does not aim to please, but to convince.

KRIS MYS
Antwerp, loft, 1987
(Bastin/Evrard)
'WAWW ! What A Wonderful World !' is the name of Kris Mys's firm. His work is a perfect illustration of this sense of wonderment. Each and every one of his realizations is a revelation, as if he had chosen his customers himself.
The warehouse in the Zuid district in Antwerp, with two galleries on the ground floor and the living quarters on the two upper storeys, shows how he has liberated an overwhelming space.

Kris Mys and Geert Clarysse
Antwerp, Coolen house, transformation, 1990-1992
(Alberto Piovano)
One of the most striking transformations by Kris Mys is that of a listed building on the Cogels-Osylei roundabout in Berchem/Antwerp. The original rear façade of the house extends into a rectangular volume and opens up towards the garden. On the inside the house is split open from top to bottom by 'the largest showcase in Belgium'.

▷ Kris Mys
Antwerp, penthouse, 1993
(Bastin/Evrard)
Up until now Kris Mys's work has consisted in more or less radical transformations of existing buildings. On top of a new block of flats near the quays of the River Scheldt he has built a splendid penthouse. In it he combines the luxury of empty space with the density of the relational patterns between the various zones of the interior among themselves, as well as between the interior and the exceptional environment created by the city and the river.

225

Ronny De Meyer (b. 1955) / Lut Prims (b. 1954)

As an ironical response to OMA, Rem Koolhaas's Office for Metropolitan Architecture, Ronny De Meyer and Lut Prims, together with Guy Steenput and José De Smet, founded OPA, Office for Postmetropolitan architecture in 1984 [in Dutch these acronyms form a pun: oma = granny, opa = grandad]. It was an act reflecting their generation's disenchantment.

We have already emphasized the extent to which large commissions in Belgium lack both an architectural tradition and architectural ambitions. Yet this is not all: young architects are probably even more the victims of the profession itself.

RONNY DE MEYER AND LUT PRIMS
Zwijndrecht, 1994
(Bastin/Evrard)
This industrial building in Zwijndrecht, right next to the Antwerp-Ghent motorway, incorporates living quarters on its roof. The geometry of its proportions transforms it into a purely architectural object without the use of any extra means.

Through the small number of their projects that have been carried out, Ronny De Meyer and Lut Prins have proved that with limited means inspiring, albeit controlled architecture can be realized. They call their own architecture 'banal' in the sense that it is 'common to all'. In their hands the commonest or most banal commission leads to works that are charged with energy. Starting out from a constructive geometry, they develop the various schemes into smooth, closed volumes that transcend their immediacy.

In the Vanderstukken building in Antwerp, which was awarded the 1988 Charles Wilford prize and combines offices and living quarters, the central volume is separated from, but again connected to the surrounding buildings via two strips of windows running along its entire height. The volume is concentrated in a white cube hanging free in the space, between the two splits containing the stairs and lifts. This cube strikingly affirms itself in the street as an independent architectural element, not only because of its whiteness, but especially through the unusual way in which the geometry of the squares in the windows creates a pattern of crosses. The play of form, which first created the field in which it takes place, occurs within this geometry. Indeed, the geometry is more than just a

covering. It is a reflection of a whole way of thought, which is also mirrored in the ground plans. The new building is situated next to a house by Walter Steenhoudt built in 1968, which interrupts the streetscape in a way that was quite daring at the time.

This geometrical order finds an even stricter application in another terraced house, no more than five metres wide, containing a medical centre and flats. The ground plan consists of three squares, the central one being set aside for services and circulation. The white façade repeats this motif and forms it into a striking composition. The form itself has become ornamentation, a precious object within which life takes place without ever getting a hold on it. Without being obtrusive, it actually transforms everyday actions into special events.

The building on an industrial site in Zwijndrecht, right next to the motorway, undergoes the same sort of metamorphosis: an industrial warehouse with living quarters has been made into a meaningful architectural object through no other means than the geometry of its proportions.

Martine De Maeseneer (b. 1962)

None of the architects mentioned in this chapter so far are men or women of words. Even Paul Vermeulen, who is an astute critic and essayist, refuses to develop any theories around his own work. Martine De Maeseneer is an exception. She has a need to put architecture, especially her own, into words. Robert E. Somol of the University of Illinois in Chicago, who wrote the introduction to Martine De Maeseneer's 1993 exhibition in deSingel, The In/di/visible Space, could not hide his urge to distinguish the structures from the words drawn around them. However, he quickly came to the conclusion that 'In the grift works of De Maeseneer and van den Brande – where "seeing" is often explicitly opposed to "knowing" – it appears no longer possible to ask whether it is honest or dishonest speech, good or bad form.' De Maeseneer's dissertations reveal the lack of space available for the development of an architectural argument as well as the danger thereof.

Martine De Maeseneer graduated from Sint-Lucas in Ghent in 1985 and set up in partnership with Dirk Van den Brande, an autodidact, in 1987. In 1988 they started on the Cabrio house on De Biest in Meise, which they completed in 1992. They have described this design as 'de-objectification', with reference to the shift in science from the Newtonian world view to a 'world view that is open to surrounding influences and pressure from outside, in which perceptional dogma is undermined once and for all'.

'In the Cabrio house the de-objectification method is rendered through the distortion of scale of elements that constitute the vernacular house. Window, porch, roof, wall, cell, and chimney are made concrete in the simple idiosyncratic, caricatural manner as seen in the infant's drawings.' However, the most striking feature of this object, no part of which has been left to chance and which is loaded with meaning, is its directness. It is as if it has left behind all forms of meaning to be perceived as something concrete, both in its open/closed figure towards the exterior and in its scenographical development inside. It is not without some irony that this house has been chosen by the advertising media to make it into a 'dream house'.

Frank Delmulle (b. 1955)

It may not have much point to look for geographical spheres of influence in an overview of young Belgian architects, but one cannot totally ignore the differences between, for instance, the Flemish scene centred around Ghent and that of Antwerp or Limburg. Moreover, there is a notable lack of Walloon counterparts.

Frank Demulle's work is unambiguously Flemish. He moves within the twilight zone between a conscious approach to architecture and architecture as a performance of villa construction. With the greatest ease, just as a master magician, he conjures the most unexpected forms of a modernist-like idiom out of his hat.

In 1987 Delmulle drew attention with a terraced house on the road to Zottegem in Oudenarde, in which he pulled out all the stops. The house is divided into an open section with the entrance to the basement containing the garage and a workshop. The living quarters are enclosed by two curved walls. The intersection and overlapping of the various surfaces and an eye-catching use of colour – e.g. yellow for the south wall, combined with blue and pink – make it a striking ensemble.

The same daring is encountered in most of Demulle's projects. For the Belgian pavilion in Seville he proposed an enormous screen to indicate the presence of the cool pavilion below the ground: 'the coolness of a cave, deep water, an immense space with just enough light to see by'. The contrasts of colour, measure, and material as well as the pursuit of effects also come to the fore in the Pijls house in Ronse (1988) and the Delmulle house in Kruishoutem.

Delmulle states that the Pijls house is nothing more than a section of the landscape. 'Partly because of transparency, the glazed façade surfaces, the house appears as an open space in the landscape. Owing to the steep sloping of the grounds, the house totals three storeys on the street side, two of which stick out above the terrain at the rear.' This transparency is contained by the seemingly floating brick sections of the side façades, one of which is even folded over as if it were a sheet of paper.

The Delmulle villa in Kruishoutem is beyond all measure. With a surface of 900 m² and a living space five metres high, it effaces all conventional proportions. The general effect is determined by the roof, which is supported by steel pillars. Below this the sumptuous ensemble is spread out, incorporating features such as a television cabin in Italian walnut set up as a house within the house. Not only does the house ignore all measure, but the use of materials too knows no bounds: a sliding partition made of Japanese paper is set off against a linen carport.

FRANK DELMULLE
Kruishoutem, house, 1994
(Bastin/Evrard)
This villa, built for a contractor on the undulating landscape of Kruishoutem, has no limits. With a surface of 900 m² and a five-metre-high living area it rejects all the conventional limitations of the private house and turns to palaces for inspiration. The flat roof disc on light steel pillars is a dominating feature of the landscape.

'The architecture of these buildings forms a totally isolated object,' Marc Belderbos comments on the existing shed. 'The architecture lies as an abandoned ship with walls around a surface of ten by sixty metres and a vault with a skylight. The second construction has arranged every section as a non-central part of an architcectural aggregation, part of reality, together with the "other".'

Marc Belderbos (b. 1954)

Its antithesis can be seen in the work of Marc Belderbos, a former student and for years an assistant lecturer at the architecture department of the Université Catholique de Louvain. He radically reopens the question of architecture and its present possibilities while insisting on the existence of a proper architectural space, 'une nouvelle architecture archaique', which is not separated from normal, everyday life. He explored the world of contemporary architecture doing practical training under Paolo Portoghesi and Alessandro Anselmi, but has consistently returned to his own fundamental notion of the 'archaic structure that precedes all ideas'. In his own words: 'Not a single reference is made to the cultural objects from the history of architecture. In this sense my design is not post-modern, even though my buildings come after modernism. Their "architecturation" (composition) is far more important than their architecture (seen as the production of finished objects or finished worlds as distinct from the world). In other words, these buildings are not situated in an aesthetic history of architecture... I have more particularly tried to take on an ethical attitude... The final aim is architecture that permits freedom and stands behind the soul rather than opposite it. These buildings therefore become an ethical part of architecture: they represent concrete authority under which people can live – freely, because this authority has no power. Its identity, which is free from meaning, is constantly based on that of its occupant.'

A house in Auderghem (1989), with 'strictly constructed walls in Paris stone like the top layer of successive plates in the earth's crust', clearly demonstrates this dramatic approach to architecture. One also encounters it in the house installed by Belderbos in the abandoned Hilaert warehouses in Astene-Deinze (1989-1991).

The architect also comments on his plans by means of drawings, photos, and texts: 'At this spot two sorts of architecture cross each other. The first is by the hand of Mr Hilaert, who after expropriation in Ghent, transported his buildings to Aspene by boat. The architecture of these buildings forms a completely closed object without any connection to the world. The architecture lies like a lost boat with walls around a surface of ten by sixty metres and a vault with a skylight. The second sort of architecture has arranged every room as a non-central part

All the dimensions of heaven and earth are revealed in the architectural object, not in order to turn it into the centre of the universe and create a closed world of its own, but rather to break through the isolation of the world and reinvest it with the originality of its beginning.

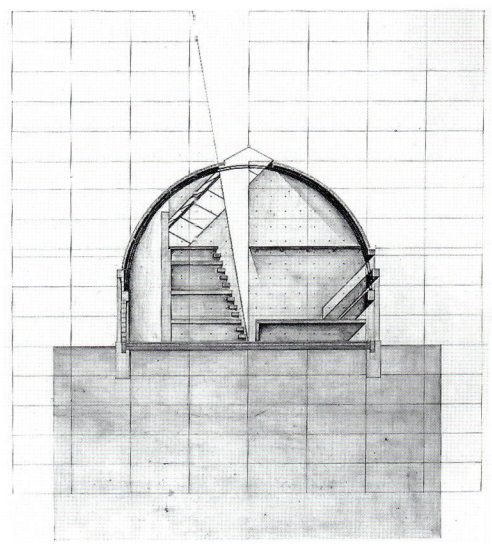

229

MARC BELDERBOS
Auderghem, house, 1989-1990

(Bastin/Evrard)

'There is not a single closed space in the form of a room in this house,' Marc Belderbos declares. 'Whoever lives here, lives behind walls in a sort of hollow at a safe distance from reality.' Marc Belderbos endues his architecture with visionary passion. His buildings are strictly autonomous creations that want to confront their occupants with the reality of existence.

MARC BELDERBOS
Astene-Deinze, own house, 1990-1991

Architecture is not a means to isolating oneself from the world or to make it aesthetic. Construction is the essential structuring of reality. 'For as long as they have existed, i.e. in an archaic way, art, science, politics, and love – all of them intimately linked with architecture – have always moved towards the other unknown with determination,' Marc Belderbos says.

of an aggregate, in reality, with the "other"... The ground plan, a cross between two plans, establishes a relation with the surroundings, so that the building no longer comes across as an aesthetic object in the world, but as an infinite structuring of the real.'

He concludes: 'Art, science, politics, and love have this in common, that they indicate that reality is not what it seems. Intimately connected with architecture, art, science, politics, and love have always – i.e. in an archaic way – approached the unkown full of confidence. They give rise to another, new truth that does not correspond to what is in all probability expected. Art, science, politics, and love are – why not say so – oblique. They go confidently to the other. In a word, this project supposes that the truth is not straight and that the closed world of certain images is finite.'

Mein erstes Haus

The exhibition held at 'deSingel' in Antwerp entitled 'Mein erstes haus' (early 1994), as reference to Adolf Loos, presented 'recent works by young Flemish architects'. In a suggestive setting designed by Xaveer De Geyter and Maarten van Severen work by no fewer than twenty-four architects was on show. We have already discussed some of them. Noteworthy names include Lieven Achtergael, with a florist's shop in Wetteren; Hans Barbier with a house in Bornem; Ralf Coussée and Klaas Goris with a bank in Staden; Lieven Dejaeghere with a house in Lokeren; Pascal François with a shop in Denderleeuw; Peter Kint with a house in Pellenberg; Johan Laethem with a house in Meulebeke; François Ponette with a house in Wilrijk; and Pascal Van der Kelen with the conversion of a house in Ghent. Indeed, the list could go on.

Such an abundance of names is not found in Wallonia or Brussels. This view does not spring from short-sightedness on the writer's part, but one wonders if this lethargy may not be due to the domination of an older generation that is still active, to the tameness of the schools where that generation still sets the tone, or to the loss of La Cambre. Whatever the case may be, there is nothing comparable to the stimulating atmosphere surrounding exhibitions such as 'Mein erstes haus'. Wallonia does not have manifestations such as 'Architectuur als buur' in Ghent (1988) or 'Konfrontaties in moderne architectuur' in Kortrijk (1990), which presented local architecture. The 'Fondation pour l'architecture' in Brussels limits itself to retrospective exhibitions of established architects' work. It comes as no surprise that the Belgian pavilion in Seville was the work of a Flemish team.

In the April 1994 issue of the French periodical *L'architecture d'aujourd'hui*, 'En Flandre', which shows the work of eleven Flemish architects, Emmanuel Doutriaux analyses the situation in Wallonia as follows: 'La longue dépression du sud du pays interdit à sa jeune garde de s'exprimer réellement. Quand elle en a les moyens, elle semble paralysée par la stérilisation du débat architectural dans sa région. Patrimonialisation sourcilleuse des centres urbains traditionnels, réglementation provinciale drastique d'instauration récente, qui préserve la campagne sans faciliter l'expression d'un langage moderne: la partie wallone est aujourd'hui très concernée par la maîtrise de la ville, son identification, son expression architecturale.' In *Bouwen in Beton 1990-1991* the German critic Wolfgang Jean Stock's article 'Jonge architecten in België' (Young Architects in Belgium) only mentions Flemish architects.

Naturally, Brussels and Wallonia could also yield a few names: besides Benoit Laloux and John Berhaut, we should mention Paul Sternfeld and Nele Huysman with a garden pavilion awarded the Maskes prize in 1984; Pierre Hebbelinck, who was included in the 'Jonge architecten in België' exhibition in 1986; and Bernard Herbecq with a house in Jehay. However, it would be hard to add any more to the list. If it is ever built, Mario Botta's new seat of the Walloon parliament will be very ambivalent in this context.

PASCAL VAN DER KELEN
Ghent, transformation, house, 1993
(Kristien Daem)
The challenge of a specific reality seems to serve as a source of inspiration to many architects. They do not blend the new and the existing, but rather transform the latter – a fact borne out by this radical, yet subtle transformation of a house in Ghent. The smooth glass wall of the rear façade adds a new sense of scale and proportion to the chaos surrounding it.

Architecture Nevertheless

Our account has turned out to be somewhat pell-mell. We have already compared the situation of architecture to a flea market where we can stroll about and find everything mixed together. This jumble is the temporary result of such a stroll, a colourful mix of individual works. Indeed, this appears to be what it is all about in the end. Inevitably general trends are defined in which the objects situate themselves in a combination of individual and common adventures. The work as a product of history is not concerned with history, but with itself, with its own truth. It produces itself.

The story of architecture in Belgium since 1945 appears – if one wants to see it as such – as a slow, gradual process of rediscovery of architecture as a spiritual adventure. It is all the more fascinating because it is inextricably linked with the immediate, heteromorphic, and coincidental nature of concrete, everyday reality. Because of this link the work is largely impervious to doctrinal lapses, despite the temptation. Whatever the myths that are invented around it, the work has to be created, conceived as matter. Whether situated in the constructive confidence of the Reconstruction period or in the hesitation of the 1970s, it can only be fascinating once it transcends this context and becomes more than an illustration of an era by directly contributing to it.

Although we have cited many quotations to give an idea of tastes at the time, they all demonstrate the pursuit of the most direct approach to the inaccessible mystery of the work of art, which interferes with the easy passage of time. This contrariness of the work acquires special significance in architecture. While confirming, it denies. While pleasing, it repulses. While protecting, it exposes. While determining, it challenges. Through its unapproachability architecture fascinates and gives rise to surveys such as this one, which has now come to its end.

Bibliographic survey

1 General

The bibliographic sources for a history of Belgian architecture are as numerous and dispersed as their subject. The most prominent ones are mentioned in the text, but we have listed them here again to provide a more practical overview.

There are no general surveys. The first half of the period discussed in this book draws on surveys of Belgian architecture after 1900. These are often pleas for a new form of architecture rather than historical texts. The volume *Belgique* in the series entitled 'L'Architecture vivante', Editions Albert Morancé, Paris, 1958, published in the wake of 'Expo '58', constitutes a first attempt at presenting post-war architecture by means of photographs. The foreword was written by Victor Bourgeois. The controversial character of historical texts is revealed in Albert Bontridder, *Architecture contemporaine and Belgique. Dialogue de la lumière et du silence*, 70 pp., Uitgeverij Helios, Antwerp, 1963. On the occasion of its 20th anniversary the 'Confédération nationale de la Construction' published *L'industrie de la construction*, 322 pp., containing an article by V.G. Martiny on Belgian architecture since 1900. Although the catalogue to the exhibition held in the museum of Ixelles in 1969, *Antoine Pompe et l'effort moderne en Belgique 1890-1940*, 192 pp., by Maurice Culot and François Terlinden, does not really belong here, it forms an important document in that it belongs to the historical context. This catalogue is complemented by *Musée des Archives d'Architecture Moderne. Fondation Robert-L. Delevoy*, 392 pp. 1986, an overview of the collection compiled by Maurice Culot, Anne Van Loo and Victor G. Martiny; and by *Académie de Bruxelles. Deux Siècles d'Architecture*, 541 pp., 1989, both published by 'Archives d'Architecture Moderne' (AAM) in Brussels. Both works contain a number of architects discussed in this book. *Bouwen in België 1945-1970 / La Construction en Belgique 1945-1970*, 384 pp., by Geert Bekaert and Francis Strauven, published in 1971 by the 'Nationale Confederatie van het Bouwbedrijf / Confédération nationale de la Construction', provides an objective collection of sources through its overview spanning 1940 to 1970. It includes main events and publications, comprehensive extracts, a series of bibliographies, as well as a complete inventory of the works and a text by each of the architects discussed. In 1970 *Architecton*, the FAB's periodical, published a catalogue entitled *Belgique. Urbanisme. Architecture. Situation 1970*. Pierre Puttemans and Lucien Hervé *Architecture moderne en Belgique*, 262 pp., Mark Vokaer Editeur, Brussels, 1974, formed the last volume in a series on Belgian architecture. Towards the end of the 1960s the linoleum factory Krommenie published a comprehensive survey of Belgian architecture, untitled and by an anonymous author. Because of its illustrations, selected by Paul Van Aerschot, Giovanni

Peers *Uit Klei gebouwd. Baksteenarchitectuur na 1945*, 198 pp, Lannoo, Tielt, 1982 / *La terre cuite. L'architecture en terre cuite après 1945*, Mardaga, Liège 1990, has to be added to this list. The catalogue *1951-1991. Een Tijdsbeeld / Image d'une époque*, 438 pp., published on the occasion of King Baudouin's 60th birthday and 40th jubilee provides a study on architecture by Geert Bekaert and on town planning by Marcel Smets. *De beschikbare ruimte. Reflecties over bouwen*, 240 pp., Lannoo, Tielt, 1990, contains specific contributions on various aspects of architecture in Belgium since 1945, apart from a few important general observations. Under the editorship of Jan Van Alsenoy, the collection *Ruimtelijke planning. Praktijkboek voor stedebouw en stadsvernieuwing, huisvesting en milieu*, 3 vols., Van Loghum Slaterus, Antwerp, has been appearing since 1981. It is complemented by *Wegwijs wonen*, 874 pp., Davidsfonds, Leuven, 1993, by André Loeckx, Herman Neuckermans and Roger Dillemans. Both works provide essential background information needed to understand the history of Belgian architecture.

The period after 1970 is dealt with in a special issue of the periodical *Wonen/TABK*, June 1983, entitled 'Op Belgische gronden', containing an article by Geert Bekaert, 'Wie over architectuur wil spreken, sta op, en zwijge', and in Francis Strauven *L'architecture en Belgique 1970-1980*, 63 pp., published on the occasion of an exhibition by the 'Centre de Recherche en Architecture', Louvain-la-Neuve, in 1981. It is discussed in more detail in Marc Dubois, *Belgio Architettura, gli ultimi vent'anni*, 166 pp., Electa, Milan, 1993, with a general introduction on the characteristics of Belgian architecture and the presentation of around fifty buildings. Marc Dubois collaborated with Christian Kieckens on a special issue of *Archis* in September 1987, entitled 'Recente architectuur in België. Gebouwen na 1970', which contains an architectural map. Dubois also worked on '1880-1890. Fragmenten van architectuur in België' in *Openbaar Kunstbezit in Vlaanderen*, no. 3, 1991. The 'Stichting Architectuurmuseum' published a number of catalogues on young Belgian architects as well: *De woning als architectuurtypologie*, 1985; *Jonge architekten in België*, 1986; *Jonge architekten (in België)*, 1987; and *Jonge Architekten (in Vlaanderen)*, 1990. For the 1991 Venice Biennale Marc Dubois compiled the catalogue *Architetti (della Fiandra)*, containing works by ten architects. In the travel guide *Langs moderne architectuur (1945-heden) Architectuurroutes in Nederland en België*, by Dorothée Van Hoof, Jouke Van Der Werf and Guy Goethals, 240 pp. Kosmos-Z&K Uitgevers, Utrecht/Antwerp, 1994, Belgium - or rather Brussels and Flanders - is considered an appendage to the Netherlands. 1986 saw the publication of *Architectura Belgica 1986*, 128 pp., Atelier Vokaer, Brussels. An excellent survey of more recent architecture appears in *Yearbook Architecture Flanders 1990-1993*, 222 pp., published by the Flemish Community in 1994. It contains contributions by Marc Dubois, who compiled it, Marcel Smets, André Loeckx, and Francis Strauven, as well as a comprehensive bibliography. It is complemented by the catalogue *Mein erstes haus. Recent werk van jonge Vlamingen*, deSingel, Antwerp, 1994, 164 pp., and by *Fundament. Architekten en hun visie*, published by the 'Henry van de Velde-instituut' in Antwerp, *s.a.*

2 Periodicals

Periodicals provide an invaluable source for the study of Belgian architecture since 1945. However, they afford an incomplete view require additional examination of records in archives, which has rarely been carried out to date. The dissertations written at schools of architecture have generally remained unpublished. A complete overview of periodicals up to 1970 can be found in *Bouwen in*

België 1945-1970 / La Construction en Belgique 1945-1970. The only surviving periodical on architecture today is *A+*, a bi-monthly publication of the 'Centre d'Information de l'Architecture, de l'Urbanisme et du Design' (ICASD) in Brussels. Until 1994 *S/AM*, the periodical published by the 'Stichting Architectuurmuseum' under Marc Dubois and Christian Kieckens, provided regular information on young Belgian architects. Until 1990 the publication by Maurice Culot and the 'Archives d'Architecture Moderne', AAM, defended its own and related views. A selection and critical analyses of contemporary Belgian architecture can be found in the Dutch-Belgian monthly *Archis*, published by the Netherlands Architecture Institute in Rotterdam. Other periodicals published abroad, such as the Dutch *De Architect*, also regularly pay attention to Belgian architecture, but this is usually limited to the presentation of new buildings. Exceptions to this are *L'Architecture d'Aujourd'hui*, 'En Flandre', no. 292, April 1994, with an essay by Emmanuel Doutriaux presenting the work of twelve architects, and *Bouwen met beton / Construire en béton* 1990/91, published by the 'Vereniging Nederlandse Cementindustrie' in 's Hertogenbosch with an essay by Wolfgang Jean Stock, 'Jonge architecten in België'. The same author has also compiled a special issue of *Baumeister*, no. 10, October 1994, dedicated to Stéphane Beel, containing essays on Belgian architecture by Marc Dubois and Geert Bekaert. The Japanese periodical *SD* dedicated an issue (no. 2, 1987) to 'Belgian Architecture and Design: The End of two Centuries'.

3 Essays and reviews

Belgium does not have a tradition of contemplative or critical writing. Most texts have been written on specific occasions by the architects themselves. The most important of these are listed under no. 7 of the bibliography, 'Monographies on Architects'. To the names mentioned in the book we may add two compilations of articles by K.-N. Elno, *Ruimte en beelding*, 140 pp., and *De vorm der dingen*, 144 pp., Heideland, Hasselt, 1965. Articles by Geert Bekaert have been collected in *Verzamelde Opstellen 1. Stapstenen 1950-1965*, 374 pp., 1985, and *2. Los in de ruimte 1966-1970*, 448 pp., 1986, published by the 'Stichting Monumenten- en Landschapszorg', Brussels. He has also written *Het einde van de architectuur*, Limburgs Universitair Centrum, 1967; *Architectuur zonder schaduw/Architecture Devoid of Shadow*, 45 pp., Uitgeverij 010, Rotterdam, 1988; *Interieur met zwembad/Interior with swimming pool*, 22 pp., Interieur, Kortrijk, 1994. *De beschikbare ruimte*, already mentioned, contains important theoretical essays. *Architecture rationnelle. La reconstruction de la ville européenne*, 214 pp., Archives d'Architecture moderne, Brussels, 1978, can be regarded as the ARAU group's theoretical manifesto. Theoretical reflections can be found in *Cahiers du centre d'Etudes architecturales*, with, amongst others, a text by Henri Van Lier, *Architecture synergique*. In 1959 Van Lier had already published *Arts de l'Espace*, 400 pp., and in 1962 *Le nouvel Age*, 232 pp., at Casterman in Tournai. The studies by Ann Van Sevenant, *Deconstructie. Een multidisciplinaire benadering*, 112 pp., Acco, Leuven, 1992 and *Poetica van de architectuur*, 176 pp., Hadewijch, Antwerp, 1994, are noteworthy in that they are not closely linked to the architectural profession itself.

The main theoretical contributions in this period do not concern architecture itself, but rather its position in society, in particular as regards its relation to living in cities. In 1965 Libert Vander Kerken published *Filosofie van het wonen*, 130 pp., and in 1970 Jacques Claes *De dingen en hun ruimte*, 373 pp., De Nederlandsche Boekhandel, Antwerp. Works that focus more directly on problems facing us today include *Omtrent wonen / Apropos de l'habitat* by G. Bekaert, B. Van Reeth and E. Van Broeckhoven, 472 pp, published by Seso, Antwerp, 1975; Jacques Aron, *Architecture et sociéte*, CIAUD, Brussels, 1976; René Schoonbroodt, *Sociologie de l'habitat social*, 348 pp, AAM, Brussels, 1979; *Essai sur la destruction des villes et des campagnes*, 188 pp., Pierre Mardaga, Liège, 1987; and Gerda Smets *Psychologie van bouwen en wonen*, 186 pp., Van Loghum Slaterus, Deventer, 1979. Among the countless contributions in general magazines, *Synthèses* published two important issues in 1968 and 1969: 'L'homme, l'urbanisme et l'architecture' and 'Interrogez l'homme. L'homme et la cité'. The legal implications of the law on town planning are considered in L.P. Suetens, *De nieuwe wetgeving. Ruimtelijke ordening*, 130pp., De Nederlandsche Boekhandel, Antwerp, 1971. It is commented upon by Evert Lagrou in *Ruimtelijke ordening... ook in België?*, 80 pp., Davidsfonds, Leuven, 1970. *Ruimtelijke Planning* has already been mentioned above.

Accusations of political abuse of power are voiced in Paul Debongnie *Les amis de Paul Vanden Boeynants et leurs affaires* and *Les amis de Paul Vanden Boeynants et leurs affaires (suite...)*, 168 pp. and 118 pp., Les Editions Vie Ouvrière, Brussels, 1970 and 1974, and *De grote stad, een geplande chaos. De Noordwijk van krot tot Manhattan*, 108 pp., Davidsfonds, Leuven, by Jozef Lievens, Nicole Brasseur, and Albert Martens. Even politicians have become involved in the debate. Their publications include Omer Vanaudenhove *Twee noodzakelijke wetten*, 166 pp., Paul Hymanscentrum, Brussels (1961); Paul Akkermans *Gaat het om stenen of mensen? Sociale stads- en dorpsvernieuwing in Vlaanderen*, 222 pp., Brussels, 2nd ed. 1983, final editing by Sieg Vlaeminck, Leonard Quintelier and Thierry Vanhecke; and Karel Poma *Knoeien met ons leefmilieu*, 196 pp., De Nederlandsche Boekhandel, Antwerp, 1972. Minister A. Califice commissioned Jan Tanghe, Sieg Vlaeminck and Hugo Vanderstadt *Wonen of wijken?*, 208 pp., ICASD, Brussels, 1978. Minister Georges Bohy published *Beginselen van de ruimtelijke ordening en van de stedebouw*, 160 pp., Editions Art et Technique, s.a. Johan Struye gave a journalist's version of the housing problem in *De pastoor wist wat goed was. Bouwen in België*, 144 pp., Knackpocket, 1974. 1965 saw the publication of *Demain, nos villes...*, 260 pp., Editions Desoer, Liège, a report of the 'Liège en l'an 2000' colloquium, which was echoed in *De Belgische stad van vandaag: waarheen? / La cité belge d'aujourd'hui: quel devenir?*, 304 pp., Gemeentekrediet van België / Crédit communal de Belgique, 1985.

4 Local history

A notable amount of attention is paid to the local history of contemporary architecture. *Bouwen door de eeuwen heen / La patrimoine monumental de la Belgique*, a series of inventories edited by Suzanne Van Aerschot-Van Haeverbeek, published at first by the 'Rijksdienst voor Monumenten en Landschappen / Service national des Monuments et des Sites', now by the ministeries of the separate communities, also contains information on buildings after 1945. The most information is found in architectural guides. Jacques Aron, Patrick Burniat, and Pierre Puttemans produced the excellent *Guide d'architecture moderne Bruxelles et environs 1890-1990*, 158 pp., Didier Hatier, Brussels, 1990, a revised edition of *Bruxelles 1890-1971 Guide d'architecture*, 1972, published by the 'Ministère de la Culture française', on the initiative of the SBUAM. These are complemented by a catalogue edited by Patrick Burniat, *50 ans architecture Bruxelles* of 1989. *Brussel. Groei van een hoofdstad / Bruxelles. Croissance d'une capitale*, edited by Jean Stengers, Mercatorfonds, Antwerp, 1979 contains a fascinating chapter on the evolution of the cityscape by Y. Leblicq. There is a large number of publications on Brussels by the 'Archives d'Architecture Moderne',

containing proposals for urban renewal. We shall mention only *La reconstruction de Bruxelles*, 1982, 184 pp., with introductions by Maurice Culot, René Schoonbroodt, and Leon Krier. Jacques Aron analyses urban evolution in *Le tournant de l'urbanisme bruxellois 1958-1978*, 122 pp., Fondation Joseph Jacqmotte, Brussels 1978.

For Antwerp the reader is referred to Tijl Eyckerman, *Gids voor Antwerpen. Moderne architectuur*, 224 pp., 1989, and *Architectuurgids Antwerpen*, 278 pp., 1993, of the Ministry of the Flemish Community, both published by Brepols, Turnhout. Jef Vanreusel edited *Antwerp. Reshaping a City*, 224 pp, Blondé Artprinting International, Antwerp, 1990, which is dedicated to the results of the 'Stad aan de Stroom' competition. The periodical *Ruimtelijke Planning*, Kluwer Editorial, Zaventem, devoted volume 3, 1994, to the theme of Antwerp. Another important publication is *Taking Sides. Antwerp's 19th-century belt: elements for a culture of the city*, Antwerpen 93, edited by Pieter Uyttenhoeve. Yves De Bondt published a catalogue, *100 jaar wonen in Turnhout*, Roularta, Roeselare, 1995 containing work of the 'Turnhout school'.

In Ghent there has been keen interest in contemporary architecture since the publication in 1988 of a book accompanying an exhibition, *Architectuur als buur. Panorama van Gent en omstreken 1968-1988*, 204 pp., Brepols, Turnhout 1988, final editing by Mil De Kooning. There also is the *Architectuurgids Gent*, in the same series as *Architectuurgids Antwerpen*, 312 pp., by Dirk Laporte, as well as *Gent & Architectuur. Trots, schande en herwaardering in een overzicht* edited by Norbert Poulain, 168 pp., Marc Van de Wiele, Bruges, 1985. 'Realisaties in Oost-Vlaanderen 1963-1993' appears in *Architectuur in de provincie*, 180 pp., published under the auspices of the 'Provinciale Raad van de Orde van Architecten, Oost-Vlaanderen'. Inspired by 'Architectuur als buur' in Ghent, 'Jonge Kamer Jaycees Kortrijk' published *Konfrontaties in Moderne Architectuur. Een 'promenade' in en rond Kortrijk*, 148 pp., 1990. Luc Verpoest, Jan Apers and Philippe Laporta edited *Hedendaagse Architectuur in Vlaams-Brabant*, 91 pp., Boek & Vorm, Herent, 1991. For the province of Limburg there is *Architectuurwijzer*, 77 pp., published and edited by Luc Vanmuysen, Louis Coolen and Francis Strauven. Karel Moerman edited *Vier architecten te Brugge*, 134 pp., Lannoo, Tielt, 1983, with an introduction by Charles Vermeersch. The review *Architecture* has recently published 'Circuit d'Architecture Contemporaine. Arrondissement de Verviers', 2nd ed., 1995.

5 Heritage and industrial archaeology

Many publications on the conservation and renovation of historical buildings or city areas are closely related to the study of local history. We have already mentioned *Bouwen door de eeuwen heen / La patrimoine monumental de la Belgique*. André De Nayer gave an overview of the problems in *Monumentenzorg*, 282 pp., De Nederlandsche Boekhandel, Antwerp, 1975. The bimonthly publication of the 'Bestuur van Monumenten en Landschappen', *Monumenten en Landschappen*, regularly offers information, also on new monuments, whether listed or not. *Les cahiers de l'urbanisme* of the Walloon administration for town and country planning focuses on urban renewal. In 1972 the Belgian Ministry of French Culture published *Namur. La ville ancienne et la rue des Brasseurs. Un problème de l'avenir* and numerous other studies. Jean Barthelemy compiled the survey *Dix ans de rénovation urbaine en Wallonie. Pour un autre urbanisme*, 124 pp., 1987, published by the Walloon Ministry of Town and Country Planning. In 1981 the 'Koning Boudewijnstichting / Fondation Roi Baudouin published *Witboek van het cultureel*

onroerend erfgoed / Livre blanc du patrimoine culturel et immobilier, 176 pp. It also publishes a series entitled 'Monografieën Bouwkundig Erfgoed'. The foundation's Guido Knops published *Stadsvernieuwing in beweging*, 168 pp., which is complemented by *Hedendaagse architectuur in historische omgevingen*, by the 'Rijksdienst voor Monumenten- en Landschapszorg', 112 pp., Brussels, 1982. In most of these publications, however, contemporary architecture comes off badly. *Monumenten: sentimenten van het post-industriële tijdperk?* is a report on the colloquium held in Antwerp on 22 March 1991, organized by the 'Koning Boudewijnstichting'.

More interesting results have been booked in the field of industrial archaeology. A first general view is afforded by Adriaan Linters *Industria. Architecture industrielle en Belgique. Industriële architectuur in België*, 232 pp., Pierre Mardaga, Liège, 1986. Paul Berckmans *et al.* published *Van Industrie tot Erfgoed*, 168 pp., Stichting Monumenten- en Landschapszorg, 1989, containing a comprehensive bibliography, and also by Patrick Viaene and René De Herdt *Industriële Archeologie in België*, 440 pp., Stichting Mens en Kultuur, Ghent, 1990. In 1994 Pierre Paquet published *La Patrimoine industriel de Wallonie*, 540 pp., Liège. Other publications have been dedicated to two important demolished monuments, namely *Elegie om een gistfabriek*, by Bruno Couwenberg and Piet Swimberghe, published by Jempie Herrebout, Bruges, 1985 and *Hommage Koninklijke Stapelhuizen Antwerpen*, published by 'Gehavende Stad' and 'Vlees en Beton', 1990. In the wake of the demolition of the warehouses ('Stapelhuizen'), Geert Bekaert and Jan Putteneers published *Gehavende stad*, 64 pp., Hadewijch, Antwerp, 1990.

6 Monographies

Monographies have been dedicated to a number of institutions and events. The 'La Cambre' school of architecture has been the focus of much interest, for instance in *La Cambre 1928-1978. L'Ecole fondée par Henry van de Velde*, 432 pp., AAM, 1978. A critical reflection is brought by Jacques Aron in *La Cambre et l'architecture. Un regard sur le Bauhaus belge*, 194 pp., Pierre Mardaga, Liège, 1982. Various issues of *Les cahiers de la Cambre. Architecture* are dedicated to the history of the school. Number 4 of 1987, 'La Cambre a 60 ans', contains a catalogue of all former graduates. Louvain-la-Neuve has also brought on a lot of comment: in October 1972 *Neuf* published a dossier on it, as did *Carré bleu* in 1987. In *Intégrations et architecture*, 290 pp., 1977, Philippe Boudon, Philippe Deshayes and Claude Nedelec present a detailed study of Louvain-la-Neuve. Jean-Marc Bodson and Jean-Pol Hiernaux devoted a photographic essay to *Souvenirs d'une ville sans cimétière...*

The results of various competitions have been published: *Sea Trade Center Zeebrugge*, 96 pp., Standaard Uitgeverij, Antwerp, 1990; *Hoog-Kortrijk*, 72 pp., Kortrijk, 1990; and *Architectuurwedstrijd Winterslag*, 48 pp., Genk, 1991. We have already mentioned *Antwerp. Reshaping a City*. André Loeckx and Marcel Smets have made a detailed study of the reconversion of the mining area in *Geschiedenis op zoek naar waardig vervolg. Studie van de Mijnnederzetting Waterschei, Winterslag en Eisden*, 166 pp., Koning Boudewijnstichting, Brussels, 1991. The report on the Prix Bonduelle 1981-1983 was published in *Bulletin de la Classe des Beaux-Arts*, 1984, no. 3-4, of the 'Académie Royale de Belgique. Françoise Robert-Jones-Popelier wrote *Kroniek van een Museum: Koninklijke Musea voor Schone Kunsten / Chronique d'un musée: Musées des Beaux-Arts de Belgique*, 152 pp., Pierre Mardaga, Liège, 1987. The commissioner general of the 1992 world fair in Seville devoted an extensive publication to the pavilion designed by Driesen, Meersman, and

Thomaes. The show town of Limal is the subject of a special issue of *Landeigendom / Propriété terienne* - the monthly publication of the 'Nationale Landmaatschappij / Société nationale ' - in 1972, entitled 'Villagexpo Limal'. In 1992 deSingel dedicated a catalogue to *Project Papeye Aalbeke. Ontwerpen voor een kijkdorp*. The catalogue *De l'Utopie au Réel. 1919-1994*, 222 pp., Les Chiroux, Liège, 1994, provides an overview of 75 years of social housing in Wallonia.

7 Monographies on architects

The monographies on architects are given in alphabetical order and only include articles in periodicals if they appear in special issues.

ALBERT BRUNO
(see: *Bouwen in België / La Construction en Belgique*)

ARNOULD PIERRE
Architecture cadre de vie. Le Bernalmont Liège, Liège, 1987

AUSIA/ MICHEL BENOIT & THIERRY VERBIEST
Pierre Loze, *Ausia. Architectures*, Didier Hatier, 160 pp. Brussels, 1990

BAELE JOHAN AND BALLIU ERIC
(see Baro: *Bouwen in België / La Construction en Belgique*)

BAINES GEORGES
(see: *Bouwen in België / La Construction en Belgique*)
Anne Van Loo, 'Georges Baines, Projets 1975-1980' in: AAM, no. 19, 1980
Norbert Trevisiol, 'Georges Baines' in: A+, no. 90, 1986

BASTIN ROGER
(see: *Bouwen in België / La Construction en Belgique*)
Art d'Eglise, no. 148, July-Sept. 1969, and no. 159, April-June 1972

BATAILLE CLAIRE AND IBENS PAUL
Marc Dubois, 'Claire Bataille and Paul Ibens' in: S/AM, April-June 1988

BEEL STÉPHANE
'Stéphane Beel. Airplanes in rice fields' in: Forum, 33/2, Oct. 1989
Wolfgang Jean Stock, 'Stéphane Beel. Ein radikaler Poet' in: Baumeister, Oct. 1994
'Provinciale zetel B.A.C. West-Vlaanderen' in: S/AM, Jan.-March 1992

BELDERBOS MARC
Marc Belderbos, *La raison de l'augure. Trois essais sur le commencement*, 1990, 492 pp.

BOGAERDE JEAN VAN DEN
Jean Van Den Bogaerde, Sint-Martens-Latem, 1989, 168 pp.

BONTRIDDER ALBERT
(see: *Bouwen in België / La Construction en Belgique*)
Albert Bontridder, *Dialoog tussen licht and stilte / Dialogue de la lumière et du silence*, Helios, Antwerp, 1963, 70 pp.
Albert Bontridder, *Gevecht met de rede. Léon Stynen. Leven and werk / Stynen, la raison révoltée; sa vie et son oeuvre*, Comité Léon Stynen, Antwerp, 1979, 238 pp.

BOURGEOIS VICTOR
Victor Bourgeois, *Charleroi, Terre d'Urbanisme*, Editions Art et Technique, Brussels, 1946, 74 pp.
Victor Bourgeois, *De l'Architecture au temps d'Erasme à l'Humanisme social de notre Architecture*, A l'Enseigne du Chat qui pêche, Brussels, 1949, 124 pp.
Victor Bourgeois, *L'Architecte et son espace*, Collection Sept Arts, Brussels, 1955, 124 pp.
Georges Linze, *Victor Bourgeois*, Monografieën over Belgische Kunst, Elsevier, Brussels 1959, 14 pp., 28 ill.
Victor Bourgeois 1897-1962, catalogue, AAM, Brussels, 1971, 62 pp.

BRAEM RENAAT
(see: *Bouwen in België / La Construction en Belgique*)
Renaat Braem, *Het lelijkste land ter wereld*, Horizonreeks, Davidsfonds, Leuven, 1968, 68 pp.
Renaat Braem, *Het schoonste land ter wereld*, Het Geheugen, Kritak, Leuven, 1987, 214 pp.

Francis Strauven, *René Braem Architecture*, AAM, Brussels, 1985, 238 pp. including a complete bibliography.

BRODZKI CONSTANTIN
(see: *Bouwen in België / La Construction en Belgique*)

CALLEBOUT PETER
(see: *Bouwen in België / La Construction en Belgique*)

COSSE JEAN
(see: *Bouwen in België / La Construction en Belgique*)
Frédéric Debuyst, *Jean Cosse. Des maisons pour vivre*, Ed. art vie esprit, Brussels, s.a., 136 pp.
Jean Cosse and Frédéric Debuyst, 'Le monastère Saint-André à Ottignies' in: *Art d'Eglise*, no. 157, Oct.-Dec. 1971

DAEM HILDE
(see: Robbrecht P.)

DELEU LUC
Luc Deleu, *Manifest aan de Orde*, Ed. Guy Schraenen, Antwerp, 1983
Luc Deleu, *Luc Deleu. Postfuturisme*, deSingel, 1987, 96 pp.
'Top Office. Floating airports and other infrastructures' in: *Forum*, 34/1, March 1990
Luc Deleu Top Office 1967-1991, Muhka, Antwerp, 1991, 125 pp.

DESSAUVAGE MARC
(see: *Bouwen in België / La Construction en Belgique*)
Carolina De Backer, Luc Verpoest and Geert Bekaert, *Marc Dessauvage*, deSingel, Antwerp, 1987, 96 pp.

DUPUIS JACQUES
(see: *Bouwen in België / La Construction en Belgique*)
Jan Thomaes, 'Jacques Dupuis 1914-1984' in: S/AM, April-June 1983

L'ÉQUERRE
Le groupe l'équerre. 40 ans d'architecture et d'urbanisme, Eugène Wahle éditeur, Liège, 1977, with mention of specific studies

EYSSELINCK GASTON
(see: *Bouwen in België / La Construction en Belgique*)
Marc Dubois, *Architect Gaston Eysselinck. Zijn werk te Oostende 1945/1953*, 96 pp., catalogue Provinciale Musea voor Beeldende Kunst, Provincie West-Vlaanderen, 1986
Gaston Eysselinck architekt en meubeldesigner (1907-1953), 70 pp., catalogue Museum voor Sierkunst, Ghent 1978

FELIX PAUL
(see: *Bouwen in België / La Construction en Belgique*)
Geert Bekaert and Ronny De Meyer, *Paul Felix Architectuur 1913-1981*, Lannoo, Tielt/Bussum, 1981, 194 pp. including a complete bibliography

GREISCH RENÉ
'René Greisch', in: A+, no. 131, Dec. 1994 - Jan. 1995

HEE MARIE-JOSÉ VAN
Paul Vermeulen et al., *M. José Van Hee/Ontwerpen 1977-1993*, 80 pp., deSingel, Antwerp, 1993

JACQMAIN ANDRÉ
(see: *Bouwen in België / La Construction en Belgique*)
André Jacqmain and the Atelier de Genval, ed. Pierre Loze, *Architecture*, Snoeck-Ducaju, Ghent, 1988, 260 pp., including a complete bibliography

KIECKENS CHRISTIAN
Christian Kieckens and Jos Vanderperren, *Crescendo*, Werkgroep Deetaaï, Brussels, 1980
Christian Kieckens, *(Form is one Function too)*, Aalst, 1993, 66 pp.
Norbert De Waele, *Christian Kieckens*, s.a.
'Christian Kieckens. Architectuur 1986-1990', in: S/AM, April-June 1990

KROLL LUCIEN
(see: *Bouwen in België / La Construction en Belgique*)
Lucien Kroll, *Composants. Faut-il industrialiser l'architecture?*, Ed. Socorema, Brussels, s.a., 134 pp.
Wolfgang Pehnt, *Lucien Kroll. Buildings and Projects*, Thames and Hudson, London, 1988, 144 pp., including a bibliography
'Conferme et perplessità nell'itinerario di Lucien

Kroll' in: *L'architettura chronache e storia*, no. 463, May 1994

KUYCK HUGO VAN
Charles E. Schelfhout, *In het kielzog van Hugo Van Kuyck. Een uitzonderlijke Belg / Dans le sillage d'Hugo Van Kuyck. Un Belge d'exception*, 152 pp., Editions de la Dyle, Bonheiden, 1988

LAMPENS JULIAAN
Juliaan Lampens 1950-1991, deSingel, Antwerp, 1991, 136 pp., with texts by Juliaan Lampens, Gerard Vandenhaute and Paul Vermeulen

LIEBAUT EUGEEN
Eugeen Liebaut, *Deconstruction. Architectuur van Stéphane Beel, Luc Deleu, Koen Deprez en Eugeen Liebaut*, Schaerbeek, 1987
Paul Vermeulen, *Eugeen Liebaut*, deSingel, Antwerp, 1991, 80 pp.

LIETAERT JOZEF
(see: *Bouwen in België / La Construction en Belgique*)

MAESENEER MARTINE DE
Martine De Maeseneer, *The In/di/visible Space*, deSingel, Antwerp, 1993, 104 pp.

VAN DER MEEREN WILLY
(see: *Bouwen in België / La Construction en Belgique*)
Mil De Kooning, *Willy Van Der Meeren*, Laat-XXe-Eeuws Genootschap, Vivekapelle, 1993, including a complete bibliography

NEEFS PAUL
(see: *Bouwen in België / La Construction en Belgique*)
Mil De Kooning, *Paul Neefs*, Laat-XXe-Eeuws Genootschap, Vivekapelle, 1992, 138 pp.

NEUTELINGS WILLEM-JAN
W.J. Neutelings, *De Ringcultuur. Een studie naar het Ringmechanisme*, Vlees en Beton 10, Mechelen, 1988
Paul Vermeulen, *W.J. Neutelings in Antwerpen. W.J. Neutelings in Ontwerpen*, deSingel, Antwerp, 1990
Stichting Rotterdam-Maaskant, *Willem Jan Neutelings Architect*, Uitg. 010, Rotterdam, 1991, 60 pp.
Neutelings & Roodbeen Architecten, *European Patent Office*, Uitg. 010, Rotterdam, 1991

PECHÈRE RENÉ
René Pechère, *Grammaire des jardins. Secrets de métier*, Racine, Brussels, 1995, 144 pp.

REETH BOB VAN
(see: *Bouwen in België / La Construction en Belgique*)
Geert Bekaert, 'bOb van Reeth. The alibi of the architecture' in: Forum XXVI/3, 1975
Mil De Kooning, *bOb van Reeth. teksten van en over*, Faculteit der Toegepaste Wetenschappen, RU Ghent, 1983, 240 pp.
Mil De Kooning, *AWG bOb van Reeth*, Marc Van Bortel, Mica Franck, Geert Driesen, deSingel, Antwerp, 1987, 96 pp.
Architekten Werkgroep. Inventaris 1965-1987, Uitgeverij Biblo, Kalmhout, 1987

RITZEN JOS
Frans De Blauwe, *Jos Ritzen*, 74 pp., De Nederlandse Boekhandel, Antwerp, 1957
Robbrecht Paul and Daem Hilde
Bart Cassiman, *Paul Robbrecht Hilde Daem. De architectuur en het beeld*, deSingel, Antwerp, 1989

SAMYN PHILIPPE
Profiel van een architect / Profil d'un architecte, 112 pp., Sint-Lukasarchief, Brussels, 1989

STYNEN LÉON
(see: *Bouwen in België / La Construction en Belgique*)
'Léon Stynen architect' in: *Plan* no. 5, 1965
Albert Bontridder, *Gevecht met de rede. Léon Stynen, leven and werk / Stynen, la raison révoltée; sa vie et son oeuvre*, Comité Léon Stynen, Antwerp, 1979, 238 pp.
Geert Bekaert and Rony De Meyer, *Léon Stynen, een architect. Antwerpen, 1899-1990*, deSingel, Antwerp, 1990, 106 pp. Trilingual edition in Dutch, French, and English
Marc Dubois and Hedwig Speliers, *Casino Memories*, Kunsthuis Loosveldt, 1994

Tanghe Jan
(see Planning: *Bouwen in België / La Construction en Belgique*)
Group Planning Partnership. Vision and Reality, Edizioni Tecno, Milaan, 1986
Vandenhove Charles
(see: *Bouwen in België / La Construction en Belgique*)
Geert Bekaert, *Charles Vandenhove*, Pierre Mardaga éditeur, Liège, 1976, 160 pp. including portfolio
Pierre Colman and Geert Bekaert, *Architecture pour Architecture. Hôtel Torrentius*, Ed. du Ministère de la Communauté française, Brussels, 1982, 96 pp.
François Chaslin et al., *Charles Vandenhove. Une architecture de la densité*, Pierre Mardaga éditeur, Liège, 1985, 160 pp.
Fondation pour l'Architecture, Charles Vandenhove. Projets choisies, AAM, Brussels, 1986, 78 pp.
Geert Bekaert, *Charles Vandenhove. Centre hospitalier universitaire du Sart Tilman Liège. A la recherche de l'unité*, Standaard/Malherbe, Antwerp, 1988
Geert Bekaert and Kim Zwarts, *Charles Vandenhove 1985-1995*, NAi-uitgevers, Rotterdam, 1994, 208 pp. Trilingual edition in Dutch, French, and English
Wirtz Jacques
Catherine Laroze e.a., *Les jardins de Jacques Wirtz*, Fondation pour l'architecture, Brussels, 1994, 176 pp.

Index

Place names

Index

Authors